Engaging Government Employees

Engaging Government Employees

Motivate and Inspire Your People to Achieve Superior Performance

Robert J. Lavigna

HarperCollins Leadership

An Imprint of HarperCollins

Engaging Government Employees

Published by HarperCollins Leadership, an imprint of HarperCollins Focus LLC.

ISBN 978-1-4003-3635-7 (TP)

This book is dedicated to the millions of public servants who, day in and day out, deliver the essential services that government provides to its citizens. It is my hope that this book will reinforce the value of effective government and also help, in a very modest way, to improve the effectiveness of the public sector.

Contents

Chapter 1

The Power of Employee Engagement and What This Book Is About

This is not an easy time to be employed in the public sector. Heated budget battles and rhetoric about the size, function, scope, and effectiveness of government have generated criticism not just of government but also of the public servants who deliver government services. Across the country—in Congress, state legislatures, city councils, political speeches and ads, the media, and elsewhere—government organizations and their employees are denigrated and stigmatized as underworked and overpaid.

In stark contrast, in the not-too-distant past, government service was a respected profession—described as a "noble calling" by President George H. W. Bush.[1] The best and brightest across our nation aspired to make a difference by devoting their careers to public service, whether it was in Washington, DC, crafting national policies, or in their local communities, protecting their neighbors, teaching their children, or helping in countless other ways.

Sadly, opinion has changed, and the public no longer views government as a noble calling.

Here's how Jay Leno described the work of government: "A survey says that American workers work the first three hours every day just to pay their taxes. So that's why we can't get anything done in the morning: We're government workers."[2]

Writer and philosopher Alex Pattakos, a strong proponent of the public service, has cited this cynical joke: "Why doesn't the civil servant look out her window in the morning? Answer: So she'll have something to do in the afternoon."[3]

And so on.

Those who criticize government, and the people who work in government, have lost sight of the critically important work of the public sector. This work affects everyone—nationally, in our states, and in our local communities. At the same time government is being castigated and hamstrung by budget cuts, the public continues to ask the public sector to solve some of the toughest and most intractable problems: fixing the economy, putting people back to work, supporting a war that has stubbornly persisted for a decade, protecting the public, maintaining the quality of life in our communities, eliminating poverty, expanding opportunity by improving the education system, providing affordable health care, and so on.

And, as we tragically learned in the aftermath of Hurricane Katrina, when government fails, people can die.

This paradox—attacking public servants while at the same time expecting them to solve problems no other sector can handle—places government leaders and managers squarely in the middle of an extremely difficult situation. Those who lead the 18,000,000-strong public-sector workforce, the nation's largest, must somehow find ways to motivate their employees despite harsh public criticism and shrinking resources.

How can these public-sector leaders, from senior-level executives to frontline supervisors, meet this challenge?

One proven solution is to improve the level of employee engagement in their organizations and agencies. After all, the primary resource we have in government is our talent—our people. If they perform well, government performs well.

But what is *employee engagement* and why does it matter? The concept has been around for decades but has come into much greater focus in the past decade. One particularly useful and actionable definition characterizes *engagement* as a heightened employee connection to work, the organization, the mission, or coworkers. Engaged employees find personal meaning and pride in their work. They believe that their organizations value them, and in return, engaged employees are more likely to go above the minimum and expend "discretionary effort" to deliver performance.[4] The consulting firm BlessingWhite sums it up even more succinctly: "Engaged employees plan to stay for what they give, disengaged stay for what they get."[5]

There is strong research-based evidence for why managers should care about employee engagement. Simply put, organizations with engaged employees outperform organizations whose employees are not engaged. This is true in both the public and private sectors.

For example, the Gallup organization, best known for its public-opinion polling, has also systematically studied employee engagement by analyzing engagement surveys of millions of employees. Gallup's research reveals that high-engagement organizations outperform low-engagement organizations in seven critical areas: profitability, productivity, customer satisfaction, retention, absenteeism, safety, and lost or stolen inventory. According to Gallup, high-engagement organizations are almost 20 percent more productive than their low-engagement counterparts.[6]

But how do these results translate to government, which usually doesn't rely on measures like profitability? The Gallup research shows that improved engagement drives outcomes that are also important in government, like productivity, customer satisfaction, and retention. Think about what a 20 percent improvement in productivity would do for your organization, jurisdiction, agency, or work unit.

Even more specific to the public sector, the U.S. Merit Systems Protection Board (MSPB) studied survey results from 37,000 federal government employees. The board found that higher levels of employee engagement across the federal government correlated with

- higher rates of success achieving strategic goals;
- higher employee retention;

- fewer days of sick leave and less lost time due to work-related injury or illness; and
- fewer equal employment opportunity complaints.[7]

A TowersWatson Consulting survey of more than 17,000 public and nonprofit employees revealed that highly engaged employees scored dramatically higher on key survey questions/statements, compared to moderately engaged and disengaged employees (Table 1.1).[8]

This and other research clearly show that employee engagement can be a powerful force for organizational change and effectiveness. Given the challenges public-sector managers face trying to succeed despite public criticism, budget cuts, layoffs, and reductions in employee compensation and benefits, building and maintaining employee engagement is more important than ever. It is also more difficult to achieve.

This book is about how to meet this challenge—by measuring employee engagement, analyzing the results of these measurements, using the data to take systematic action to improve engagement, and then sustaining it over time in government—the nation's largest and perhaps most important employer.

There are many other books about employee engagement, and some are excellent. But this book departs from the others in three ways.

Table 1.1. Results From the TowersWatson Consulting Employee Engagement Survey

Statement	Highly engaged (% who agree)	Moderately engaged (% who agree)	Disengaged (% who agree)
I can positively impact quality.	86	61	32
I can positively impact cost.	59	37	21
I can positively impact customer service.	72	50	28

First, I focus on the science of employee engagement—that is, what the research clearly proves about the power of engagement to improve individual and organizational performance. Instead of relying on my insights "culled from my many years of experience" or "my work with many different types of organizations," I emphasize what the engagement research has proven empirically and how these results apply to government organizations.

Sure, I have experience with engagement, and I will cite some of these experiences as examples, but I don't trust purely anecdotal experiences and don't believe they necessarily apply to the situations or challenges other managers face. I don't rely exclusively on my personal experiences to make the case for why government leaders, managers, frontline supervisors, and employees should focus on engagement. Instead, I rely on the research and empirical evidence.

Second, my focus is government. There are other fine works on the science of engagement, but they don't emphasize the public sector. In Chapter 4, I highlight the unique challenges government faces, the fundamental differences between the public and private sectors, and the implications of these differences for managers—and for employee engagement. I argue that, in some respects, these differences make it harder to manage in the public sector. As a result, public-sector leaders, managers, and frontline supervisors must approach engagement differently than their private-sector counterparts.

In addition to the hostile environment the government operates in today, other key factors that distinguish the public sector from the private sector include political leadership that changes frequently; hard-to-measure goals and impacts; complicated, rule-bound, and sometimes irrational decision making; multiple external stakeholders with power and influence; an older, more educated, and more white-collar workforce; strong civil-service rules and employee protections; heavy union influence; limited financial tools to influence and reward employee behavior; public visibility of government actions; and, more positively, a workforce that is intrinsically motivated toward public service. I believe that government leaders and managers need to understand these differences and their implications for employee engagement. This argument is a key focus of this book.

The third way in which this book departs from many other works on engagement is that I don't present a one-size-fits-all approach to improving engagement. There are many engagement models and approaches that their designers maintain can be adopted just about anywhere. In contrast, I don't see how any single employee-engagement model can apply to all organizations and situations, particularly in government. Just in the United States, there are more than 85,000 government jurisdictions and agencies, and each has its own mission, strategy, values, and culture.

Instead, I believe that every organization needs to measure its own level of employee engagement, analyze the results to identify specific areas to improve, set priorities for action, and then act on the data. While there are some broad principles that apply generally to engagement (which I'll discuss), there is no single solution that will automatically improve engagement across all organizations.

I do present a model in Chapter 7, but it is an engagement *process* model—that is, a model that a public-sector organization can adapt and adopt to assess its level of employee engagement. The organization needs to then act on these results to improve engagement. The model is intended to help each agency generate the data it needs to draw conclusions about what its employee-engagement issues are and how to deal with them to improve engagement, but it does not prescribe generic solutions. In Chapter 12, I describe what some government agencies have done to improve engagement, but I present these actions as examples, not prescriptions.

From the start, it is important to understand that there is no silver bullet to achieve high levels of employee engagement. Instead, what's needed is silver buckshot—an integrated series of actions, specific to each government jurisdiction or agency, to measure and then improve engagement.

Here's a quote that I think sums up the power of employee engagement. According to Jim Goodnight, CEO of SAS, a leading business software company that is also a perennial member of *Fortune* magazine's annual "100 Best Companies to Work For," "My chief assets drive out the gate every day. My job is to make sure they come back."[9]

Goodnight's statement is just as applicable (or maybe even more applicable) to government. And improving engagement is one clearly documented way to make sure that when the chief assets of government leave at the end of the day, they *do* plan to return tomorrow.

Chapter 2

So What Is Employee Engagement, Exactly?

I'm sure most readers are familiar with LinkedIn, the social networking site for professionals that, among other things, hosts online discussion groups. One of these groups focuses on employee engagement, and a discussion question was, "In ten words or less, name what you believe are or could be the three most effective drivers of engagement." (Oddly, this was posted next to another question, "Are you sure your employees are washing their hands?" But that's a topic for another day.)

As I write this, 124 LinkedIn members have posted answers to the engagement question, and the range of responses about engagement is both interesting and instructive. Here are some responses:

- Creating conversations where none existed
- Work gratification
- Purpose
- Compelling vision
- Camaraderie
- Personal connection
- Inclusion
- Feedback

- Caring
- And last (but never least)—love

Aside from the fact that we need to love our employees (platonically, I assume), what else can we conclude from this baffling range of responses? As one of the LinkedIn commenters said, "Clearly from the comments above there is no consensus . . . Every possible positive quality is seen to be a driver. No wonder many people working in this field don't know where to start, and how."

This commenter isn't the only person confused about what *employee engagement* means exactly. According to a report on engagement prepared for the United Kingdom government, "There is no one agreed definition of employee engagement—during the course of this review we have come across more than 50 definitions."[1]

Another analysis of public-sector engagement prepared for the European Group of Public Administration concluded that

> almost every scholar, every organization, and every consulting firm active in this corner of the human resource management field has used their [*sic*] own particular set of concepts and vocabulary. Some measure employee "satisfaction," some measure employee "commitment," some employee "loyalty," some employee "engagement," or a distinctive combination of these and other concepts . . . The result is a state of high confusion, with little consistency or consensus. Cutting through this confusion will be one of the first conditions of progress across the public sector, not to mention the private sector.[2]

So, despite all the discussion about employee engagement, there isn't much agreement on what it is, exactly. We're in a "state of high confusion." Reminiscent of what Supreme Court Justice Potter Stewart famously wrote about his threshold test for pornography: "I know it when I see it."[3]

In fact, this same view was expressed in the U.K. report on engagement:

> You sort of smell it, don't you, that engagement of people as people. What goes on in meetings, how people talk to each other. You get the sense of energy, engagement, commitment, belief in what the organisation stands for . . . As a number of business leaders told us, "You know it when you see it."[4]

But we have to devise a better method than the "smell test" to help public-sector managers understand why employee engagement is important and how to engage their employees. Fortunately, there is science that helps us define what engagement is; why it's important; how to measure it; how it applies to government in particular; and how to build, maximize, and maintain it.

According to the definition I cited in Chapter 1, developed by the U.S. Merit Systems Protection Board (MSPB), employee engagement is a heightened connection to work, the organization, the mission, or coworkers. Engaged employees find personal meaning and pride in their work. They believe that their organizations value them; in return, engaged employees are more likely to go above the minimum and expend "discretionary effort" to deliver performance and support their colleagues and the organization. Engaged employees have made a choice to go above the minimum job requirements.[5]

The U.S. Office of Personnel Management (OPM), the central HR office for 2.1 million federal government employees, has a more succinct definition: Engaged employees are passionate, energetic, and dedicated to their job and organization.[6]

According to other research, while there may not be a standard definition of employee engagement, there is broad agreement that engaged employees

- feel personally and emotionally bound to the organization;
- feel pride in recommending their workplaces to others as good places to work;

- get more than just wages or salary from their work and are attached to the intrinsic rewards they gain from being with the organization; and
- feel a close attachment to the values, ethics, and actions the organization embodies.[7]

In a study of employee engagement in the Canadian federal government, engagement was defined in a much broader context: "As a higher-level outcome, engagement can be used as a synonym or proxy for overall people management [because] it is the cumulative effect of leadership, workforce, and workplace efforts that drives engagement."[8]

According to this study, engagement is "the level of satisfaction and commitment that employees feel for their job and their organization. The more employees are engaged in their organization and the work it does, the more likely they are to remain with the organization, recommend the organization to others, and perform at higher levels." Based on this definition, engagement has three specific components:

- **Job satisfaction.** The level of contentment or happiness people assign to their jobs
- **Commitment to the organization.** The level of pride people feel for their organization and the degree to which they intend to remain with the organization, perform at high levels, positively recommend the organization to others, and improve the organization's performance
- **Satisfaction with the organization.** The level of contentment or happiness people feel about their organization and their employment

The consulting firm BlessingWhite offers another definition—one that helps agencies actually identify engaged employees. According to this, engaged employees

- go the extra mile for colleagues and customers;
- work hard—and smart—to deliver what matters most to the agency;
- aren't thinking about leaving;

- volunteer their best ideas; and
- drive innovation to move the organization forward.[9]

Engagement also links to the concept of *flow*, as developed by Mihály Csíkszentmihályi. Employees who are in the flow are fully immersed in a feeling of energized focus, full involvement, and success. Like engaged employees, employees in the flow feel a strong connection to their jobs. Achieving the state of flow drives higher levels of workplace satisfaction and accomplishment.[10]

One writer describes *flow* as involving "good work" in which one "enjoys doing your best while at the same time contributing to something beyond yourself." This requires full involvement and the challenge of a task that matches one's ability.[11]

In order to achieve flow at work, Csíkszentmihályi specifies several conditions:

- Clear goals
- Immediate feedback
- Balance between opportunity and capacity
- Deep concentration
- The belief that the present is what matters

According to Csíkszentmihályi, organizations that create a workplace atmosphere that stimulates flow and growth can increase employee achievement.

> When the deepest part of you becomes engaged in what you are doing . . . you are doing what you were meant to be doing.
>
> Gary Zukav[12]

While most employee-engagement definitions do not distinguish between the public and private sectors, there are important differences between the sectors. One is the role of public-service motivation. As described in more detail in Chapter 4, a stream of research has uncovered strong evidence that public servants are motivated differently than private-sector workers. In large part, government employees are attracted to public service primarily by the opportunity to make a difference in the lives of the people government serves. Thus the employee-engagement challenge for public-sector organizations is to hire employees who have this gene, nurture it even when public employees feel undervalued or devalued, and then build on public-service motivation to promote engagement.

LEVELS OF ENGAGEMENT

As discussed in Chapter 6, there are different ways to assess the level of employee engagement in a government organization, jurisdiction, or agency. Consulting firms and other organizations that focus on engagement have developed their own descriptions of the different levels of employee engagement.

For example, Gallup has identified three levels of engagement (or disengagement):

1. **Engaged.** Employees work with a passion and feel a profound connection to their company. They drive innovation and move the organization forward. Note the focus on the private sector ("company"), which will be addressed later.
2. **Not engaged.** Employees are essentially "checked out." They're sleepwalking through their workday, putting time—but not energy or passion—into their work. I sometimes describe these employees as having retired; they just haven't told anyone yet.
3. **Actively disengaged.** The most disturbing of the three, these are employees who aren't just unhappy at work; they are busy acting out their unhappiness. Every day, these "workers" are ticking time bombs who undermine what their engaged coworkers are trying to accomplish.[13] Too many of these in the private sector, and you're out of business. Too many in the public sector, where

the actions of government are played out very publicly, and an agency can become the object of public ridicule and find itself on the political chopping block.

Other companies and organizations in the engagement business have their own takes on how to define and categorize engagement. The consulting firm BlessingWhite, for example, slices and dices engagement levels into five smaller pieces:

1. **Engaged.** With high levels of contribution and satisfaction, these employees are at the "apex" where personal and organizational interests align, and they therefore contribute fully to the success of the organization and find great satisfaction in their work. They are known for discretionary effort and commitment.
2. **Almost engaged.** With medium to high levels of contribution and satisfaction, these employees are among the high performers. Although they may not have consistent "great days at work," they at least know what those days look like. Organizations should invest in them for two reasons: They are highly employable and more likely to be lured to greener pastures, and they have the shortest path to reach full engagement, with a potential big payoff for the organization.
3. **Honeymooners and hamsters.** With medium to high levels of satisfaction but low levels of contribution, honeymooners are new to the organization or their role. They have not yet found their stride or don't yet clearly understand how they can best contribute. Hamsters may be working hard but are in effect spinning their wheels, working in nonessential tasks and contributing little to the success of the organization. Some may even be hiding out, curled up on their cedar shavings.
4. **Crash and burners.** With medium to high levels of contribution but low levels of satisfaction, these employees are disillusioned and potentially exhausted; they are top producers who aren't achieving their personal definition of success. They can be bitterly vocal that senior leaders are making bad decisions or that

colleagues are not pulling their weight. If left alone, they can slip on the contribution scale to become disengaged, often bringing down those around them.

5. **Disengaged.** These employees are disconnected from organizational priorities, feel underutilized, and are clearly not getting what they need from work. They may indulge in "contagious negativity." If they can't be coached to higher levels of engagement, their exit benefits everyone, including themselves.[14]

More specific to government, the U.S. Merit Systems Protection Board (MSPB) has identified three levels of engagement, based on a survey it administered to about 37,000 federal employees. The MSPB survey uses a scale of 1 (low engagement) to 5 (high engagement) for each survey question. The "not engaged" employees have average survey scores of 1–3 on the MSPB five-point scale, "somewhat engaged" score between 3 and 4, and the "engaged" score between 4 and 5. There are no clever descriptions of engagement levels for MSPB—just the numbers and the facts.

Thus there is quite a taxonomy of employee engagement, or lack of engagement, including some clever descriptors. Do you have hamsters in your organization, spinning their wheels or peacefully curled up on their comfortable wood shavings? Probably—we all do, unfortunately.

ENGAGEMENT: HAPPY AND SATISFIED EMPLOYEES?

Improving engagement in government is not necessarily about making employees happy. John Palguta is vice president of the nonprofit Partnership for Public Service and one of the driving forces behind "Best Places to Work in the Federal Government," which, since 2003, has rated and ranked federal agencies on employee satisfaction. According to Palguta, "It's not about happy employees, it's about effective government, and the potential for engaged employees to deliver consistently high-quality, efficient, and responsive service."[15]

While there is undoubtedly a correlation between employee happiness and employee engagement, they are not the same concepts. Employees can be happy because their jobs are easy or not challenging, and they have job security, good wages, and benefits. (In other words, they can be happy living down to the negative stereotypes associated with government that we hear too often.) In contrast, engaged employees drive improved organizational performance. Some government agencies with high levels of employee engagement demand a great deal from their employees—sometimes even while running the risk of making them unhappy.

Employee satisfaction and engagement are also often used interchangeably but are not precisely the same concepts. Many organizations focus on satisfying their employees, believing that a satisfied employee is a productive employee. However, studies have shown that employee engagement is a better measure of productivity than satisfaction. Employees who are engaged, and therefore feel a close connection to their agencies, will deliver the discretionary effort that drives organizational success.

Just as happy employees can be happy for the wrong reasons (e.g., a high-paid, unchallenging job with good benefits), so too can satisfied employees. Engagement goes beyond mere satisfaction, rising to the level of personal commitment to the organization's mission and the employee's colleagues. According to the consulting firm Kenexa, "Satisfaction depends primarily on job security (while) engagement measures how committed employees are to the workplace and how connected they feel."[16]

But employee satisfaction shouldn't be completely dismissed as a component of employee engagement. Researchers (including Gallup) have proven that satisfaction and engagement are correlated. If an organization's pay, benefits, and work environment are not good enough to satisfy employees, then it is unlikely that they will take the next step and become engaged—that is, form a stronger bond with the organization. When employees are engaged, they will accept periods of dissatisfaction and still remain committed.[17] But when employee satisfaction is low to begin with, employees are likely to be disengaged and ultimately leave the organization—not just physically, which can be good for both the employee and employer, but mentally and emotionally, which can be bad. I like to think of satisfaction as necessary but not sufficient for employee engagement.

Employee Engagement and Employee Well-Being

The Gallup organization has expanded the scope of its employee-engagement research to focus more broadly on the larger issue of employee well-being. Gallup has identified five dimensions of employee well-being:

1. **Career well-being.** How people occupy their time and like what they do at work each day
2. **Social well-being.** Having strong relationships and love in their lives
3. **Financial well-being.** Effectively managing their economic life to reduce stress and increase security
4. **Physical well-being.** Having good health and enough energy to get things done daily
5. **Community well-being.** The sense of engagement and involvement people have with the area where they live

The Gallup research shows that career well-being may be the single most important element of overall well-being, and career well-being is driven by the extent that employees are engaged.[18]

ENGAGEMENT LEVEL CAN VARY BY TYPE OF EMPLOYEE

The level of engagement across a government jurisdiction or organization can also vary by type of employee. In general, the higher an employee is in the organization's pecking order, the more engaged that person is likely to be. In other words, employees who do the pecking are typically more engaged than employees who are being pecked on.

The reasons for this should be obvious: In most organizations, including government, executives, managers, and supervisors have the lion's share of power, authority, and flexibility. They're also likely to be more closely connected to the organization's mission and strategy since they either helped create it or are directly accountable for achieving it. This organizational placement usually results in higher levels of engagement, compared to employees who don't have this authority or empowerment.

For example, the MSPB engagement study of federal employees revealed the following:

- Members of the Senior Executive Service (the highest level of the federal civil service) are more engaged than supervisory employees who are, in turn, more engaged than nonsupervisory employees.
- Federal employees with higher incomes tend to be more engaged than employees who earn less.
- The more education federal employees have, the higher their engagement levels.

MSPB also found differences in engagement by racial and ethnic groups. Federal government employees of Asian descent were most engaged followed by, in order, white, Hispanic, African American, and Native American employees. The largest and most significant difference, therefore, was between employees of Asian descent and Native Americans. According to the MSPB, levels of education and salary may account for some of these differences. Specifically, Native American employees had less education, and African American and Native American employees earned less than employees in the other groups.

The percentage of engaged employees also varied widely by federal agency, ranging from 25 to 50 percent. The highest-scoring agency was NASA, followed by the Department of State, U.S. Air Force, U.S. Army, and the EPA. (Army and air force results include only civilian employees.) The lowest five were the Departments of Energy, Education, and Transportation; the Federal Deposit Insurance Corporation; and, bringing up the rear, the Department of Homeland Security.[19]

In state government, a 2011 employee survey of state of Washington employees revealed that supervisors scored higher than nonsupervisors in all 16 survey questions.

Another survey of public-sector employees revealed different levels of engagement by age. While engagement levels were low across the board, older workers were more engaged than younger workers.[20]

This can perhaps be explained in several ways. First, most public-sector agencies have low turnover and, therefore, older workers in government are more likely to be in leadership positions. As explained previously, this often translates into higher engagement. It's also well documented that older workers—baby boomers in particular—have different views about careers and work than their younger colleagues. Many baby boomers have spent their entire working lives in government—a commitment that is inconceivable to many younger workers. These younger workers have been described as the "disengaged generation," in part because workplace conditions often don't meet their needs. Older workers who are more invested in their public-sector careers may also be more tolerant of how difficult it can be to get things done in the complex environment of government.

Another engagement analysis by Gallup shows that, among the U.S. working population, 20 percent of employees in unions are engaged, while 28 percent of those not in unions are engaged. Across the more than 500 organizations Gallup consults, this gap holds up: 38 percent of union employees are engaged and 45 percent of nonunion employees are engaged.[21]

Despite these types of differences, engagement can exist throughout an organization, across demographic and employee groups. In fact, the thesis of this book is that high levels of engagement can exist across the entire organization. In most government organizations, however, this is more a goal than a reality.

Table 2.1. Public-Sector Employee Engagement by Age Group

Age group	Highly engaged (%)	Disengaged (%)
29 or younger	15	24
30–44	14	21
45–54	18	15
55 or older	22	14

To summarize, while there are different definitions of employee engagement, I think MSPB characterizes it best, particularly in government: Engaged employees have a heightened connection to work, the organization, the mission, or coworkers. Engaged employees find personal meaning and pride in their work. They believe that their organizations value them and, in return, are more likely to go above the minimum and expend "discretionary effort" to deliver superior performance.

The level of engagement in an organization can be measured, and results show that engagement usually varies across the organization. Measuring engagement reveals different levels of engagement in most organizations (some even with clever descriptive titles). Later, we'll explore the various ways that engagement can—and should—be measured, particularly in government. Just as important, we will also focus on how to use the measurement results to take action and improve engagement across the jurisdiction or agency.

Chapter 3

Why Engagement Matters

The Business Case for Improving Engagement

Having defined what employee engagement is, the logical next question is, Why does it matter? While it may seem like common sense that managers should strive to engage their employees, common sense isn't always common practice.

When I speak about employee engagement, managers and supervisors often react that they just want their employees to do their jobs. Engagement is the touchy-feely stuff they don't have time for. Plus, isn't engagement HR's job? In Chapter 13, I discuss HR's role in measuring and improving engagement. However, improving engagement should be a shared responsibility across the entire organization, including leaders, managers, supervisors, and rank-and-file employees themselves. Engagement takes a village.

But why bother with employee engagement? The answer is that engagement matters: There is a clear and compelling research-based business case for improving engagement. Simply put, organizations with engaged employees perform dramatically better than organizations whose employees are not engaged, including in government.

For example, the Gallup organization has assembled an employee-engagement database built on 30 years of research involving more than 17 million employees.[1] Gallup's analysis of the engagement-survey results from 23,910 business units reveals that high-engagement organizations outperformed low-engagement organizations in seven critical areas: profitability, productivity, customer satisfaction, retention, absenteeism, safety, and lost or stolen inventory.

Figure 3.1, based on Gallup research, shows the differences in key business results between high-engagement organizations (that scored in the top quartile based on the Gallup employee-engagement survey) and low-engagement organizations (that scored in the bottom quartile). The contrast is dramatic, including more than 10 percent higher profits and almost 20 percent higher productivity.

Another study of 50 global companies, by the consulting firm TowersWatson, found that firms with high levels of employee engagement produce dramatically better bottom-line results than companies with low levels of engagement. The data cover 664,000 employees from 50 companies of all sizes, around the world, representing different industries. In three key metrics—income, income growth, and earnings per share—the high-engagement organizations performed dramatically better. Notably, companies with highly engaged employees had

Figure 3.1. High-engagement (top-quartile) work groups compared to low-engagement (bottom-quartile) work groups.[2]

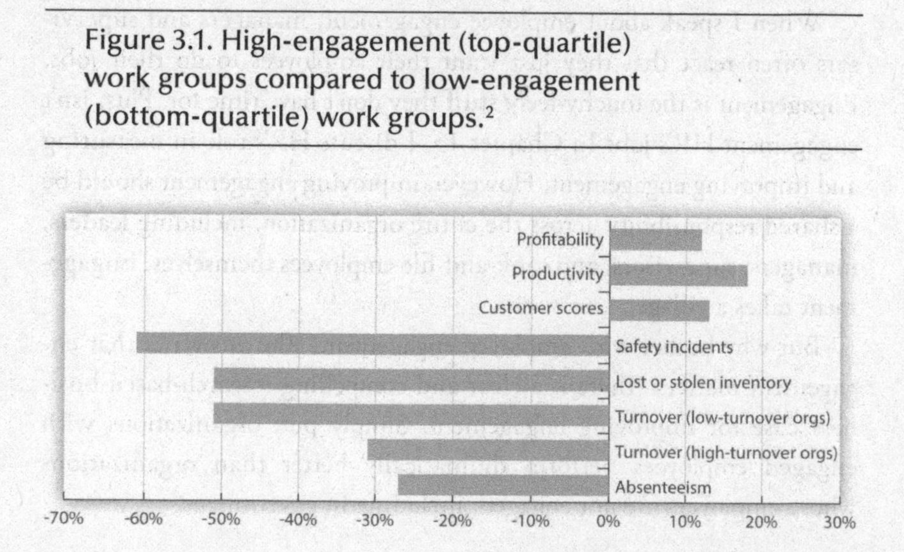

a 52 percent advantage in operating income change over companies whose employees had low engagement scores. The firms with high levels of employee engagement had a 19.2 percent increase in operating income, while low-engagement companies' operating income declined by 32.7 percent.[3]

Other research-based examples of the value of engagement abound:

- The Corporate Leadership Council (CLC) reports that highly engaged organizations increase profits up to three times faster than their competitors. The CLC also reports that highly engaged organizations could reduce staff turnover by 87 percent and improve performance by 20 percent.[4]
- Another CLC research study found that companies with above-average employee commitment were, in 71 percent of cases, achieving above-average performance in their sectors. In contrast, only 38 percent of low-commitment companies achieved above-average performance.[5]
- A Watson Wyatt study of 115 companies shows that companies with highly engaged employees achieved financial performance that was four times better than companies with poor engagement. Watson Wyatt also reports that the highly engaged firms were more than twice as likely to be top performers—almost 60 percent of them exceeded/far exceeded expectations for performance. Plus, the highly engaged firms had 43 percent fewer days off work due to illness.[6]
- A British study of manufacturing companies shows that people management practices, especially employee engagement, are better predictors of company performance than strategy, technology, or research and development.[7]
- A study of 20,000 employees shows that high engagement correlates with lower levels of employee stress and higher levels of work-life balance.[8]
- Employee *dis*engagement in the United States is estimated to cost American businesses from $287 to $370 *billion* annually due to low productivity.[9] In Germany, Gallup estimates that actively

disengaged employees cost the economy up to 109 billion euros per year in lost productivity alone. This does not include additional costs of absenteeism, lack of innovation and customer orientation, high turnover, and negative word of mouth.[10]

- Gallup research also suggests that higher levels of engagement are strongly related to higher levels of innovation. Fifty-nine percent of engaged employees said that their jobs bring out their most creative ideas—compared to only 3 percent of disengaged employees.[11]

The research showing the impact of engagement goes on. The U.K. government report "Engaging for Success: Enhancing Performance Through Employee Engagement" summarizes dozens of studies and examples demonstrating how improved engagement has improved business results.[12] Another U.K.-based research study found that engaged employees are more likely to be advocates for the organization,[13] which can be a big advantage when recruiting and retaining talent.

Less empirical but still compelling is an anecdote told to me by a Gallup executive. As he tells it, Gallup was approached by a national firm that wanted a customer-satisfaction survey. The Gallup executive told the firm that he would be happy to do the survey; however, he suggested, if the firm really wanted to get the most return on its investment, they should conduct an employee-engagement survey instead and then act on the results. His logic is that when organizations, in the public or private sectors, pay attention to employee engagement, other key business outcomes, including customer satisfaction, can follow.

EMPLOYEE ENGAGEMENT IN GOVERNMENT

There is a large body of research demonstrating the value of employee engagement in the private sector. But this book is about engagement in government. How does the engagement research translate to the public sector, where we don't usually measure results like profit and earnings per share? Is there comparable research that matters to government and to the taxpayers who finance government?

The answer is that there *is* research that links engagement directly to public-sector performance. It's thinner than the private-sector results but is compelling nonetheless.

For example, the U.K. Civil Service has made a strong commitment to measuring and improving engagement across the British government, including by conducting the annual Civil Service People Survey of British civil servants. The survey results show that government departments with high engagement levels perform well on department capability reviews—a key metric of departmental performance.[14] In the U.K. government, 78 percent of highly engaged public servants say they can have an impact on service delivery or customer service—against only 29 percent of the disengaged.[15] According to a British government leader,

> The Civil Service faces unprecedented challenges tackling complex policy issues every day. In order to meet these challenges we must harness the talents of all our staff to the full. Our employee engagement programme enables us to do this by understanding and improving civil servants' experience of work, helping to ensure that they have access to the opportunities they need to achieve success in their roles. This, in turn, supports our drive to deliver improved public services and better outcomes for citizens.[16]

Research on employee engagement in Canada also shows that engagement drives outcomes that are important to government. Heightened employee engagement is one of the three building blocks in the "public-sector service value chain." According to this model, employee engagement in government leads to citizen/client satisfaction, which then leads to citizen trust and confidence in public institutions—an outcome that is increasingly rare but critically important to the health of public service.[17] The government of British Columbia found that work units with high levels of employee engagement scored higher in customer satisfaction than low-engagement work units. Also in Canada, an Ontario public-service study of an information technology work group found that employee engagement was linked to customer satisfaction.[18]

The Ontario public service also inserted a performance link into the value chain: Increased employee engagement leads to better organizational performance, which then leads to increased customer satisfaction and promotes public trust and confidence in government. Several Canadian public-sector organizations are using this service value chain concept as a management tool for improving organizational performance.[19]

The province of Alberta, which has been conducting employee-engagement surveys since 1996, included engagement as a critical element of its strategic workforce vision for 2012–32. As part of its bold attempt to predict what the workplace will look like 20 years from now, the Alberta plan includes this strong assertion: "The advantage for organizations in the competition for talent will be directly linked to the level of engagement of its employees."[20]

Research on the value of engagement to government is not just limited to the British Commonwealth. As mentioned earlier, the U.S. Merit Systems Protection Board (MSPB) has done a series of studies on engagement in the federal government, the nation's largest employer (with a workforce of about 2.1 million, excluding the postal service). MSPB found the following:

- Employees who reported that they were very *unlikely* to leave their agency were much more engaged than those who reported they were very *likely* to leave. This pattern was the same for both retirement-eligible employees and those not yet eligible for retirement. If employees are not engaged, many will look for better opportunities elsewhere. It's also revealing that MSPB found that most of the employees who said they were very likely to leave their agency (i.e., those who were not engaged) nevertheless had received high performance ratings. So the disengaged were not necessarily low performers. Thus, federal agencies are at risk of losing high-performing but disengaged employees to more engaging employment elsewhere.

- Higher levels of employee engagement correlated with fewer average days of sick leave and less lost time due to work-related injuries or illness.
- Higher levels of employee engagement were linked to fewer workplace discrimination (equal employment opportunity) complaints.
- Perhaps most important, higher levels of employee engagement correlated with higher scores on agency program results, as measured by the U.S. Office of Management and Budget (OMB) Program Assessment Rating Tool (PART).[21]

This last finding is particularly significant because it links engagement directly to agency performance, which can be elusive to measure in government. As the MSPB emphasizes, pinning down whether federal agencies (or most government agencies, for that matter) are producing successful outcomes is not easy—government doesn't have outcome measures like revenue, profit, stock price, earnings per share, or related financial outcomes.

In an attempt to measure federal agency performance, OMB required agencies to use the PART to track whether they were achieving annual and long-term performance goals. This tool, later discontinued by the Obama administration, required agencies to report their goals and results using consistent data, therefore improving performance measurement. PART assessed how well agency programs were operating compared to similar programs in other federal agencies and how effective the programs were overall. Because OMB used the PART results to help decide agency budgets, these were high-stakes measurements.

The MSPB used data from the results section of the PART to determine whether higher levels of employee engagement were linked to better program results. The board found that there was indeed a positive and statistically significant correlation between the levels of employee engagement in an agency and program results, as measured by the PART. In other words, the higher an agency's average employee-engagement score, the higher the PART results score. Specifically, the agencies with the five highest employee-engagement scores had an average PART score of 65 (out of 100) on the results section. In contrast, the five agencies with the lowest engagement scores had an average PART score of 37.

Since this correlation is statistically significant, we can expect that if a federal agency's engagement level increased, so would its PART results score. Presumably, agency results themselves would therefore improve. We would also expect that if engagement decreased, the performance measure would also suffer.

Also in the federal government, the annual Federal Employee Viewpoint Survey reveals a strong link between engagement/satisfaction and retention. Among the 687,000 federal employees who responded to the survey in 2012, those classified as moderately engaged and with low satisfaction were five times more likely to say that they plan to leave the federal government than employees who were highly engaged and satisfied.

In state and local governments, a 2012 engagement survey jointly conducted by the payroll firm ADP and the nonprofit International Public Management Association for Human Resources revealed the following about engaged public-sector employees:

- They are twice as likely to stay in their current jobs.
- They are 2.5 times more likely to feel they can make a difference.
- They are 2.5 times more likely to recommend their workplace to others.
- They are three times as likely to report being "very satisfied" in their jobs.[22]

Deloitte Consulting, which has also done research on public-sector employee engagement, sums it up by arguing that enhanced employee engagement can help leaders do the following:

- Improve employee performance that supports mission-related outcomes.
- Engage employees to foster collaborative, innovative work environments.
- Lower the costs associated with disengagement.[23]

EMPLOYEE ENGAGEMENT IN HEALTH CARE AND EDUCATION

There is also research demonstrating that hospital employees who are highly engaged help produce better patient outcomes. Research conducted on hospitals in both the United Kingdom and the United States, for example, revealed that high levels of employee engagement are linked to the following outcomes:

- Better patient outcomes
- Lower hospital mortality rates
- Higher patient satisfaction
- Higher service quality
- Better financial performance
- Improved employee health and well-being
- Lower absenteeism[24,25]

Since many hospitals in both countries are government operated, this research has important implications for employee engagement in government.

Engagement is also a critical issue in another public-sector work environment: public education. Our nation continues to be embroiled in a high-stakes debate about how to most effectively educate our children. There is perhaps no issue more important to our long-term future. Central to this debate is the role of teachers and how to measure the educational results they help produce. The engagement of this workforce of teachers—3.3 million strong—needs to be part of that debate.

For example, a 2011 survey revealed that education is one of the five industries in the United States with the "most disengaged" employees (32 percent disengaged).[26] In another study, of three school districts, the schools with high staff engagement had almost 12 percent more students passing all tests.[27]

The need for improved employee engagement applies to higher education as well. According to another study, "The employee engagement discussion should be front and center for higher education leaders.

Engagement should be just as important as enrollment budget reallocation, infrastructure/facilities development, academic focus, fundraising, faculty governance, rising healthcare costs and all other top-of-mind issues."[28]

The bottom line is that a wealth of evidence makes a clear and compelling case that employee engagement matters, including in government. Engagement matters to the organization, the manager/supervisor, and the individual employee. According to one extensive study of public-sector engagement, "Our conclusion from the evidence available, including our own first-hand observations of the impact of successful employee engagement in practice, is that the correlation between engagement, well-being and performance is repeated too often for it to be a coincidence."[29]

Or, as one local government official put it more bluntly, "If you don't start with the workforce, how can you reach the public? 18,000 ambassadors are better than 18,000 assassins."[30]

HOW ENGAGED ARE MOST EMPLOYEES? NOT VERY

So far, we've discussed what engagement is and why it's important, focusing on the research that has demonstrated the benefits of engagement in both the private and public sectors. With all this evidence, we might expect that organizations in all sectors would focus on employee engagement and, as a result, engagement levels would be high. Right?

Well, not exactly. The reality is that across the public and private sectors, and around the globe, employee engagement is generally low.

For example, Gallup's data, based on 17 million employee-engagement surveys, paints a disturbing picture. According to Gallup, only 29 percent of employees are "engaged," while 54 percent are "not engaged," and 17 percent are "actively disengaged."[31]

The consulting firm BlessingWhite surveyed 11,000 employees worldwide in 2011 and found 31 percent were engaged. Engagement levels by country ranged from 17 percent in China to 37 percent in India. Among North American employees, only 33 percent were engaged and 17 percent were disengaged.[32] In North America, BlessingWhite found that 22 percent of government employees were disengaged.[33]

Also in government, the consulting firm TowersWatson surveyed more than 17,000 public and nonprofit sector employees and found that only 16 percent were "highly engaged," with 65 percent "moderately engaged" and 19 percent disengaged.[34] In the United Kingdom, only 12 percent of public-sector employees were "highly engaged."[35]

Among U.S. federal government employees, the MSPB survey revealed that 35.3 percent of federal employees were "engaged," 47.2 percent were "somewhat engaged," and 17.5 percent were "not engaged."[36] These results are more positive than the other survey results but certainly not where we want the nation's largest employer to be.

The U.S. Office of Personnel Management (OPM), the federal government's central HR office, conducts the annual Federal Employee Viewpoint Survey. In 2012, for the first time, OPM expanded the survey to almost the entire workforce of federal permanent-civilian employees. More than 687,000 federal employees completed the survey—a 46 percent response rate. The Federal Employee Viewpoint Survey measures federal employees' experiences with their jobs and work environments and does not directly measure employee engagement. However, OPM uses survey results to calculate composite scores: an employee satisfaction index and an employee-engagement index. The latter represents the "conditions likely to lead to employee engagement" (e.g., effective leadership, meaningful work, the opportunity for employees to learn/grow on the job).

The OPM "conditions for employee engagement index" score for 2012 was 65 percent positive, down two percentage points from 2011. Individual agency scores ranged from 56 to 76 percent. While this result may seem more positive than other engagement survey results, an overall engagement score of only 65 percent positive in the nation's largest workforce is still troubling, as are the declines in both the satisfaction and engagement indices. OPM also uses the survey data to calculate a "satisfaction index." In 2012, the government-wide satisfaction index was 63 percent, also down from 66 percent in 2011 and 67 percent in 2010.[37]

The "Best Places to Work in the Federal Government" rankings produced by the nonprofit Partnership for Public Service are even less encouraging. The Partnership annually rates and ranks more than 300 federal agencies and their subcomponents (e.g., the Department of Justice as well as its subcomponents like the FBI) on an employee satisfaction scale of 0–100. These scores are also based on questions and results from the OPM Federal Employee Viewpoint Survey.

According to Partnership calculations, the government-wide employee satisfaction score for 2012 was 60.8 out of 100, a decline of 5 percent from the 2011 government-wide index (which also declined from the 2010 index). Scores declined in two out of every three agencies in 2012. The Partnership summary of the results concluded the following:

> The 2012 results tell a troubling story about a workforce whose satisfaction and commitment levels have dropped to the lowest point since 2003, when the rankings first launched. The 3.2-point drop is the largest change in the history of the rankings . . . The declining job satisfaction levels across the federal government come during turbulent times, with employees buffeted by many uncertainties and feeling the effects of a two-and-a-half year pay freeze . . . hiring slowdowns, buyouts, increased retirements and budget constraints.[38]

A McKinsey study of midlevel federal government professionals and managers also produced alarming results. The research compared employee engagement in the federal government to the private sector and revealed:

- only 29 percent of survey respondents felt they were consulted on issues that affect them, compared to 40 percent in the private sector;
- only 34 percent of respondents said they operate in an open and trusting environment, compared to 49 percent in the private sector; and

- only 34 percent said they are encouraged to provide honest feedback to each other, compared to 48 percent of private-sector respondents.[39]

In state and local governments, research conducted in 2012 by the payroll firm ADP and the International Public Management Association for Human Resources revealed that 58 percent of survey respondents were engaged. Even though this percentage is higher than in some other surveys (e.g., Gallup and MSPB), the survey methodology is different, and this survey still shows that more than 4 of 10 state and local government employees are not engaged. Plus, nearly all respondents to this survey described a sharp decline in employee morale and engagement in the last few years.[40]

This conclusion was supported by the results of the biennial employee survey of state of Washington employees. The 2011 results showed that scores for all 13 questions included in both the 2009 and 2011 surveys declined in 2011. According to the report on the results, "Having the scores go down in all 13 of those questions is similar to 13 tails in a row in a coin toss." The report explained that the decline was likely the result of several "environmental factors":

- A 3 percent pay cut for all state employees effective three months before the survey
- Ongoing layoffs and reorganizations for many state agencies
- A large gap in the state budget, which will have an unknown impact on many state employees
- Negative focus on state workers from the media and the public
- A high state unemployment rate[41]

WHY ISN'T EMPLOYEE ENGAGEMENT HIGHER?

The various engagement surveys have different methodologies, and therefore results are not entirely comparable. However, all the surveys and research suggest that there is substantial room for improvement in the engagement of government employees. The question of why employee engagement is low is puzzling but critical to answer, especially in government, given the strong empirical evidence that engagement is linked to individual and organizational success plus the government's extreme reliance on its workforce to produce results.

One answer, as I've argued and the state of Washington employee survey report explicitly cites, is that this is a difficult time to work in government. It should not come as a surprise, therefore, that the attacks on government and government employees are damaging morale and employee engagement.

But the answer goes beyond attacks on government. Many managers are unaware of the potential benefits of improving employee engagement. A 2012 survey of HR professionals by the Society for Human Resource Management revealed that the HR community believes that engagement is the number one human-resources challenge, yet most organizations aren't measuring it.[42] Maybe line managers haven't had time to read the email from HR about the importance of engagement. Or maybe HR hasn't sent it yet.

The empirical evidence and my personal experience both suggest that managers *haven't* gotten that email, in part because many HR departments haven't sent it yet. The fact that managers don't understand the power of engagement, and therefore don't focus on it, is a key reason employee engagement is low, especially in government.

This disconnect may stem from the perception that employee engagement is synonymous with employee happiness, and many managers just don't feel particularly obliged to make their employees happy. As mentioned previously, these managers believe all is well in their organizations and think it's a waste of time to focus on employee engagement.

These views, while shortsighted, sometimes come through when I speak about engagement with government managers. Responses range from disinterest to a feeling that employee engagement might be worthwhile, but improving it is HR's job, of course.

My counter is that focusing on employee engagement should be a critical part of every supervisor's and manager's job. It is not just "HR stuff." But this can be a tough sell, especially to public-sector managers who are already overloaded and don't feel that they have the time to devote to (i.e., waste on) improving employee engagement. They're just too busy. That's especially true in today's tough budget environment, in which public-sector managers and employees are being asked to do more with less.

As a journalist friend of mine who covers government likes to describe it, government is asked to do more with less, then asked to do even more with even less, and ultimately asked to do everything with nothing. This somewhat cynical description does, however, seem to jibe with what many Americans believe—that is, when it comes to government and the government workforce, less is definitely more.

The British study I referenced earlier, "Engaging for Success," also attempted to answer the question of why engagement levels in government are low:

- Some public-sector leaders are simply unaware of the concept of employee engagement.
- Others do not believe it is worth considering or do not fully understand the concept and the benefits it can deliver for their organizations.
- Managers may be interested in engagement but don't know how to address it.
- Even when senior leaders emphasize employee engagement, managers may not support it or may be ill equipped to implement engagement strategies. As a result, the organizational culture is unable to improve engagement.
- Even among leaders who are concerned about employee engagement, there is great variability in the views on and commitment to engagement. Often the potential of employee engagement is underestimated. For some, engagement is an annual staff survey whose results might be acted on. For others who understand the power of engagement, a survey is just one tool in an overall approach that places employee engagement at the core of the organization's strategy.[43]

Disinterest in employee engagement is likely a symptom of a larger problem in government: the failure to truly focus on talent management as a key to organizational performance and success. Despite the common refrain, especially in the public sector, that "people are our most important resource," government organizations consistently fail to back this up with investments in their human capital. Downsizing and layoffs, leaving vacancies unfilled, eliminating training and development, and cutting back on employee benefits are all symptoms of the implicit belief, despite all the human-capital rhetoric, that employees are actually costs to be minimized, not assets to be invested in. That's one reason, according to the American Society for Training and Development, government agencies usually rank near the bottom in training expenditures as a percentage of payroll.[44]

This laissez-faire attitude also applies to managers and supervisors who are often too busy with their own work to make sure their employees understand their roles and jobs and have the support and resources to develop their capabilities. Too often, particularly in government, we promote good performers into supervisory positions because of their technical skills and performance as individual contributors—not their potential to be strong leaders. The outcome is poor leadership, leading to an increasingly disaffected and disengaged public-sector workforce.

IT'S ABOUT LEADERSHIP

It comes down to leadership. Leaders need to take action to attract, develop, and retain talent and drive higher levels of employee engagement. Study after study has reached essentially this conclusion. Even though the way in which specific drivers of engagement are described and operationalized differ depending on the research and the organization that has conducted it, these drivers (sometimes called *enablers*) all revolve around leadership. For example, the Partnership for Public Service's analyses of the key drivers of federal government employee satisfaction have consistently shown that the number one driver of employee satisfaction (which, as we discussed earlier, is correlated with engagement) is leadership. In six separate sets of rankings over a nine-year period, leadership has been, by far, the number one key driver each time.

Yet some managers seem to be blissfully unaware of the sad state of employee engagement. A British study found that "although nearly three in four leaders rate their levels of staff engagement as above average, it appears that the vast majority of them are guessing."[45] The results from large surveys conducted by organizations like Gallup, the MSPB, and OPM clearly show that managers believe that employee-engagement levels are higher than they actually are. Sort of like Garrison Keillor's Lake Wobegon, where every child is above average.

In a U.S. case study, for example, the director of a city government department explained that the department formerly conducted employee surveys to gauge employee engagement and satisfaction but doesn't any more. According to the director, employee surveys are not necessary in his department, mainly because employee retention is excellent. Employees are happy and morale is good, and leaders interact with all employees regularly to gauge their satisfaction. The director gave his department an "A" for employee engagement and satisfaction, based on employee retention and personal feedback he gets from employees (but not on any real data).[46]

Meanwhile, a county government executive estimated that her county's engagement score *would be* roughly 85 percent, based on interactions with county employees. According to her, a high proportion of workers appear to want to do a good job and achieve a particular level of excellence and pride in their day-to-day responsibilities.[47] She might be right but, in the absence of real data, how can she be sure?

Jack Welch, the legendary former CEO of General Electric, identified employee engagement as the most important barometer of organizational performance.[48] According to Welch, who said he spent half of his time on people issues, "You need to take the measure of employee engagement at least once a year through anonymous surveys in which people feel completely safe to speak their minds."[49] As part of his commitment to people issues, Welch prepared handwritten, two-page evaluations of every one of his direct reports—his three vice chairs plus each of the operating heads of GE's 12 businesses.[50] If Jack Welch could successfully run one of the largest and most successful corporations in the world and still find time for employee development, why can't the rest of us, who probably have a little less responsibility than he did?

The evidence clearly shows that employee engagement is low in most organizations, and the managers who "don't get it" are the ones who must act to improve it. For example, let's take a look at the employee survey statements the MSPB used to assess employee engagement across the federal government (see box). Employees in high-engagement agencies agreed with these statements more often than employees in low-engagement organizations. The 16 statements are divided into 6 categories.[51]

U.S. Merit Systems Protection Board Employee-Engagement Survey Statements

Pride in One's Work or Workplace

1. My agency is successful at accomplishing its mission.
2. My work unit produces high-quality products and services.
3. The work I do is meaningful to me.
4. I would recommend my agency as a place to work.

Satisfaction with Leadership

5. Overall, I am satisfied with my supervisor.
6. Overall, I am satisfied with managers above my immediate supervisor.

Opportunity to Perform Well at Work

7. I know what is expected of me on the job.
8. My job makes good use of my skills and abilities.
9. I have the resources to do my job well.
10. I have sufficient opportunities (such as challenging assignments or projects) to earn a high performance rating.

Satisfaction with the Recognition Received

11. Recognition and rewards are based on performance in my work unit.
12. I am satisfied with the recognition and rewards I receive for my work.

Prospects for Future Personal and Professional Growth

13. I am given a real opportunity to improve my skills in my organization.

Positive Work Environment with Some Focus on Teamwork

14. I am treated with respect at work.
15. My opinions count at work.
16. A spirit of cooperation and teamwork exists in my work unit.

An agency's leaders, managers, and supervisors can influence most of the factors embedded in these statements. In addition to the direct statements about satisfaction with supervisors and managers, the statements in the other categories—pride in the organization, opportunity to perform well at work, satisfaction with recognition, prospects for future personal and professional growth, and positive work environment with focus on teamwork—can all be influenced by the manager or supervisor.

The OPM engagement index is based on 15 statements in three areas—leadership, supervision, and "intrinsic work experience" (see box).[52] The OPM engagement statements (like the statements in the MSPB and other engagement surveys) focus, directly or indirectly, on the role, influence, and behaviors of managers and supervisors.

U.S. Office of Personnel Management Engagement Index Statements

Leaders Lead: Employees' Perceptions of the Integrity of Leadership, as Well as Leadership Behaviors Such as Communication and Workforce Motivation

1. In my organization, leaders generate high levels of motivation and commitment in the workforce.
2. My organization's leaders maintain high standards of honesty and integrity.

3. Managers communicate the goals and priorities of the organization.
4. Overall, how good a job do you feel is being done by the manager directly above your immediate supervisor/team leader?
5. I have a high level of respect for my organization's senior leaders.

Supervisors: The Interpersonal Relationship Between Worker and Supervisor, Including Trust, Respect, and Support

6. Supervisors/team leaders in my work unit support employee development.
7. My supervisor/team leader listens to what I have to say.
8. My supervisor/team leader treats me with respect.
9. I have trust and confidence in my supervisor.
10. Overall, how good a job do you feel is being done by your immediate supervisor/team leader?

Intrinsic Work Experience: Employees' Feelings of Motivation and Competency Relating to Their Role in the Workplace

11. I feel encouraged to come up with new and better ways of doing things.
12. My work gives me a feeling of personal accomplishment.
13. I know what is expected of me on the job.
14. My talents are used well in the workplace.
15. I know how my work relates to the agency's goals and priorities.

Florida International University, a public university, evaluated engagement challenges and opportunities and found that supervisors were often the greatest impediment to increasing morale. The university concluded that supervisors and managers simply didn't have the skills to be effective leaders and therefore were not equipped to improve engagement.[53]

Therefore, if a government organization decides that engagement is a priority, taking action must start with top leadership and then extend to managers and supervisors. They should be held responsible and accountable for achieving and maintaining high levels of engagement. Leaders must also understand how to make this happen.

The overall low level of engagement in government, accentuated by the apparent lack of interest by many managers in improving engagement, is alarming. However, my glass-is-half-full take on this situation is that it's really a bad news–good news story. The low levels of engagement in government coupled with the power of high engagement creates a huge potential to improve engagement and therefore performance.

We'll explore *how* we can achieve this later in the book. First, however, we need to focus on *why* the public sector is different from the private sector and what that means for employee engagement.

Chapter 4

The Special Case of Public Service and How This Affects Engagement and Efforts to Improve It

I began this book by emphasizing that this is a particularly tough time to work in government. Persistent attacks on government can't help but affect the morale and engagement of public-sector employees. Despite well-publicized private-sector fiascos such as Enron, the BP oil spill, and the subprime mortgage meltdown, we don't see similar attacks on rank-and-file private-sector employees.

I've worked in or with government for almost 40 years, at federal, state, and local levels, and now at a major public university—the University of Wisconsin. I've devoted my career to public service because I believe in government and the ability of government to help the people we serve improve their lives. Even at the University of Wisconsin, our teaching and research mission is grounded in the "Wisconsin idea": Our university should be a resource for the public and enhance the quality of life in our state, nation, and world.

In my view, very few—if any—other careers offer the same kinds of opportunities to make a difference as careers in the public sector.

Yet public opinion surveys clearly show the negative impact of attacks on government. According to the Pew Research Center, in April 2012 the favorable rating for the federal government fell to just 33 percent, the lowest in 15 years, with nearly two-thirds of the public having an unfavorable view.[1] Ratings of state governments remained barely positive (52 percent favorable). The public's opinion of local government was more favorable (positive by a roughly two-to-one margin).

While state and local governments polled better than the federal government, the trend for these sectors has been steadily downhill since 2002. At that time, roughly two-thirds of Americans had favorable opinions of federal, state, and local government.

Digging deeper, the 2012 Pew survey showed that most Americans believed their state government was not careful with their money (56 percent) and was generally inefficient (51 percent). While more said their state government was honest rather than corrupt (49 percent versus 37 percent), a majority (54 percent) said the federal government was mostly corrupt—not just inefficient or ineffective or bloated, but corrupt! Very disturbing.

According to Max Stier, CEO of the nonprofit Partnership for Public Service, as a result of attacks on government, "employee morale is in decline, the desirability of public service has diminished and trust in government is at an all-time low."[2]

Consider this other evidence:

- According to an article on the Society for Human Resource Management website, the criticism directed at public servants—and its impacts on government budgets—is leading to a "storm of disengagement" among government employees.[3]
- In a 2012 survey by the Center for State and Local Government Excellence, state and local government officials reported that the number one issue they faced was the public perception of government workers.[4]
- According to an online survey of state and local government agencies conducted in 2012 by the payroll firm ADP and the International Public Management Association for HR, nearly

all survey respondents reported that employee morale and engagement have sharply declined in the last few years.[5]

- A 2012 survey by the National Association of Colleges and Employers (NACE) revealed that just 6 percent of college students surveyed plan to work in local, state, or federal government. This is the lowest percentage since NACE first started asking this question annually in 2008.[6] This result clearly shows the harmful impact of government bashing on the public service's ability to attract talent.

Where Did the Expression "Close Enough for Government Work" Come From?

Those of us who work in government cringe when we hear someone use this clearly derogatory term. But where did it come from? Although the etymology of this expression is not entirely clear, one explanation is that it originated during World War II, when the industrial sector began to produce large quantities of war-related materials for the federal government. At that time, so the story goes, "close enough for government work" meant that government had the highest and most-exacting standards. If the work could pass government inspection, it could meet any benchmark. In other words, "Finally, it's close enough for government work."

Ironically, however, over time the expression has taken on a highly negative connotation.

MISCONCEPTIONS ABOUT GOVERNMENT

The criticism of government has also resulted in (or perhaps resulted from) some fundamental misconceptions about the size and function of government. For example, as President Obama noted, "I got a letter the other day from a woman. She said, 'I don't want government-run health care. I don't want socialized medicine. And don't touch my Medicare.'"[7]

Here's another example:

> A 59-year-old man who earns $39,000 a year said he does not need any help from the federal government. He says that too many Americans lean on taxpayers rather than living within their means. Yet for four years, this guy has counted on a payment of several thousand dollars from the federal government, a subsidy for working families called the earned-income tax credit. He has also signed up his three school-age children to eat free breakfast and lunch at federal expense. And Medicare paid for his mother, 88, to have hip surgery twice.[8]

Another misconception is that the size of the government workforce has exploded. The fact is that, since 2009, government workforces across the United States have shed a total of 642,000 jobs.[9] And since 1975, the percentage of all jobs in the United States that are in the public sector has fallen from 19.2 to 17.3 percent.[10]

Take the federal government, for example—the nation's largest employer and the target of much of the criticism about "bloated government." Excluding the postal service, there were about 2.1 million federal employees in 2012. This workforce is actually smaller now than it was in 1967, at the height of Lyndon Johnson's Great Society, even though today the federal government serves 100 million more Americans than it did in 1967.[11]

Despite federal hiring fueled by the war on terror (e.g., creation of the Department of Homeland Security), the per capita ratio of federal government employees to the general U.S. population has actually declined in the last 50 years.

In state government, there are slightly fewer employees now than there were 20 years ago.[12] The size of the local government workforce has also been declining. According to the 2012 survey by the Center for State and Local Government Excellence, more than half the survey respondents (most of whom are local government officials) reported that their workforces were at least 5 percent smaller in 2012 than they were in 2008.[13]

The shrinking of government is partially the result of increased retirements as baby boomers head toward the exits. For example, federal government retirements in 2011 jumped 24 percent compared to 2010[14] and increased again in 2012.[15]

In state government, according to the Center for State and Local Government Excellence:

> Local governments are experiencing a wave of retirements in an era of sustained fiscal constraints. They recognize that they . . . also need to identify any looming skills gaps and develop workforce strategies for the future. Such strategies includes professional development for current workers so they can fill certain key positions, as well as adjustments in human resources practices that will appeal to the next generation of public servants.[16]

While the size of the public-sector workforce has not grown, the size of the workforce of contractors who support government has expanded dramatically. In fiscal year 2011, for example, federal agencies spent $496 billion on contracts (and that was less than the previous years, when the value of federal contracting was as high as $537 billion). Only a decade earlier, federal contracting was "only" $206 billion. And these totals don't include contracts awarded by state and local governments. So, in essence, much of the work of government has been privatized.

PUBLIC VS. PRIVATE—SAME OR DIFFERENT?

In response to the criticisms of government and the misperceptions about the growth of government, we often hear the refrain, "run government like a business." This regularly comes from politicians calling for reform of what they consider to be government waste, inefficiency, and ineffectiveness.

And when scandals erupt in government, like the indefensible waste and behavior by U.S. General Services Administration (GSA) officials who put on a series of over-the-top conferences in Las Vegas in 2011, voices for reform reach a fever pitch. One congressman's reaction to the GSA misdeeds was to propose privatizing some of the agency's work. Aside from the very legitimate concerns about wasting taxpayer dollars, the implication seems to be that if government operated more like the private sector, these kinds of behaviors wouldn't occur.

There is evidence to the contrary, however, including private-sector scandals like the mortgage meltdown or JP Morgan Chase's $2 billion hedge fund loss in 2012, which its CEO admitted was an "egregious failure" to manage risk. And remember the disgraced head of Tyco, Dennis Kozlowksi, who put on a million-dollar birthday bash for his wife—paid for by his company and its stockholders—that included a personal Jimmy Buffett concert? Government can do without this type of "efficiency."

As one observer said about state government, "When I hear people talk about how they are going to run the state like a business, my response is that you have to run the state better than you run a business, because you have to do so much more with less resources."[17] Government leaders also have less unilateral power to make decisions and implement change than private-sector leaders.

In *If We Can Put a Man on the Moon*, the authors compare getting things done in government to the Greek myth about Sisyphus, who was doomed to a lifetime of pushing a boulder up a hill, only to have it roll back down again before it reached the top. The book's authors refer to a "Sisyphus trap" in government:

> Public sector leaders fall into the Sisyphus trap when they fail to fully comprehend the special challenges of the public sector terrain. [They] believe they can achieve results simply by devising the right strategy or passing the

> right law. They miss a critical ingredient for success because the problem of getting things done in government isn't merely a systems problem. It isn't merely a policy problem. It's a human problem as well.[18]

In other words, to my way of thinking, this is an employee-engagement problem.

The National Performance Review in the 1990s was an attempt to reinvent the federal government and create a government that "works better and costs less." As a result of the review, the size of the federal workforce was reduced by 330,000 positions between 1993 and 1998.[19] However, as Paul Light (formerly of the Brookings Institution and a longtime observer of government) has pointed out, the services previously provided by these federal government employees were not eliminated.[20] Instead, this work was transferred to contractors (the shadow government, now a $500-billion-a-year business) or state and local government (i.e., largely through "unfunded mandates"). Because, after all, the public wants leaner and more efficient government (who wouldn't?) but balks at cuts that would produce real service reductions.

While the "reinventing government" movement achieved some successes, mostly shedding federal government employees, there is no consensus that it actually produced a government "that works better and costs less."

Where Did the Term Bureaucrat Originate?

Another negative term tossed around about government is *bureaucrat* (often preceded by *faceless* or *nameless*). Max Weber (1864–1920), a German sociologist, political economist, and administrative scholar, first coined the term *bureaucracy.* He defined *bureaucracy* as an organizational structure designed to follow the rules, laws, ideas, and functions of the institution it serves. According to Weber, bureaucrats are expected to be loyal to the state and the public good rather than to any particular ruler. In addition, bureaucracies follow rules and patterns of administration that separate them from the rest of society. Weber idealized the bureaucracy as the most efficient form of organization—a far cry from what the term has come to mean today.

The answer to the question about whether private-sector management practices can seamlessly translate to government has important implications for employee engagement. If the leadership challenges in the public and private sectors are essentially the same and the solutions are also the same, then approaches to improving employee engagement should also be the same, or at least very similar.

By now, you probably know where I'm headed. I agree that there are lessons government can learn from the private sector about how to operate more effectively and efficiently. (Do we really need to have seemingly endless meetings in government about *everything*?) However, I also think the reverse is true: The private sector can also learn from government, perhaps about persevering to accomplish critical missions despite facing serious challenges and obstacles.

I also believe there are some fundamental and important differences between the public and private sectors. These differences make managing in government different (and in some ways more difficult) than in the private sector. The differences also have important implications for employee engagement, including my view that an engaged workforce is actually more critical in government. This is especially true now, with government being demeaned while at the same time also being challenged to handle the toughest jobs and under pressure to operate more effectively and efficiently despite shrinking budgets and workforces.

That may be why one of the cover articles in the October 2012 issue of *Fortune* magazine was titled, "Does Ray Kelly Have the World's Toughest Job?" The *Fortune* writer said this about Kelly, the New York City police commissioner (who, by the way, I've met briefly twice and is a very gracious guy):

> Kelly may have the toughest job there is. The NYPD is the biggest police force in the country. Running it is not unlike running a midsize Fortune 500 company—except that the stakes are much, much higher. Kelly manages a $4.9 billion budget, 250 buildings, 7,000 pieces of rolling stock, and 50,000 employees, most of whom carry handguns. One of his operating units is devoted to fighting terrorism. Like a CEO, he contends with a vast and varied cast of stakeholders who scrutinize his every move, but the metrics by which his performance is measured all have to do with life and death.[21]

So, according to this article, the toughest job in the world is a government job where the stakes are "much, much higher" than running a corporation. Quite a tribute to public service from *Fortune*, a publication focused on the private sector. It's worth emphasizing that Kelly operates in perhaps the toughest fishbowl environment possible—a high-visibility job where even small mistakes will generate intense criticism in the media, in city hall, and on the streets of New York City.

In a 2013 *New York Times* op-ed piece, David Rothkopf, who has served in senior-level positions in both the private and public sectors, wrote, "Public sector management poses its own unique challenges. Great business leaders and great governmental leaders require different personalities, skill sets, tactics and backgrounds."[22]

KEY DIFFERENCES BETWEEN THE PUBLIC AND PRIVATE SECTORS

If government is indeed different from the private sector, then public-sector managers must approach engagement differently than their private-sector counterparts. I believe managing in government is different from managing in the private sector in at least 11 key dimensions that affect employee engagement and therefore efforts to improve it:

1. An environment of broadscale attacks on government and government employees
2. Political leadership that can change frequently
3. Hard-to-measure goals and impacts
4. Complicated, inefficient, rule-bound, and sometimes irrational decision making
5. Multiple external stakeholders with power and influence
6. An older, more educated, and more white-collar workforce
7. Strong civil-service rules and employee protections, plus superior benefits
8. Limited financial tools and incentives to influence employee behavior
9. Strong union influence
10. Public visibility of government actions
11. Different employee motivations (i.e., public-service motivation)

As we review these differences, it's also important to keep in mind the fundamental elements of employee engagement—specifically, according to U.S. Merit Systems Protection Board research, how employees feel about their workplaces. This includes pride in the workplace or work, satisfaction with leadership, the opportunity to perform well at work, satisfaction with recognition received, prospects for future personal and professional growth, and a positive work environment. Each of the 11 public-private differences affects the key dimensions of engagement. In the rest of this chapter, I outline these differences and how they affect employee engagement. Then, more important, and more optimistically, in Chapter 5 I discuss how managers can address these issues and therefore improve employee engagement.

ATTACKS ON GOVERNMENT AND GOVERNMENT EMPLOYEES

First, foremost, and most harmful to employee engagement are attacks on government. Critics include politicians, the media, the public, and other organizations—all of whom repeatedly characterize public servants as overpaid and underworked bureaucrats. This almost constant drumbeat of criticism is disheartening to public servants and can be deadly to employee engagement, as illustrated by the survey data provided earlier in this chapter.

These attacks erode employees' pride in their agencies—a strong element of engagement. It's hard to be proud of your work or organization and by extension yourself when your employer and your work are being repeatedly criticized. It's also hard not to take these criticisms personally. Who wants to go to a social event, explain to someone you've just met that you work for the government, and then worry about how the person will react? That is, with an awkward silence or a tirade about waste and inefficiency in government? I recall a conversation I had with an accountant who asked me what I did for a living. At that time, I worked for the Partnership for Public Service, so I replied that I was vice president of a nonprofit dedicated to improving the effectiveness of government. His reply? "That can't be too hard." In other words, it was a target-rich environment.

Attacks on government have also morphed into tangible impacts—delays in passing budgets, cuts when budgets do pass, mandatory furloughs, reduced pay and benefits, and downsizing and layoffs. Here in Wisconsin, government employees have taken a verbal beating and had their collective bargaining rights drastically curtailed. Moreover, increases in Wisconsin public employees' contributions to benefits program resulted in the equivalent of an 8 percent pay cut. The national debate now continues over public-sector pensions (namely, if they are too rich for taxpayers to afford).

No wonder organizations like the Society for Human Resource Management, the International Public Management Association for Human Resources, the Center for State and Local Government Excellence, and the Partnership for Public Service have all concluded that the criticism leveled at public servants across the country—and the budget impacts of these attacks—leads to disengagement among government employees. For example, as cited previously, the number one concern identified in a 2012 survey of state and local government agencies was the public perception of government workers.

It's easy to see how attacks on government and government employees (and resulting cuts in budgets and staff) can affect engagement. For example, antigovernment animus and its tangible impacts can negatively affect key engagement factors like pride in the work or workplace, satisfaction with leadership, the opportunity to perform well at work, satisfaction with recognition received (especially with pay and benefits cuts), prospects for future personal and professional growth, and especially a positive work environment.

Moreover, attacks on government are usually outside the organizations' and managers' control, and government is often not adept at responding. Many agencies lack public relations savvy and fear that PR efforts will be counterproductive anyway, viewed by the public as waste of taxpayer money. This inability to portray a positive image about government work can cause employees to feel ineffective, disengaged, and even hopeless.

Despite the critical need for new talent in government, the attacks on government also discourage talented people from entering public service.

My own daughter is an example. Like many in her millennial generation, she is committed to public service. However, she chose to act on that commitment by working for Teach for America, a nonprofit organization. After her two-year stint with Teach for America, she was interested in applying to the U.S. Department of Education, a logical step, but was frustrated and repelled by the virtually impenetrable language used to describe the department's work and job opportunities. Instead, she went to work as a government consultant for a large consulting firm.

Moving the Needle of Public Opinion About Government, One Person at a Time

Research jointly conducted by the Partnership for Public Service and Gallup showed that when public servants deliver responsive service to individual citizens, those citizens are significantly more likely to have positive views about government in general.[23] In this research, Gallup surveyed a random sample of Americans and found that more than three-quarters said they had some type of direct contact with a federal agency, with 69 percent reporting that the interaction occurred in the past six months. Those who came into direct contact with the federal government were much more likely to view that interaction favorably (32 percent) than unfavorably (18 percent).

While this is good news for government, the more important finding from this research is that Americans who are satisfied with their individual interactions with federal agencies are three times more likely to give a positive rating to the federal government *overall* than those who were dissatisfied with their interactions (41 percent versus 14 percent).

The take-away is that individual public interactions with government are therefore key touch points for creating positive experiences that then translate into more positive feelings about government overall. In other words, public servants who are engaged and committed to delivering responsive service can move the needle of public opinion about government in general—more evidence that employee engagement matters and that public-sector managers should focus on improving it.

POLITICAL LEADERSHIP THAT CAN CHANGE FREQUENTLY

Many government agencies are led by elected or politically appointed leaders with brief tenures, short-term perspectives, and politically driven policy goals and agendas. It's not unusual for political appointees to serve for only a year or two, enhance their résumés, and then leave, often frustrated by their inability to quickly implement large-scale change. In the federal government, for example, the average tenure of a political appointee from 1969 to 2000 was fewer than 30 months.[24]

Compared to the private sector, this temporary political leadership in government makes it harder to build and sustain initiatives like employee engagement. In particular, leadership changes can affect engagement triggers like satisfaction with leadership, pride in the work or workplace, input to decisions, and opportunity to perform well at work.

Leadership that comes and goes puts extra pressure on career executives and managers (the levels below political appointees) to provide organizational stability and create an environment conducive to employee engagement. Sure, there is turnover in the executive suites in business too, but it's less frequent than in government and rarely drives the kind of 180-degree change that occurs when the other political party takes control of a government agency. Plus, in the private sector, leadership transition is often the result of succession planning that has intentionally and carefully groomed the next leader(s). This is not possible with political changeovers in government. Policies put in place during the tenure of one political party usually change, often quickly and dramatically, when the other party takes over.

One writer titled his analysis of federal government political appointees "Amateur Government" to reflect the reality that many political appointees have little, if any, experience running large government operations or, for some, any large operation at all.[25]

Even at the career levels of government, succession planning is rare, in part because of the fear that this kind of planning would amount to "preselection" for promotions and would therefore violate civil-service rules that mandate open competition for vacancies.

Succession Planning in Government: Can It Be Done?

Many public-sector organizations shy away from succession planning because of fears that developing successors for key positions would be considered preselection and therefore violate civil-service rules requiring open competition for vacancies. For most government organizations, the version of succession planning common in the private sector, often involving identifying high-potential employees and then grooming them for advancement, would likely run afoul of civil-service principles.

But there are succession-planning approaches that can work within the rules and culture of government. In fact, given that the government workforce is older, on average, than the private-sector workforce, it's not a stretch to argue that succession planning is at least as important in government as in other sectors.

Public-sector succession-planning programs are typically designed as leadership development programs that allow candidates to apply to be selected. Those selected then go through development programs that can include approaches such as competency assessments, formal training sessions and workshops, job rotations inside and outside the home organization, feedback, mentoring and coaching, and perhaps even an "action learning" project that enables the prospective executives to apply what they have learned to actual challenges in their organizations.

One example is the federal government's Senior Executive Service (SES) Candidate Development Program, which competitively selects midlevel managers and then prepares them to compete for positions in the federal civil service's highest career level. There are no guarantees of promotion—after completing the program, which can last for up to two years, graduates must apply for specific SES positions. Some state and local governments have comparable programs. The key differences between public- and private-sector succession planning are that government programs typically require competition to be selected and then don't guarantee that graduates will be promoted. But these programs are still designed to prepare the next generation of government leaders.

In government, frequent top-level turnover makes engagement of the rank and file critically important to smoothly maintain effective operations despite new leaders and new policies. But the irony is that political turnover also makes it more difficult to implement and sustain long-term workforce initiatives such as employee engagement. A critical factor in successful employee-engagement initiatives is sustained top-level support.

In the federal government, the Securities and Exchange Commission's (SEC) score in the 2010 "Best Places to Work in the Federal Government" rankings dropped by 6.4 percent, plummeting the SEC to rank 24 out of 32 large federal agencies. SEC's scores declined in dimensions that included employees' perceptions of senior leaders and their own sense of empowerment. A factor that likely contributed to the drop in SEC's score was that nearly every division underwent a change in senior leadership between 2009 and 2010, and several of these leadership changes were accompanied by major reorganizations. SEC continues to struggle, ranking 19 out of 22 midsize agencies in the 2012 "Best Places" rankings.[26]

Elected or appointed political leaders (even if competent and well-intentioned) often focus on near-term results, which means new agency priorities, policies, and agendas. In the city of Minneapolis, which has conducted employee-engagement surveys since 2004, frequent turnover in appointed department directors was a big challenge to sustaining the long-term focus on the engagement action plans developed in response to survey results. Frequent leadership changes meant virtually restarting the engagement initiative every time a new director was appointed. Political turnover like this makes it difficult to connect the dots that are critical to engagement, which include the following:

- Linking the work of individual employees to agency mission/goals and long-term agendas
- Clearly articulating employee expectations/goals
- Involving employees in decision making
- Building and maintaining pride in the organization

Newly installed political leadership can also put career managers and supervisors in difficult situations by pressuring them to advocate and quickly implement policies that are major shifts from the previous administration's (or leader's) policies. Examples include situations where regulatory agencies have abruptly morphed from strictly enforcing rules to advocating for the industry they regulate. Shifts like these erode key drivers of engagement such as confidence in and respect for leaders and supervisors, pride in the organization, and input to decisions.

In Wisconsin, for example, this type of scenario played out at the state Department of Natural Resources (DNR), when a probusiness governor took office in 2011. The mission of the Wisconsin DNR is to preserve and enhance the natural resources of Wisconsin, in part by enforcing laws that protect the people and resources of the state. During the first year of the new administration, DNR's issuance of violation notices reached a 12-year low. Referrals to the Wisconsin Department of Justice for prosecution were also down dramatically, from a 12-year annual average of 65 to 21. The newly appointed department secretary explained that the department's new philosophy was to emphasize cooperating with business and bringing violators into voluntary compliance, making them "self-regulators."[27]

Almost literally overnight, this regulatory agency's posture abruptly changed as the new administration took over. Whether you agree with the new philosophy or not, imagine the impact on the engagement of the rank and file who were committed to implementing the "old" strategy.

Another factor working against employee engagement is the unfortunate but seemingly inherent mistrust between elected/appointed officials and career employees. The political figures who take charge often see the career folks as intractable bureaucrats who resist change, no matter what. Career employees, on the other hand, often view new political leaders as novices and opportunists eager to make their mark quickly, who are here today and gone tomorrow and therefore don't really care about the career public servants in their agencies. This conflict filters down to frontline supervisors versus rank-and-file employees. The result can be antagonism and employee disengagement.

Dwight Ink, a retired civil servant who served seven presidents, puts it this way:

> The career civil service is the only vehicle through which a president can govern. Yet we continue to see instance after instance of White House staff and agency (politically appointed) leaders not only failing to reach out to the men and women on whom their political success will

largely rest but also quickly alienating them through distrust and marginalizing their roles.[28]

This atmosphere of mistrust extends to other levels of government. Craig Benson, a multimillionaire high-tech CEO, was elected governor of New Hampshire in 2002 by promising to run the state like a billion-dollar corporation. On his first day in office, he hosted an inauguration-day breakfast attended by hundreds of state employees. During this event, he told this audience of public servants, "I bet you that not many people in this room have been asked to bring their brains with them to work in a long time."[29] According to the authors of *If We Can Put a Man on the Moon*, with these words, the new governor managed to achieve a rare political trifecta—he was insulting, condescending, and arrogant, all at the same time. Two years later, Benson was defeated in his reelection bid.

This mistrust between elected and appointed officials and career public servants can also result in minimal investments in employee development—another critical aspect of employee engagement. In contrast to private-sector leaders who have longer-term time horizons, elected and appointed officials are often reluctant to invest in developing agency staff. That's because helping employees develop their long-term capabilities does not help political leaders achieve their short-term policy or political agendas, even though employee development is a key driver of employee engagement. That may be one reason government has trailed the private sector in training expenditures.[30]

GOALS AND IMPACTS OF GOVERNMENT THAT ARE HARD TO IDENTIFY AND MEASURE

The goals of public-sector organizations are harder to articulate and measure than in the business world. While most private-sector organizations need to focus on generating revenue and profits, thereby delivering returns to their owners and shareholders, government's goals are often hard to clearly identify and measure in transparent and meaningful ways. The purpose of most public-sector organizations is not to generate revenue but to achieve goals that collectively provide for the common good. This can mean defending the nation, enforcing laws, educating our children, putting people back to work, caring for an aging population, or solving problems like poverty and homelessness. It can also mean more mundane chores like collecting trash, fixing potholes, removing snow, or making sure that sewer systems operate the way they should. These tasks are mundane but essential to the quality of our lives and often go unnoticed and unappreciated by the public—until something goes wrong.

While the axiom "what you measure is what gets done" also applies to government, developing valid measures is much more elusive in the public versus the private sector. Take corrections (prisons), for example. How do departments of corrections measure their impacts? How do we measure the public's satisfaction with prisons? Should we count the number of successful prison breaks? Can corrections departments be held accountable for high recidivism rates, which are driven by many factors, including socioeconomic conditions that corrections departments can't influence?

Another public-sector measurement challenge is in education. It seems as if the entire nation is embroiled in a highly charged debate about the goals of our educational system, particularly in K–12, and how to measure success. What are students learning, how well are our teachers teaching and how do we measure the quality of our schools?

The No Child Left Behind Act was designed to help answer these questions, but now, a decade after the law was enacted, there is still disagreement about how to measure the quality of the education our children are receiving and how to make teachers accountable. If students, particularly from low-income and disadvantaged homes, come to school hungry after escaping from difficult, often single-parent home environments, how can we hold teachers accountable for overcoming these barriers to educational progress?

My intent here is not to try to answer the questions surrounding how to measure the quality of government services or public education. Others are working on that. Instead, I simply mean to point out how difficult it can be to agree on, and then measure, the desired outcomes of government.

Ambiguous, changeable, and hard-to-measure goals create barriers to individual employee commitment and motivation, and therefore engagement. Specifically, it is difficult to clearly link individual employees' jobs, tasks, and performance goals/expectations to the agency mission and goals when the latter are not clear, or they abruptly change. Plus, because it is often hard to empirically demonstrate that the work of a government agency is making a real difference, employees may question if they're really having an impact. They often don't have a line of sight between their work and what their agency is accomplishing.

Despite calls for more efficiency in government ("run it like a business"), the public sector was not built for efficiency. Instead, government was expressly designed with checks and balances to achieve consensus and compromise. This takes time, is difficult to measure, and is often inefficient.

COMPLICATED, INEFFICIENT, RULE-BOUND, AND SOMETIMES IRRATIONAL (I.E., POLITICAL) DECISION MAKING

The political agendas that drive government agencies also drive decision making. This results in an often complicated and seemingly subjective decision-making process that challenges efforts to improve employee engagement.

Decision making that is politically based and sometimes may even seem irrational affects drivers of engagement such as employee confidence in, and satisfaction with, supervisors, managers, and senior leaders; involvement in decisions ("my opinion counts"); and pride in the agency. The government decision-making process also dampens employee creativity and risk taking because of uncertainty about (and mistrust of) how decisions will ultimately be made—and the high price of failure.

Government agency decisions are also influenced by the "optics" of how decisions will play out with the media, the public, and the other political party. I often think of when a state government executive told me that his marching orders from the governor in the months leading up to a gubernatorial election were to "make no waves."

I also recall when I was the administrator of the Wisconsin civil-service system and a colleague and I were discussing with a state senator our proposal to amend the civil-service "rule of five" law that limited all hiring managers to interviewing only the five highest-scoring candidates from civil-service exams. The law was so restrictive that if the applicants with the fifth- and sixth-highest scores were tied, even to the one-hundredth of a point, we had to figure out a way to break the tie.

We gave this senator what we thought was a very logical and compelling argument that this highly restrictive law needed to be changed. After patiently listening to our pitch, he told us that he absolutely agreed. However, he couldn't support us because the governor who had proposed this change was in the other political party. It took three legislative sessions before we were finally able to convince the legislature to eliminate that ancient rule.

Laws concerning freedom of information and open meetings also allow the media and the public to have broad access to information not only on government decisions themselves but also on how these decisions are made. More on this later.

This decision-making environment is further constrained by government red tape and rules that restrict actions and flexibility in areas like personnel, including civil-service laws that strictly control hiring and firing. Restrictions also cover procurement, which someone who knows once described to me as "the only thing in government more screwed up than HR." Consider the Federal Acquisition Regulations: more than 2,000 pages of requirements and processes about what to buy and how to buy it.

This environment makes it hard to get things done, and employees who feel they can't get things done are not likely to be engaged. They must constantly consider all the rules and various stakeholders, assessing possible pitfalls. This sacrifices results for process. A state government executive once remarked to me, "I like process." Compare that to what *Fortune* magazine described as the need for businesses to hire people with a "bias for action."

For many reasons, including rules, politics, and the openness of government decisions to the public and media, public managers have to think twice—and sometimes more than that—before making decisions. They have to assess not only the business benefits and risks but also the political impacts and optics of what they're about to do. Private-sector decision makers are not as encumbered by these factors.

At the University of Wisconsin, the state legislature gave us the unprecedented freedom to design an entirely new HR system for our public university—that is, the opportunity to design a personnel system to meet the needs of a world-class higher education institution, free from the often-rigid restrictions of the state civil-service system. Our initial enthusiasm was dampened, however, when we realized how many stakeholders with decision-making authority or influence we had to convince to sign off on our HR redesign plan.

First we had to navigate through our shared governance system, which, by law, gives three separate groups—faculty, nonfaculty academic staff, and students—the right to formally weigh in on major changes like this. We also had to vet the proposal with multiple labor organizations; civil-service employees; deans and department directors; the University of Wisconsin System administration, which governs our 26-campus state system; the board of regents; and, finally, the state legislature. Each of these stakeholders had its own, often conflicting, agendas. As one of our colleagues described it, "A university is the only place where a 10–1 committee vote is a tie." Plus, this entire process played out under close media scrutiny.

As we repeatedly told our chancellor, if the goal was to create a system that would please everyone, we'd be wasting our time.

Here's one example of the complexity of our decision making. Some faculty members were lobbying for more market- and performance-based compensation to attract, reward, and retain world-class talent in areas like stem cell research, which University of Wisconsin scientists helped pioneer. According to these faculty members, we needed new and more flexible compensation tools to attract and retain these researchers.

On the other hand, our labor groups, still reeling from the governor's actions to limit their collective bargaining rights and increase their members' benefits contributions, resisted performance-based pay. They were particularly wary about giving their supervisors authority over their pay raises. The labor groups lobbied hard (including in the press) for across-the-board pay raises to make up for years of no pay raises, as well as recently enacted increased contributions to retirement and health care that effectively reduced base pay by about 8 percent. Then, if there was any money left over, it could go for performance-based raises or bonuses. Threading the needle between these two diametrically opposed views was a tough challenge.

The complicated and sometimes irrational decision-making process makes it harder to legitimately involve employees in decision making, a key driver of engagement. Employees' opinions about how to achieve agency goals and how to get the work of their organizations done more efficiently and effectively can be trumped by political considerations. This makes it far more difficult to explain and justify decisions and therefore harder to get employee buy-in—and engagement.

MULTIPLE EXTERNAL STAKEHOLDERS WHO HAVE CONTROL AND INFLUENCE

The inherent complexity of government decision making is further complicated because public-sector organizations often find themselves in the eye of a hurricane of external forces they have little or no control over. Agencies can be influenced by pressure from external constituencies who often have conflicting goals and agendas and can drown out employees' voices. This can result in disengagement, with employees feeling their leaders lack authority and/or are ineffective and perhaps even unethical.

In addition to the appointed political officials who lead their agencies, public servants have to implement the policies and agendas of their chief executives. These executives include the president, governors, county executives, mayors, and so on, who, along with their staffs, don't hesitate to directly intervene in agency affairs. Outside forces also include the legislative branch (Congress, state legislatures, city councils, and even school boards), as well as external audit organizations like the Government Accountability Office in the federal government and legislative audit bureaus for states.

Government agencies have little or no control over the influence these leaders and organizations have, but they can nevertheless drive policies, processes, budgets, and even downsizing and layoffs. As described earlier, regulatory agencies are particularly vulnerable to these conflicting demands, both by those who want stronger regulation and by those who chafe at regulation and believe aggressive regulation constrains business and limits job creation.

Because employee engagement is driven by factors such as satisfaction with leadership and the ability to make a difference, the impacts of these outside forces can block efforts to improve engagement.

There are also the outside nonprofit watchdog organizations that exist primarily, or solely, to scrutinize government. These mostly well-intentioned groups span the political spectrum, from liberal-oriented organizations like the American Civil Liberties Union to middle-of-the-road organizations like Common Cause to conservative groups like Citizens Against Government Waste, whose mission is to "eliminate waste, mismanagement, and inefficiency in the federal government."

Each state also has its own set of government watchdog organizations. The Citizens for Responsibility and Ethics in Washington maintains a website of state government watchdog organizations that includes state-by-state listings of dozens of these organizations.[31]

In addition to the direct impacts of external organizations, especially on budgets and the workforce, there is a more subtle, but perhaps even more pernicious, impact: Employee creativity and risk taking can be hampered by fear that outside organizations—including and especially political opponents—will criticize and publicize mistakes. It's hard for leaders to improve, or even maintain, engagement (e.g., "my opinions count") when employees know their decisions and actions are subject to this kind of second guessing.

AN OLDER, MORE EDUCATED, AND MORE WHITE-COLLAR WORKFORCE

Government's chief assets are its people. In most government organizations, employee pay and benefits account for 70 percent or more of budgets. Unlike private-sector firms that can leverage assets like raw materials, machinery, patents, and other proprietary intellectual property to drive business results, most government organizations don't have these resources. What they do have is people—the public sector's main asset. This makes leadership and employee engagement more critical in government. Plus, there are major differences between public- and private-sector workforces that affect engagement.

Demographically, the government workforce is, on average, older, more educated, and more white collar than the private-sector workforce. For example, federal, state, and local government agencies have higher percentages of employees over the age of 45 than private-sector employers.[32] In local government, which employs more than 14 million workers, almost 36 percent are over the age of 50, compared to just 26 percent in the private sector.[33] Likewise, government has lower percentages of workers under the age of 30. The average age of a newly hired state government employee in 2010 was 37.[34] While I don't have anything against thirtysomethings, this is hardly a youth movement.

There are reasons why the public-sector workforce is older, including golden handcuffs like generous pension plans and retiree health care that reward longevity. At the other end of the career life cycle, government hiring qualifications often emphasize job experience, even for entry-level jobs, thus disadvantaging recent college graduates who may have great potential but not much real work experience.

Public-sector employees are also more educated than their private-sector counterparts. Specifically, in 2010, 52 percent of public-sector workers had a bachelor's, advanced, or professional degree, compared to 34 percent in the private sector. This is largely because a higher percentage of government jobs are white collar and require more education. About 55 percent of public-sector employees are employed in "management, professional, and related occupations," compared to 37 percent in the private sector.[35]

These workforce differences affect efforts to improve engagement in several ways:

- Employees who are more educated and employed in professional occupations have higher expectations about their ability—and need—to make a difference. This can be a huge advantage for government agencies committed to improving engagement.

However, it also means that government managers must work hard to satisfy their employees' need to be engaged by involving them in decisions and helping them clearly see the line of sight between their work and their agencies' results.

- Older workers tend to be more skeptical about (and therefore less willing to endorse and support) what they may perceive as fads like employee engagement. It's harder to convince them that engagement isn't just another passing fancy; instead, it is a long-term strategy worth actively supporting.
- An older workforce also means a higher percentage of older managers and supervisors who can be reluctant to give new (and younger) employees real responsibility and a voice in decision making.
- Likewise, a higher proportion of older workers can mean more friction between generations in the workplace and can also mean fewer opportunities for younger workers to develop and advance—key factors in engagement. Although I'm skeptical about the generational stereotypes that writers and consultants seem to peddle relentlessly, the research clearly shows that younger workers generally prize work-life balance above most other job characteristics. This tends to grate on baby boomer managers who question younger workers' commitment because they don't seem to want to work as hard, or as long, as "we did when we were their age."

While these demographic factors also exist in some private-sector organizations, the government workforce is older, more educated, and more white collar than the private sector. As a result, these demographic realities present higher hurdles to engagement in government than they do in the business world.

STRONG CIVIL-SERVICE RULES AND EMPLOYMENT PROTECTIONS, PLUS SUPERIOR EMPLOYEE BENEFITS

Most public-sector managers do not have the tools that private-sector managers have to influence employee behavior and performance. For example, public-sector managers can be strictly limited in how they can deal with poor performers; these restrictions don't exist in most private sector organizations. While these limitations exist for good reasons, they can also be barriers to employee engagement.

In particular, public employees have stronger job protections, even in nonunion organizations, than their private-sector colleagues. In fact, courts have ruled that most civil-service employees can only be dismissed from their jobs "for cause" (i.e., for a valid and job-related reason) unlike most private-sector employees who are "at will" and can therefore be fired for any reason except discrimination. Plus, most government employees have the right to pursue lengthy, highly legalistic processes, including appeals, when they've been dismissed (or even when they feel they've been mistreated in the workplace).

Rather than try to deal with marginal performers or disengaged employees, many public-sector supervisors/managers often tolerate them. It's not good management, but it's reality. Anyone who's worked in government personnel has stories of managers who come to HR because they want to fire an allegedly poor performer. The first question HR asks is about the employee's performance appraisals. The answer, too often, is that there aren't any appraisals for the alleged poor performer, or the appraisals are positive because "everyone around here gets good evaluations."

On the other hand, I'm not a naive defender of HR. The flip side of this poor performer kabuki occurs when a manager comes to HR with a well-documented case of poor performance, yet HR is reluctant to take action for fear that the employee will make a fuss and generate bad publicity and maybe a lawsuit.

Failing to deal with poor performers can also magnify conflicts between older and younger employees because the latter want the organization to deal with ineffective workers (who may even be their bosses). This lack of management flexibility to take swift action against poor performers creates workforce calcification that makes it harder to drive change. Employees feel they can simply wait out any change efforts. This frustrates leaders who want to make big changes fast and also frustrates rank-and-file employees who are solid performers and don't want to work with those who aren't.

At the other end of the employee life cycle, hiring in government is often a lengthy and arduous process with many hurdles that tend to discourage the best talent from competing for government jobs. Rigid civil-service hiring requirements, often involving the dreaded civil-service exam, create a double whammy: The best candidates likely have other job options and may not wait around for government agencies to make hiring decisions after lengthy processes. A public-sector HR "professional" once confided in me that the many hurdles in government hiring were intentionally designed to screen out the candidates who are not fully committed to finding a government job. In other words, only the strong—and truly patient—should survive.

The public-sector hiring process also gives experienced candidates an advantage because the candidates with the most work experience usually get the job interviews, even for entry-level jobs. This poses a disadvantage to younger candidates, including recent college graduates.

One observer wryly characterized this decidedly user-unfriendly government process as resulting in hiring "the best of the desperate."

In addition, despite attacks on public-sector benefits, most government employees still have better benefits than most private-sector workers. These include guaranteed pensions, more paid time off, and health care that is heavily employer subsidized, even for retirees. These generous benefits tend to limit government turnover, which is generally lower than in the private sector. While low turnover can be healthy, it also limits the infusion of new talent and ideas.

Rigid civil-service policies and rules can also stifle employee development, including limited opportunities to perform work that is more fulfilling and engaging; restrictions in job descriptions ("it's not in the job description"); and limits on employee advancement, job movement, and succession planning. In fact, as I described earlier in this chapter, we *can* do succession planning in government if it's designed as an inclusive development opportunity (open to qualified candidates) and not an exclusive process (preselection of the anointed).

LIMITED FINANCIAL TOOLS AND INCENTIVES TO RECOGNIZE PERFORMANCE AND INFLUENCE BEHAVIOR

For reasons that include budget cuts, pay freezes, union contracts, and strict rules on how pay is distributed, government managers do not have the same compensation and related tools to drive behavior as their private-sector peers. Government agencies usually can't provide incentives like substantial pay raises and bonuses, not to mention perks like stock options, fitness center club memberships, and car services.

Compensation inflexibility is a barrier to improving engagement because a key driver of engagement is employees' satisfaction with the recognition they receive—and compensation is an important way to recognize good performance. According to the U.S. Merit Systems Protection Board engagement survey and model, key issues to measure engagement include the following:

- "Recognition and rewards are based on performance in my work unit."
- "I am satisfied with the recognition and rewards I receive for my work."

Most public-sector employees have not received raises in years due to difficult budgets. In Wisconsin, state government employees haven't had an across-the-board pay raise since 2009. In addition, because of the criticism of public employees (underworked and overpaid with gold-plated benefits), agencies are reluctant to give pay raises for fear of political and public backlash.

For example, I was interviewed by a television news reporter about the University of Wisconsin's decision to provide modest raises and bonuses to exceptional performers. One of the questions the reporter asked me went something like this: "Why are you giving raises and bonuses? Shouldn't these employees just be happy they have jobs?"

Even when money for raises is available, union and other restrictions often prevent managers from using pay raises or bonuses as rewards or incentives. Unlike private-sector firms, few public agencies can provide meaningful pay raises or bonuses linked to performance. When there is money for raises, the more common way to distribute it is through across-the-board pay raises, often per union contracts. But how much does an across-the-board pay raise of 1 or 2 percent (when that is even possible in today's highly constrained budget environment) provide recognition or drive behavior? Not much.

STRONG UNION INFLUENCE

Unlike in the private sector, where union membership is at an all-time low (7 percent of employees in 2011[36]), union membership in the public sector reached an all-time *high* (37 percent) in 2011 (but declined slightly to 36 percent in 2012). In 2009, for the first time, the overall total number of union members in the public sector exceeded the number of union members in the private sector.[37] This was the inevitable outcome of the decades-long erosion of organized labor's influence in the private sector; at the same time, labor's influence in the government workplace has dramatically increased. Public-sector unions are therefore formidable forces that must be reckoned with, including in efforts to improve employee engagement. Even in states with laws that do not allow public employees to form unions, employee associations can exert considerable power and influence.

The relationship with public-employee unions is particularly sensitive today. In some public-sector environments, there is strong antilabor animus that, in turn, has further hardened labor's attitude toward management.

In addition, there is the danger that organized labor can view employee-engagement efforts as attempts to co-opt employees and therefore minimize union influence and power. Organized labor also has its own allies and influence (including with elected officials whom unions support financially and politically). Much more than in the private sector, public-sector engagement efforts must bring unions inside the tent.

PUBLIC VISIBILITY OF GOVERNMENT

The work of government is complex but also uniquely visible. Open meeting laws in most jurisdictions, for example, require that legislative sessions be open to the public. These meetings are even routinely televised, from congressional proceedings shown nationally on C-SPAN to city council and school board meetings on local cable networks. Besides turning our elected and appointed officials into actors and actresses, this visibility is in stark contrast to private-sector deliberations (such as board meetings), which play out largely behind closed doors.

Freedom-of-information and open-records laws also force government agencies to provide, on request, material that includes meeting minutes, memos, decision documents, emails, and even text messages.

This public visibility of government can affect employee engagement in several ways, including dampening employees' appetites for taking risks and being creative for fear that failures will be publicized and pilloried. It also has a chilling effect on interactions between supervisors and their direct reports, because documentation of these interactions, such as performance appraisals and even emails, can become public records.

I'm not arguing against government transparency. As Supreme Court Justice Louis Brandeis said, "Sunlight is said to be the best of antiseptics."[38] But the result is that the work of government is highly visible and highly scrutinized.

Imagine the impact on large corporations if the deliberations of their leaders and managers, including board members, were as transparent and available to the public. That would certainly make for interesting and revealing reading.

The public visibility of government decision making and activities has a chilling effect on risk taking and innovation. Engaged employees are the most likely to contribute innovations, according to a Gallup survey of U.S. workers.[39]

In government, however, innovation is not often rewarded. In fact, creativity can actually be penalized. In the 2012 Federal Employee Viewpoint Survey of more than 1.6 million federal employees, only 38.5 percent of respondents said creativity and innovation were rewarded in their agencies. And this percentage is down from 2011, when 41 percent responded positively to this statement.[40]

When a government agency or employee tries something new and creative and it fails (an often critical step in innovation), the failure is likely to be publicized. This creates disincentives to risk taking and innovation. The sad reality is that it's highly likely that politicians, the media, and the public will seize on and publicize government failures.

In the private sector, while failure is certainly not intentional, healthy companies look at failure as a learning opportunity that can lead to improvements and eventual success. This principle has been called "failure value" or "intelligent fast failure." While private-sector failures are not routinely publicized, unless they're enormous (e.g., JPMorgan Chase), government failure is often seen as fatal, especially by political leaders. There is not much perceived "failure value" in public-sector failure.

A Partnership for Public Service analysis concluded that six factors must be present in government agencies to stimulate innovation:

- Employees are recognized for providing high-quality products and services.
- Employees are given real opportunities to improve their skills.
- Employees are involved in decisions that affect their work.
- Employees are given a sense of personal empowerment with respect to work processes.
- Employees are provided with opportunities to demonstrate their leadership skills.
- Leaders work to gain employees' respect.[41]

If these look like the factors that drive engagement, that's because they are quite similar.

The potential visibility of managers' and supervisors' actions can also stifle candid interactions with their employees. Experienced public-sector managers understand that virtually anything they say or do is subject to freedom-of-information or open-records requests. The sad result can be a reluctance to provide candid feedback and openly discuss performance issues, even with direct reports. Given that two key drivers of engagement are "I know what is expected of me on the job" and "I am given a real opportunity to improve my skills," the absence of candid performance feedback is a barrier to improving employee engagement.

PUBLIC-SERVICE MOTIVATION

The public-private differences do not always put government at a disadvantage when it comes to employee engagement. There is strong evidence that public servants are motivated differently than private-sector employees. This public-service motivation (PSM) research suggests that government employees are attracted to public service primarily by the opportunity to make a difference in the lives of the people they serve. In psychological terms, they are "other-regarding."[42]

PSM research shows that this willingness to help others and serve the common good is a stronger motivator in the public sector than in the private sector. Public servants find meaning in work by making a positive difference in the lives of the citizens government serves. This concept is a counterweight to the assumption that people—including when they're at work—make decisions primarily to maximize their personal benefit.

That's not to suggest that our colleagues in the private sector are motivated solely by greed. I reject this kind of stereotype just as much as I reject negative stereotypes about government.

This PSM research, however, suggests that employees with high levels of public-service motivation are more likely to be satisfied and engaged than those who do not have this predisposition. To the extent that they see their agency's mission as satisfying their basic need to help others, they will commit to that mission. These public servants are more likely to be motivated by intrinsic, not extrinsic, incentives.[43]

As one county government employee put it, "I love the job I have because every day I can look back on at least one project that is going to make someone else's life safer, someone's property safer, someone's community more secure."[44]

This is good news for government. The challenge, however, is to recruit and retain employees who have a high degree of PSM and then build on this gene to drive high levels of engagement. Even though engaged employees can be made, not born, government agencies can get a head start by recruiting, hiring, developing, and retaining employees with PSM.

However, this also means that employees with public-service motivation have higher expectations about their involvement in and impact on important policy issues and socially desirable outcomes. This puts pressure on managers who want to improve engagement to (1) help employees see directly how their work contributes to the agency mission, (2) involve employees in decision making, and (3) help them grow and develop in ways that will contribute to agency mission/goals.

So the differences between the public and private sectors, while distinctive and important, are not all negative in terms of driving higher levels of engagement in government. Despite the attacks on and declining public trust in government, there is still cause for optimism. The PSM factor, in particular, can be an important asset in efforts to improve public-sector employee engagement.

CHAPTER 5

How Managers Can Respond to the Differences Between the Public and Private Sectors and Improve Engagement

The differences described in Chapter 4 have important implications for employee engagement and how to achieve and maintain it. First, and critically important, government agencies have an extreme dependence on their human capital—their talent—and this means that public-sector managers must make engagement a top priority, even more than their private-sector counterparts.

This is particularly true in today's environment of budget cuts, downsizing, attacks on public-sector benefits, very limited pay raises (or even pay cuts), and the general demand for government to do more with less. Because government managers have fewer tools to deal with these challenges, employee engagement should be front and center. And this is true across the globe, not just in the United States. The British report "Leading Culture Change: Employee Engagement and Public Service Transformation" concludes,

> In one sense, the challenge facing all local service organisations is essentially the same: to do "more with less."

The latest and most urgent version of the challenge was set by the Government's Comprehensive Spending Review in October 2010, which cut £83 billion from public spending over the next four years and required local authorities to reduce current spending by 27 percent.[1]

To fully leverage the power of engagement to help address these challenges, government agencies and managers must approach engagement—and efforts to improve it—differently than private-sector employers and managers.

For example, let's take a more detailed look at the 2012 survey by the Center for State and Local Government Excellence, which revealed that the top issues facing state and local governments are as follows, in order. (Note that 65 percent or more of respondents rated these as "important"):

- The public perception of government workers
- Retaining staff needed for core services
- Managing workloads when current staff is stretched thin but new staff cannot be hired
- Reducing employee health care costs
- Staff development
- Employee morale[2]

All but one of these issues, health care costs, are clearly linked to employee engagement. And even that issue can affect engagement if employees continue to be asked to shoulder a higher proportion of health care costs. At the University of Wisconsin, some of our lowest-paid employees gave up their health care coverage because they couldn't afford it after employee contributions were increased.

Compare the center's results to a survey of the top business challenges private-sector firms say they face: sustained and steady top-line growth, excellence in execution, and consistent execution of strategy by top management.[3] These are important challenges, to be sure, but they are different from the challenges faced by government and have different solutions. For the public sector, the top issues line up around talent and employee engagement. Small wonder, then, that in the 2012 online survey referenced earlier, conducted by ADP and the International Public Management Association for HR, nearly all survey respondents (all of whom work in state and local government) reported that employee morale and engagement have sharply declined in the last few years.

But I believe that low engagement in government is not just a bad-news story. The good news is that there is tremendous potential to improve government performance by improving employee engagement. To achieve this potential, however, government managers must act aggressively to improve engagement. They must also understand the differences between the public and private sectors, what these differences mean for engagement (as outlined in the previous chapter), and how to respond to them.

The following sections describe how public-sector managers who want to improve employee engagement can address these challenges. As you read this, however, you may recall that I said earlier that there is no one-size-fits-all approach to improving engagement. I believe that each organization, jurisdiction, and agency needs to measure and then analyze its own level of engagement, identify specific areas to improve, and then act on the data.

That process notwithstanding, however, there are also some broad principles that apply generally to employee engagement. For example, the engagement questions in the surveys developed by the U.S. Merit Systems Protection Board and others can serve as veritable management checklists and provide a framework to help meet the challenges that public-sector managers, in particular, face as they attempt to improve employee engagement. Many of the engagement research studies (and the surveys that often accompany them) have identified engagement "drivers." These are factors that lead to high levels of engagement. These drivers are often described differently, and therefore sorting through them can be confusing. But most of them focus on similar factors.

For example, the U.S. Merit Systems Protection Board survey includes questions that fall into six areas that drive employee engagement:

1. Pride in the work or workplace
2. Satisfaction with leadership
3. Opportunity to perform well at work
4. Satisfaction with recognition received
5. Prospect for future personal and professional growth
6. Positive work environment with some focus on teamwork[4]

Generally speaking, if these conditions exist in an agency, that organization should have a high level of employee engagement.

OVERCOMING THE IMPACTS OF ATTACKS ON GOVERNMENT

Persistent attacks on the public sector and public-sector employees create serious problems for government managers who are trying to improve the engagement of their workforces. Because "pride in the work or workplace" is an important driver of engagement, public-sector managers have to find ways to overcome the demoralizing impacts of government bashing.

Government agencies and their leaders need to aggressively and publicly advocate for government and the public service, including to elected and appointed officials and in the media. This includes identifying and publicizing—both to employees and to external audiences—agency successes and the resulting benefits to the public. This also means directly confronting critics to explain and emphasize the value of government and public service. Rank-and-file employees need to be involved in this process to put a face on government and counteract the "nameless, faceless bureaucrat" stereotype.

In other words, government agencies need to get into the public-relations business to educate the public about what government does and what it accomplishes—in press releases, in public forums, on websites, in the social media, and even in our schools. Too often, government does not do this well, or at all.

That's unfortunate, because government agencies should have a lot to say. In its 2007 annual report, the Partnership for Public Service included a "Government's Everyday Impact Index" to illustrate the role of the federal government in the day-to-day lives of Americans. The index included data (mostly from 2006 to 2007) such as the following:

- Number of people who travel on federally funded highways each day: 190,000,000
- Number of people who visit a national park each day: 750,000
- Number of students who received federal student aid for college: 10,000,000
- Number of people who received Social Security benefits: 49,122,831
- Number of people who received health care through Medicare: 44,067,816
- Percentage of children receiving free or reduced-cost school lunches funded by the federal government: 56
- Number of families who received federal assistance to heat or cool their homes: 5,800,000
- Number of criminals successfully prosecuted by U.S. attorneys: 72,585
- Number of businesses counseled by the Small Business Administration (SBA): 1,520,000
- Number of U.S. businesses operating with the assistance of an SBA loan: 190,000
- Number of workplace safety regulations prosecuted by federal officials: 88,846
- Average number of patents granted each day: 476
- Phone numbers on the Federal Trade Commission's "Do Not Call" list: 145,000,000
- Number of patients treated at Veterans Affairs medical facilities: 4,200,000
- Number of people in foreign countries who received U.S. disaster relief: 173,000,000
- Number of passports issued annually by the State Department: 12,000,000[5]

These examples, while providing compelling evidence of the impact of the federal government, only tell part of the story. The public also needs to understand the many ways that state and local governments affect them every day—work that includes maintaining our parks and roads, providing police and fire protection, educating our kids, delivering social services, maintaining water and sewer systems, licensing professionals who work in fields such as health care and law, passing zoning laws to make sure our neighborhoods are attractive and livable, and collecting trash. Most Americans take these services for granted. According to Dick Armey, the former House of Representatives majority leader, "I don't want to give the impression that most government programs are designed, even ostensibly, to help families with the needs of everyday life. Most government programs don't even pretend to do that, and very few American families would notice their disappearance."[6]

His remark is as outrageous as it is untrue.

In addition to damaging morale and employee engagement, attacks on government have limited the public sector's ability to attract talent. The public sector needs to aggressively recruit new talent by marketing what government does, the value of public service, and the opportunities to make a difference by working in government, including early in the careers of new hires.

SUSTAINING ENGAGEMENT DESPITE FREQUENT LEADERSHIP CHANGES

The revolving door of top leadership in government, accompanied by shifting policy priorities, makes employee engagement in government more important—but more difficult—to maintain and improve. Temporary political leadership can short circuit engagement initiatives. So the pressure is on career managers and supervisors to make the case for employee engagement, up and down the organization, as a long-term strategy.

Leaders with short-term agendas that dramatically change agency priorities and policies can (perhaps unintentionally) block fundamental engagement drivers such as employee pride, satisfaction with leadership, input to decisions, and the feeling that employees have the opportunity and tools to perform well at work.

To overcome these barriers, career managers and supervisors, in particular, must provide strong and stable leadership, managing not just down but also up. They must also be politically astute.

Specific strategies include onboarding new political leaders to help them understand—and buy into—the agency's values, mission, and goals (not just their political agendas). Newly appointed political leaders need to understand how to translate and link their political goals to their agency's mission, goals, and operational activities. Career public servants can help political leaders understand how to make this happen. This also means establishing positive relationships, right from the start, with these elected/appointed leaders, including helping them understand that good policies and laws do not automatically translate into good outcomes. Results depend on engaging the public servants who must implement these policies and laws.

The National Academy of Public Administration and the IBM Center for the Business of Government collaborated on *Speeding Up the Learning Curve: Observations from a Survey of Seasoned Political Appointees*. This study summarized the results of a survey of a group of Senate-confirmed appointees of former President George W. Bush. According to these appointees, their success depended heavily on building positive relationships with career employees and understanding the agency's internal culture.[7]

Metro, the regional government for the Portland, Oregon, area, conducts employee-engagement surveys every two years. Metro's current chief operating officer (COO) was appointed in 2011. According to Mary Rowe, the Metro HR director, the new COO quickly bought into Metro's employee-engagement strategy because she was presented with a strong business case for continuing the initiative.

In the 2009 "Best Places to Work in the Federal Government," the Federal Labor Relations Authority (FLRA) received the lowest score that an agency had ever received: 16 on a scale of 0 to 100. (For comparison, the lowest score of any agency or agency subcomponent in 2012 was 32.7.) I was managing "Best Places" when we calculated that FLRA score. We were so surprised by the low score that I called the HR director to ask him if there was any way we had miscalculated the score. His response went something like, "Nope, you got it right. We were expecting a low score."

One year later, the FLRA score skyrocketed to 68.3, and in 2012, it was 74.3. The authority took a series of aggressive actions that drove these improvements. These steps included the authority chairwoman bringing senior career and political leaders together in regular meetings to share information and discuss mission performance, what policies to develop, and how to implement them. These meetings helped create a more collegial environment among political and career leaders and also improved communication.

The province of Alberta, Canada, has been conducting employee-engagement surveys regularly since 1996. During this time, the province has had had three different elected premiers, the province's head of government. These changes in political leadership have not diminished Alberta's commitment to engagement, largely because the deputy ministers in each department, who are career (i.e., not elected or appointed) executives, have continued to support the survey strategy.

Career managers and supervisors must also work hard to foster direct and positive interactions between political leaders and rank-and-file employees to help them understand each other's interests and agendas. This includes being the liaison between elected/appointed officials and front-line employees—for example, avoiding the disastrous initial interaction New Hampshire governor Craig Benson had with his career employees. Compare what the governor said on his first day ("Not many people in this room have been asked to bring their brains with them to work") to what President George H. W. Bush told 200 federal career senior executives when he gathered them at Constitution Hall shortly after he was inaugurated in 1989:

> Well, I'm honored to be with you, to work with you, you here in Washington, your colleagues in the federal service around the nation. They're some of the most unsung heroes in America. The United States is the greatest nation in the world because we fulfill that mission of

> greatness one person at a time, as individuals dedicated to serving our country. And as we embark on this great new chapter in our nation's history, I want to tell you—came over here to tell you—that I am proud of you and very glad that we will be working to write this chapter together. Thank you all, and God bless you in your important work. Thank you very, very much.[8]

Many of the career executives who were there still talk about how inspiring it was to see and hear the new president speak to them, very personally, about the value of public service.

To further overcome the negative impacts of frequent leadership changes on engagement, career managers and supervisors must also insulate rank-and-file employees, as much as possible, from political maneuvering.

Managers should also advocate to senior leadership on behalf of employees. This includes making a commitment to, and supporting, long-term employee development by providing the time and money for training and other development activities.

OVERCOMING THE CHALLENGE OF HARD-TO-MEASURE AGENCY GOALS

Highly engaged employees have a clear "line of sight" between their jobs and the mission, goals, and impacts of their organizations. However, it's often difficult for public-sector organizations to clearly define goals and measure their impacts. That makes it more difficult to have this line of sight and also puts government managers in a double bind. That is, the public-service motivation research has shown that line of sight is particularly important for public servants, yet it is harder to connect these dots in government because of goal ambiguity.

Government managers must respond by clearly articulating the long-term mission, values, goals, and impacts of the agency (i.e., in contrast to short-term political goals). Then managers must work with employees to make sure they see the connections between their work and these goals—and the agency's impact on the public it serves. A key way to do this is to connect employees directly with the citizens they serve. Here's the way one public servant put it: "When I found myself getting down, I would head to the front lines. Being among the citizens we served reminded me why I was there and why it was important to keep fighting."[9]

INVOLVING EMPLOYEES IN DECISION MAKING AND SURVIVING THE INFLUENCE OF EXTERNAL STAKEHOLDERS

An important element of employee engagement is input to decision making (i.e., "my opinion counts"). That's why the complicated, inefficient, and sometimes even irrational government decision-making environment is a barrier to managers who are trying to improve and maintain high levels of engagement. More than their private-sector peers, government managers who want to maintain and improve engagement in the complex environment of government must work hard to involve rank-and-file employees in operational decisions in the areas they *can* influence. To achieve this end, public-sector managers and supervisors should do the following:

- Involve employees in making operational (implementation) decisions about how to implement policies and improve work processes.
- Explain the context for political decisions even when they seem illogical, and then translate these decisions into operational steps. Employees need to understand the basis for, and nature of, political decision making—that is, understand the "why" of these decisions as well as fully appreciate the realities of the how government is designed and operates. Elected officials (and their appointees) pledge to implement certain policies, and the job of career employees is to help implement these policies.
- On the other hand, also try to make sure senior leaders understand frontline employee views and perspectives.

- Create an environment that encourages employees to take risks and then insulate them from negative consequences.

The Federal Deposit Insurance Corporation was number one on the "Best Places to Work" rankings for large federal agencies in 2011 and again in 2012. One reason for the high score was a dedication to soliciting staff input and communicating how and why decisions have been made. Even if employees don't agree with decisions, explaining them can go a long way toward maintaining and improving engagement.

ENGAGING AN OLDER, MORE EDUCATED, AND MORE WHITE-COLLAR WORKFORCE

Government managers can leverage the unique demographics of the public-sector workforce to improve engagement, but these demographics also present challenges. Since, in general, government workforces are more white collar than private-sector workforces, public-sector managers can build on this natural engagement advantage. The flip side of this is that more educated and professional workers have high expectations about making a difference and being involved in decision making.

Managers striving to improve engagement can leverage the upside and minimize the downside of government workforce demographics in the following ways:

- Make the engagement business case, to managers and supervisors in particular, to demonstrate that engagement should be a way of life in the workplace—that is, not a fad but a proven strategy that can help leaders, managers, and supervisors achieve their goals and therefore succeed. In the words of a manager in the Air Force Materiel Command, make engagement a mind-set, not just a buzzword.
- Hold managers/supervisors accountable for improving engagement and achieving measurable results (that an engaged workforce can help them deliver).

- Understand that different generations have different needs and perspectives (e.g., for work/life balance and input to decisions) and then create workplace conditions that meet these needs as much as possible.
- Train managers on how to deal with—and leverage the talents of—multiple generations in the workforce.
- Openly discuss retirement and help older employees ease gracefully into the next phase of life. Several years ago, the Tennessee Valley Authority (TVA) asked employees approaching retirement age (and there were many) what their retirement plans were. TVA was concerned that employees would be reluctant to answer this question for fear that the authority would use the answers to somehow discriminate against older workers. However, TVA employees responded very positively, including many who said, "What took you so long to ask?" TVA used the data to develop a succession-planning program.
- Implement a succession-planning process that conforms to civil-service restrictions against preselection. This can be accomplished by implementing succession planning as a career-development program open to all eligible employees.
- At the other end of the employee life cycle, prepare to recruit replacements for the baby boomers who are beginning to leave government. This means putting in place effective recruiting and hiring systems to attract talented people who are already motivated to consider public service.

Part of the solution is also to provide younger employees with opportunities to make a difference and excel. For example, the U.S. Office of Management and Budget (OMB; which has done consistently well in "Best Places to Work") has a much younger workforce than most public-sector organizations—one-third of its employees are under the age of 35. OMB attracts this talent because it has built a reputation as a place where talented young people can make their mark. OMB gives young staff members responsibility for critical agency assignments, even at the beginning stages of their careers. And it doesn't hurt the agency brand to be located in the executive office of the president of the United States.

OVERCOMING CIVIL-SERVICE RULES AND FINANCIAL LIMITATIONS AND USING OTHER APPROACHES TO INFLUENCE BEHAVIOR

Public-sector managers do not have many of the financial tools that most private-sector managers have to link rewards to performance and therefore drive behavior and performance. Plus, government personnel systems are famously (or infamously) inflexible ("you can't hire or fire anyone in government").

Faced with limited ways to reward and recognize their employees, managers in government need to emphasize agency mission and impact and also provide nonfinancial recognition. Money is not the only way to recognize superior performance. Sometimes simply thanking an employee for a job well done can go a long way.

In fact, the good news is that nonfinancial rewards can be an effective way to reward and engage public-sector employees. A recent survey of federal government employees revealed that federal employees are not motivated solely, or even primarily, by monetary rewards. The survey respondents rated eight nonmonetary reward options as more important than monetary awards and bonuses. The higher-ranked recognition approaches included "personal satisfaction," "interesting work," "job security," and "being able to serve the public."[10]

Here are some other approaches government managers should consider to overcome rigid personnel rules and limited financial tools and improve engagement:

- Adopt workplace flexibility practices, such as allowing employees to work remotely and adopt alternative work schedules (e.g., four 10-hour days).
- Involve employees in decision making.
- Use the new hire probationary period to weed out bad fits. Too often, marginal performers in government are "passed" through

probation and then become far more difficult to deal with and/or remove.

- Clearly articulate employee performance expectations and recognize good performance, but also use the performance management process to deal with employees who do not perform and/or resist change. Although dealing with performance problems can be difficult in government, it *is* possible to fire a poor performer.
- Push human resources to do its part in dealing with performance problems, including making sure that managers understand HR policies and processes and receive the support they need to deal with poor performers.
- Advocate for broad personnel/civil-service reforms to create more flexibility (e.g., in hiring, job movement, and dealing with poor performers).

INVOLVING LABOR UNIONS

Public-sector managers must also involve labor organizations as partners—and therefore as advocates—in measuring and improving engagement. This means reaching out aggressively to unions, making the business case for engagement, and then involving labor in measuring engagement and taking action to improve it. It also means making it clear to labor organizations that employee-engagement initiatives are not a strategy or conspiracy to co-opt employees and wring more work out of them or to cut pay and benefits.

Employee engagement, if done carefully and collaboratively, offers the potential to break through labor-management antagonism and partner with organized labor to improve working conditions, but this relationship must be approached with care and sensitivity. In particular, it is important to deal with labor-union leaders and only deal directly with the rank-and-file as a last resort.

The city of Minneapolis, which has conducted employee-engagement surveys four times since 2004, has 23 separate collective-bargaining agreements and a workforce that is more than 90 percent unionized. Before conducting employee-engagement surveys, HR staff met with a board of union representatives to discuss the survey strategy and timeline and ask for their support in increasing the overall response rate. After the survey results were received, HR staff again met with the unions to review the results, including areas of strength and opportunities for improvement.

Similarly, the Air Force Materiel Command reviewed its engagement survey with labor unions and explained the command's plans for collecting the survey data and using the results. This process paved the way for working with the unions in later implementation strategies. The Oregon Metro Board has also worked closely with its unions and shares engagement survey results with all employees and labor organizations.

The U.S. Government Accountability Office (GAO) consistently ranks near the top in the "Best Places to Work" rankings despite having to deal with GAO's first-ever employee union. This relationship is unusual for a federal agency because the new union was granted the right to negotiate with GAO over wages (and most federal government unions cannot do this). GAO worked hard to create the basis for a strong labor-management partnership. For example, the agency's executive committee (which includes the comptroller general of the United States, the GAO CEO) meets quarterly with union leaders. GAO also formed a diversity committee, which includes representatives from the employee advisory council, the union, nonunion members, and representatives of liaison groups such as Blacks in Government.

In Alberta, Canada, the province's union views the engagement survey as a way for its members to provide direct and anonymous feedback to the province's senior management.

In some jurisdictions, laws prohibit labor unions from representing public-sector employees. In some of these locations, employees may join employee associations, which serve as a substitute for unions. These organizations also need to be brought into the engagement process.

DEALING WITH PUBLIC VISIBILITY AND SCRUTINY

The visibility of government, including laws requiring open records and meetings, means that public-sector managers committed to improving engagement need to take extra measures to make employees feel as safe and secure as possible. This includes helping employees feel comfortable voicing their opinions, taking risks, and innovating. Managers should strive for a culture that encourages innovation and insulates employees from adverse publicity as much as possible. My approach has always been to tell the people who report to me that if we're successful, they get the credit. If we fail, it's on me.

Public-sector managers also need to be particularly careful about how they relate to, communicate with, and most importantly, treat employees. Even emails and texts are subject to release to the media and the public. This transparency can be positive, however, because it accentuates the need for managers to treat their employees in ways that promote high levels of engagement. This involves having interactions and discussions about the following:

- How to create the workplace conditions and opportunities that enable them to excel
- How they can grow personally and professionally
- Whether they are satisfied with the recognition they receive
- How to build pride in their work and organization
- Whether they are satisfied with supervisors and leaders and, if not, why

LEVERAGING THE PUBLIC-SERVICE MOTIVATION

As described previously, public servants are motivated more by mission than financial or other extrinsic rewards and are therefore predisposed to respond to public-service missions, goals, and motives. Government agencies need to find these people, hire them, and then leverage their intrinsic motivation through engagement strategies. This involves the following:

- Identifying, aggressively recruiting, and then hiring job candidates who are motivated by public service

- After hiring these motivated employees, leveraging their public-service motivation as a strong driver of change by involving them in decision making and helping them see and appreciate their individual impacts (especially if financial rewards are limited)

ATTRACTING TALENT TO GOVERNMENT

Today, more than ever, government agencies need to very intentionally design recruiting and hiring strategies that will attract these public-service-motivated candidates. Hiring top talent is becoming a heavier lift for the public sector in part because the criticism of government has diminished interest in government careers.

Government has a lot of work to do to become an employer of choice, particularly on college campuses. As noted earlier, young people have become an endangered species in many public agencies. In the federal government, for example, only 3 percent of the workforce is under the age of 25. In the 2012 Federal Employee Viewpoint Survey, only 43 percent of the 687,000 federal employees who responded agreed that their "unit is able to recruit people with the right skills." And that percentage was down from the previous two years.[11]

Today's college graduates are more attracted to jobs in other sectors because employers in the private and nonprofit sectors have made the commitment to aggressively court top talent from campuses across the country. Plus, these organizations have refined their hiring approaches to make them inviting, efficient, user friendly, and timely.

Government's failure to recruit new talent aggressively is particularly frustrating because, according to a survey of 8,000 college students, the top two most important criteria these students are using to make decisions about where to work are "career advancement opportunities" and "interesting, challenging work."[12] Government can deliver these opportunities.

However, too many public-sector agencies are still in a time warp, relying on user-unfriendly hiring methods that can take months.

Government also has not focused enough on helping students who have public-service motivation recognize the opportunities government offers to satisfy their need to make a difference. To successfully compete for talent with the private and nonprofit sectors, government must understand the attitudes and expectations of college students about the world of work and about careers in government. Then agencies need to bring more to the table than a vague hint of a job opportunity, a complicated and confusing job application, and a lengthy hiring process.

The Partnership for Public Service conducts research on what it takes to attract new—and particularly young—talent to government.[13] The Partnership's research has shown that few college students (only 13 percent) are knowledgeable about federal job opportunities. As one student put it,

> I am a student leader and senior here on campus and I have been sought out by companies as well as . . . Teach for America. Why can't the government do the same? If I am being pursued and contacted on a regular basis by groups like Conoco and Teach for America it makes me feel very wanted and piques my interest.[14]

Some other key findings are as follows:

- When students were asked what might make them want to work in government, the highest-rated responses were "working on interesting issues" (82 percent), "good benefits" (77 percent), and "the opportunity to make a difference" (74 percent). In other words, aside from benefits (which, as we have noted, are already generous in government), the responses link to the public-service ethic.
- On the other hand, when asked about the biggest reason *not* to work in government, students said "too much bureaucracy"

(53 percent), "don't know what careers are available" (43 percent), and "salaries not high enough" (40 percent).

The Partnership has gone on record with a series of conclusions/lessons learned about how to attract today's college graduates (and other candidates) to government:

- **Publicize job opportunities.** When candidates know about government job opportunities and how to apply for them, they are much more likely to be interested. Sounds self-evident, but government agencies often do not do a good job publicizing their job opportunities. Government must clearly communicate the benefits of public service and make a long-term investment in on-campus recruiting, including building long-term relationships with faculty, academic advisors, and career center professionals.
- **Stress opportunities in government.** A huge deterrent to government service is the widely held perception that government is overly bureaucratic and stifles individuality and creativity. To overcome this belief and tap into those who are motivated by public service, agencies need to stress the unique opportunities in government to do good *and* do well—that is, interesting work, an unparalleled ability to make a difference even early in their careers, competitive pay, and good benefits.
- **Understand that high touch is as important as high tech.** Although most students use the Internet to search for job leads and details about jobs, the most effective recruiters are the people students directly relate to—parents, friends, faculty, and advisors.
- **Give students what they want, where they want it.** Private-sector firms and many nonprofits work hard to reach students and faculty where they live—both literally and figuratively. Government agencies should follow suit (e.g., by holding events where students are already gathered such as in classes, student organizations or clubs, or academic departments). It's also

important to include "people like me" in recruitment ads, fairs, and information sessions by featuring younger employees and alumni, as well as the diversity of the workforce. This puts a face on public service so students will see people with similar characteristics, talents, interests, and backgrounds working in government.

- **Educate and enlist faculty and advisors as allies.** To be effective, these potential allies must be equipped with pertinent and current information. Once faculty members are sold on government careers and have the information and tools they need, they will continue to highlight the public sector in their discussions and advice and even invite government speakers into their classrooms.

Government agencies need to recruit aggressively, including using technology efficiently. And that doesn't mean just posting vacancies on the agency website ("post and pray"). It means aggressively promoting the mission of the agency and the potential to make a difference. It also means using technology such as LinkedIn, Facebook, and Twitter.

A recruiter from the National Institutes of Health described effective recruiting, perhaps somewhat indelicately, as being like the difference between trapping and hunting. Trappers put out a trap and wait for the prey to show up, while hunters aggressively seek out what they want. Government recruiters need to hunt, not trap.

Attracting young talent who have public-service motivation also means streamlining government application and hiring processes. This includes eliminating lengthy written submissions and the dreaded civil-service exams, which many of the best and brightest are loath to take. The days when a government agency could post a job announcement on a few bulletin boards or a website and then sit back and wait for the stream of qualified applicants to come flowing in are long gone. Even in a slow economy, the best candidates have options. Young people with public-service motivation are out there—government agencies must aggressively recruit and hire them. And when the economy does turn around and jobs are again plentiful, government needs to be ready to compete aggressively for the best talent in a tighter job market.

Teach for America: A Model for Recruiting and Hiring Talent

Founded in 1990, Teach for America (TFA) annually places more than 5,000 new teachers in 46 urban and rural areas across the country—all low-income and underserved. Its founder, Wendy Kopp, has executed on her belief that teachers, by going above and beyond traditional expectations, can enable students in low-income communities to achieve at high levels.

In just two decades, TFA has created a "brand" that the best and brightest want to be a part of, despite the enormous challenge of trying to educate children in the nation's toughest environments. The nonprofit organization has become a premiere employer of choice. In 2011, TFA received 48,000 applications,[15] many from top universities. At 55 colleges and universities—including Yale, North Carolina, Berkeley, Howard, Arizona State, and Washington University in St. Louis—TFA is the top employer of graduating seniors.[16] TFA is also among *Fortune* magazine's 2012 "Best Companies to Work For."

How has TFA built such a strong brand?

The Mission

TFA has defined a mission that is clear, compelling, and actionable:

> Our mission is to build the movement to eliminate educational inequity by enlisting our nation's most promising future leaders in the effort. We recruit outstanding recent college graduates from all backgrounds and career interests to commit to teach for two years in urban and rural public schools. We provide the training and ongoing support necessary to ensure their success as teachers in low-income communities.

Aggressive, Strategic, and Coordinated Recruiting

Each year, TFA recruiters, who are often former corps members, meet one on one with up to 30,000 students at hundreds of colleges. According to the TFA director of recruiting, "We are not in the business of just going after anybody. We are looking for a very specific person." TFA doesn't just put its opportunities on its website ("post and pray"). It understands that inspiring the best and brightest young people to devote two years to a tough job requires a high-touch approach including marketing, communicating, and relationship building.

Trained recruiters develop and implement marketing plans; cultivate high-potential students on campus; and build relationships with student leaders, faculty, administrators, corps members, and alumni.

Timely and Rigorous Timely Applicant Assessment Process

The process, from application to job offer, usually takes eight weeks. When it does take longer, TFA lets candidates know why. The organization's website specifically outlines the entire hiring process—online application, phone interview, day-long interview, and assessment center. The TFA website posts specific milestone dates—not just the application deadline but also the date candidates can go online to find out if they're going to get an interview, dates for phone interviews, and when candidates can go online again to find out if they've been invited to an in-person final interview. The site also includes projected dates for final offers and candidate decisions. Applicants know—in advance—what's going to happen and when.

Comprehensive Onboarding and Continuous Training and Development

Because TFA primarily hires recent grads who were not education majors, the onboarding process is crucial to preparing new hires for the enormous challenges they will face.

The onboarding process starts when a new corps member accepts the TFA job offer. The day after my daughter said yes to TFA, a recruiter called her to discuss her new job and answer questions. The next week, a local rep arranged a conference call with the parents of the new Washington, DC, corps members to explain what their sons and daughters were getting into and answer questions.

Onboarding continues when each incoming corps member attends a five-week summer training institute. Corps members, my daughter included, describe the summer training institute as intense, challenging, and rewarding. Some corps members quit or wash out during training. (But it's better to find this out during training than in the classroom.) The training institute is followed by a week-long induction in the location where each TFA teacher is assigned.

The TFA regional support network then provides professional development throughout each new teacher's two-year commitment. Each corps member is assigned a regional program director who provides support, guidance, and feedback. Every month or so, my daughter joined other DC corps members in a day-long professional development session. Although she complained about having to give up a Saturday, this program demonstrates TFA's commitment to its new teachers' development.

TFA corps members also must become certified as teachers in their jurisdictions. TFA arranges with local universities to enable corps members to earn master's degrees, funded in large part by AmeriCorps grants, which lead to certification.

Focus on Impact

The Teach for America model—putting talented new college grads in classrooms even though they didn't major in education—is still controversial. But a growing body of research shows that corps members have a positive impact on student achievement. Research like this, which provides a direct line of sight between the work TFA teachers do and the TFA mission to eliminate educational inequality, is a powerful driver of recruiting success and employee engagement.

Commitment to Long-Term Career Support

A key TFA goal is to not just attract talent to education but also retain that talent. But TFA also understands that many of its corps members will go on to other careers after their initial two-year teaching commitment. No matter where alumni wind up, TFA tries to lay the foundation for a lifetime of advocacy on behalf of the Teach for America mission. Instead of fighting the inclination of millennials to move on to other things, TFA embraces this new reality with programs designed to help corps members make transitions and also create a strong alumni network.

A Model for Government

Many aspects of the TFA approach to acquiring and managing talent are transferable to government. The fundamentals—aggressive recruiting, clear communication about the hiring process, rigorous but timely candidate assessment, solid and thoughtful onboarding, continuous training and development, and a focus on measuring results and commitment to long-term career development—should be applied to public-sector hiring as well as building employee engagement.

As I've emphasized, the low level of employee engagement in the public sector is a good news–bad news story—the good news being that there is a huge upside to improving engagement in government. We've discussed the barriers to improving engagement and some ways to deal with these obstacles. Next, we'll review how to assess the specific level of employee engagement in a jurisdiction or agency and then how to act on the results to improve it.

Chapter 6

Measuring Employee Engagement

The first step for a government organization that commits to improving employee engagement is to understand the current level of engagement in the organization. There are a wide range of available approaches and tools that purport to help with this.

Employee engagement is a hot topic. This strong interest has created a sort of engagement cottage industry. A Google search on "employee engagement" produces more than 4.5 million hits, including a very authoritative-sounding Wikipedia entry. The Google searcher is also bombarded with engagement tools, reports, white papers, training sessions, lists, awards programs (including the "I Love Awards" organization's 50 most engaged employers), seminars (learn how to "do" employee engagement for only $1,000), blogs, networks, and so on. One ad asks, "Is your company engaged?" No, but we're dating.

It's an employee-engagement jungle out there. One comment posted on an online discussion about the value of employee engagement referred to the "engagement racket."

While I wouldn't go that far, it is true that some of the advertised engagement solutions and measurement tools are unsupported by any apparent science and are often geared toward the private sector.

There is hope, however, for government agencies that are sifting through this blizzard of employee-engagement information. First, as we have discussed, there are approaches to measuring and building employee engagement in government that *are* based on strong scientific evidence. These include public-sector surveys developed by the U.S. Merit Systems Protection Board (MSPB) and Office of Personnel Management (OPM) and the United Kingdom and Canadian governments. These scientific approaches also include other engagement surveys such as the Gallup survey, known as the "Q12," which is based on 30 years of research involving more than 17 million employees.[1] Gallup's results have been reported in publications, including the *Harvard Business Review* and in books such as *First, Break All the Rules* and *12: The Elements of Great Managing.* Gallup's research has isolated 12 survey questions that predict employee engagement and therefore workgroup performance.[2] The Gallup survey focuses on issues such as ensuring that employees understand their job expectations, receive regular feedback, and have the opportunity to perform well.

While Gallup has worked with government agencies, most of its Q12 data are from the private sector. Plus, you have to pay Gallup to conduct the Q12, but public-sector agencies that have contracted with Gallup for employee-engagement support report that Gallup delivers very solid value.

Consistent with my argument that government is different from the private sector, however, I believe it's also reasonable that measuring engagement in the public sector should also reflect these differences.

Surveys of public-sector managers reveal that maintaining an effective and productive workforce is perhaps the most critical issue government jurisdictions and agencies face today. Yet it's ironic that most agencies do not have formal processes, such as employee surveys or other research tools, to measure and then improve employee engagement.[3]

There are two basic ways to assess employee engagement—indirectly or directly.

The indirect approach involves trying to assess the level of engagement using data like employee turnover, employee performance evaluations, missed work time, accident rates, and the results of exit interviews. Some organizations are also even beginning to track their employees' attitudes and views about their jobs and organizations by monitoring their social media activity on sites like Facebook. It's not a big leap of faith to conclude that an agency with a lot of poor performers, high turnover, excessive employee sick time, or a high accident rate (or a lot of nasty comments on Facebook) may have some engagement issues. After all, we've already said that a high level of employee engagement is linked to lower turnover, less missed time, better performance, and so on. Case closed, right?

Well, not exactly, especially in government. Public-sector organizations are usually low-turnover organizations because of "golden handcuffs" that include generous benefits such as guaranteed retirement annuities and employer-paid health insurance, even in retirement. Therefore, turnover may not be a good indicator of employee engagement in government agencies.

However, even in a public-sector agency that has high turnover, this metric doesn't necessarily relate to employee engagement. Sure, it could be that low employee engagement is driving high turnover. It could also be that an agency with high turnover is losing its employees to competitors who pay better, the agency has a poor selection process that results in bad job fits, or it has a lot of baby boomers who are retiring because it's time for them to move on to the next stages of their lives. No harm, no foul. And so on.

Analyzing Turnover: Do You Know Who's Leaving Your Agency?

Employee attrition in government is generally low. As a result, agency turnover data—when it's available—can be easy to ignore. According to research conducted by the Partnership for Public Service, overlooking employee turnover and failing to understand exactly who is leaving, and why, is a mistake.[4]

On the plus side, attrition can create space for an agency to add new talent and skills, enable an agency to say farewell to marginal performers or disaffected employees, and provide promotional opportunities for less-senior employees.

On the minus side, the loss of experienced employees due to retirement or greener pastures can damage an agency's capacity and performance if these employees leave with institutional knowledge and organizational savvy that up-and-coming staffers don't yet have. The same goes for attrition of recently hired talent or employees with critical and/or hard-to-find skills.

High turnover can also indicate employee dissatisfaction with the agency; its leaders, managers, and supervisors; the workplace environment; or organizational systems and processes. For example, attrition of recently hired employees means wasting the considerable investment to recruit and hire them, as well as suggesting weaknesses in recruiting, hiring, onboarding, and supervision. According to some estimates, the cost of replacing a departed employee ranges from 30 to 50 percent of the annual salary of entry-level employees, 150 percent for midlevel employees, and up to 400 percent for specialized, high-level employees.[5]

Beyond replacement costs, agency leaders also need to clearly understand whether, and how, attrition affects operational capacity, the health of the workplace, and the agency's ability to achieve its organizational mission. This includes analyzing turnover data to understand who is leaving and why. For example, while overall turnover might be low, what is the turnover rate for new hires; superior performers; and employees in mission-critical jobs, in specific demographic groups, and in individual work units? The "why" is also important and can be assessed through exit interviews as well as engagement-survey results.

Assessing employee engagement through the lens of performance appraisal data also has limits, particularly in government. It's an unfortunate truth that the public sector is notorious for not providing employees with candid performance appraisals or, in some cases, not providing employees with appraisals at all. For example, in the federal government, performance appraisal systems do not effectively differentiate different levels of employee performance.[6] Fewer than 1 percent of federal employees are rated as less than fully successful.[7] While I'm an unabashed fan of public servants and the contributions they make, this absence of poor-performing federal employees defies logic in a workforce of two million plus.

Employee interviews and focus groups can also provide information on the level of employee engagement. An agency can, for example, conduct "engagement interviews" with employees to subjectively assess their level of engagement. Sometimes these discussions are also referred to as "stay interviews" (in contrast to exit interviews). While this approach can reveal how the individual employees interviewed feel, it is labor intensive and puts employees on the spot. Thus these interviews may not be candid. In addition, the results of these interviews, unless the interviewed employees are identified through statistically sound sampling techniques, can't be generalized to the entire workforce.

The same goes for exit interviews to find out why employees have decided to leave and whether their departures suggest an employee-engagement problem. I think conducting exit interviews is a sound practice that organizations should use to collect data on why employees are leaving. However, exit interviews are the ultimate lagging indicator of workforce health (after all, these employees are already headed for the exits) and also suffer from the other limits of interviews: They are not anonymous and it can be difficult to generalize the data to the entire workforce.

Another, even more indirect strategy is a "diagnostic checklist"—a sort of self-assessment to assess engagement. According to its proponents, a "yes" answer to specific issues and concerns like the following can indicate an engagement problem:

- The credibility of leadership is routinely questioned: "We've heard *this* one before."
- People often come to meetings and nod in agreement but limited or no progress is made.

- Employees are unclear about the priorities and expectations of leadership: "What's the direction of the business? How does *my* role contribute?"
- There is a lack of information sharing across business units and a lack of collaboration toward common goals and results.
- Superior performance is often undefined, unrecognized, and/or unrewarded.
- Turnover among top performers is high while overall turnover remains flat.
- Rates of absenteeism and short-term disability are on the rise.
- Employees often arrive late and leave early.
- Training and development initiatives are poorly attended.
- Employees feel far removed from the results of the business and have little understanding of how they can contribute toward the organization's strategy.
- There is a lack of a "higher cause" or "shared mission," with people simply doing their eight hours so they can go home.[8]

These are issues that managers should reflect on. However, while this may lead an agency to conclude that there are workplace problems, these concerns won't necessarily identify causes, including whether there are employee-engagement issues.

While some of these items do focus on data (turnover, absenteeism), most are subjective. For example, as discussed previously, the reasons for turnover might not link directly to employee engagement. The same goes for boring, unproductive meetings and low attendance at training sessions, which could result from poorly planned meetings and ineffective training programs.

Another approach, perhaps the most clever, is the "cheap climate survey." This is billed as "something to try before launching into those expensive, time-consuming climate surveys." Employees are asked to post happy or sad faces on a bulletin board to show how they feel about their jobs and the organization.[9] While clever and undeniably low-cost, I'm not sure how confident I'd be about taking the "data" to senior management to advocate for an engagement initiative or anything else.

For these reasons, I believe that direct measurement, through employee surveys, is the most valid and reliable way to assess employee engagement, particularly in government, where other measures like turnover and performance evaluations are problematic. While surveying is a more complex solution than simply looking at already existing data or trying to brainstorm answers to diagnostic questions (or posting happy or sad faces), it's a long-term strategy worth the time and effort to accurately measure engagement. In the words of Mila Cosgrove, the HR director of the city and borough of Juneau, Alaska, "you have to ask" your employees to truly assess their level of engagement.

As I suggested in my listing of the engagement "resources" available on the web, there is a wide variety of surveys—and firms that will conduct them—to measure employee engagement. Many of these firms are highly reputable and will not only help conduct the engagement survey but, just as important, be there to help analyze the results and then act on the data. The question is how to select the approach that is right—and affordable—for a government jurisdiction and agency.

Unfortunately for us in government, many engagement surveys and follow-up approaches are designed for employees in the for-profit world. For example, one company that offers engagement surveys advertises that organizations with the highest levels of engagement achieved the following results:

- 87 percent had increased revenue in the following three years.
- 86 percent reported increased market share.
- 90 percent of the publicly traded clients reported higher stock prices.
- 57 percent reported lower employee turnover.[10]

While this is impressive, except for turnover, these metrics don't translate well to most government agencies. Plus, when it's time to use the survey data to develop and implement a strategy to improve engagement, the world of government is far different from the world of business.

That's why I suggest using a survey that's been validated for use in the public sector. What does *validated* mean? It means the survey has been proven, through statistical techniques, to measure what it's supposed to be measuring. Among other things, this usually means that the survey has been administered to a large sample of employees.

The Q12, for example, while not designed expressly for government, has been validated through millions of administrations to employees, some in the public sector. Gallup has been on the leading edge of the engagement movement, and its work is hugely valuable even though it does not focus primarily on government.

There are also engagement surveys that have been developed expressly for the public sector. For example, the 16 U.S. Merit Systems Protection Board (MSPB) engagement index questions I've cited are based on a survey of almost 37,000 federal government employees. This survey has been statistically validated and the responses generalize to the entire federal workforce.[11] Although the results are based on surveys of federal government employees, the MSPB methodology can also be applied to other public-sector workplaces.

The U.S. Office of Personnel Management (OPM) has also developed an engagement index based on the annual Federal Employee Viewpoint Survey of federal employees. The survey includes 84 questions covering work experience, work unit, agency, supervisor/team leader, leadership, satisfaction, and work/life. Through statistical analysis, OPM identified 15 questions from the survey that it uses to construct an index that represents the "conditions likely to lead to employee engagement."

The nonprofit Partnership for Public Service uses the OPM employee-engagement survey results to annually rate and rank more than 300 federal agencies in "Best Places to Work in the Federal Government."[12] Although employee satisfaction (what the Partnership measures) is not the same concept as employee engagement, research has shown that both satisfaction and engagement are linked to organizational performance.[13]

Similar in some ways to the OPM survey, the U.K. Civil Service People Survey is a comprehensive survey of U.K. government employees. The 2012 survey was completed by almost 300,000 British civil servants working in 97 central government organizations. The survey includes 49 "engagement driver" and 5 "engagement index statements" that respondents are asked to agree or disagree with:

1. I would recommend (name of department) as a great place to work.
2. I feel a strong personal attachment to (name of department).
3. (Name of department) motivates me to help achieve its objectives.
4. (Name of department) motivates me to help achieve its objectives.
5. I am proud when I tell others I am part of (name of department).[14]

In Canada, 12 of the 13 provincial and territorial governments collaborate, along with the federal government, on the Employee Engagement Interjurisdictional Initiative survey. The survey has 19 common questions, used by all participating jurisdictions, including 6 questions that compose an engagement index. The participating jurisdictions adhere to a usage and data-sharing protocol that outlines eligibility requirements for using the common questions and specifies the principles and operational procedures for collecting, storing, and reporting data and for the confidential sharing of results that enables benchmarking across the participating jurisdictions. The interjurisdictional team compiles the survey responses into a national index, which each participating organization can compare to its results. Employees are asked to rate the following six engagement index statements:

1. I am satisfied with my ministry/department.
2. Overall, I am satisfied in my work as a(n) (name of ministry/department) employee.
3. I am proud to tell people I work for the (name of ministry/department).
4. I would prefer to stay with the (name of ministry/department), even if offered a similar job elsewhere.
5. I am inspired to give my very best.
6. I would recommend (name of ministry/department) as a great place to work.[15]

The U.S. Postal Service (USPS) conducts perhaps the largest single-employer engagement survey in the world, public or private sector. Every three months, the USPS invites one-quarter of its almost 550,000 employees to take the Voice of the Employee Survey. The survey has 33 statements including eight key statements that form the "performance index":

1. I am aware of current business conditions facing the postal service.
2. I am confident in the ability of senior management to make the decisions necessary to ensure the future success of the postal service.
3. Rate the quality of the service provided by your office/facility to your customers.
3. Rate your immediate supervisor on communicating regularly to keep you informed.
4. The postal service values diversity of backgrounds, talents, and perspectives.
5. I feel personally responsible for helping the postal service succeed as a business.
6. I receive information to perform my job safely.
7. I understand how the work I do impacts the service the postal service provides.[16]

As these examples illustrate, there is a range of engagement surveys available. However, looking closely at them reveals that they share a few key dimensions. Although these engagement dimensions may be described differently in different surveys and analyses, they generally link to the six question areas in the MSPB survey:

1. Pride in the work or workplace
2. Satisfaction with leadership
3. Opportunity to perform well at work
4. Satisfaction with recognition received
5. Prospect for future personal and professional growth
6. Positive work environment with some focus on teamwork

A major advantage of the MSPB, OPM, and other public-sector-developed surveys is that they're in the public domain and therefore can be administered without paying to use them. American taxpayers have already paid for the MSPB and OPM surveys.

Chapter 7

A Process Model for Measuring and Improving Employee Engagement

Figure 7.1 depicts an employee-engagement process model with five steps: (1) plan the engagement survey, (2) conduct the survey, (3) report and analyze the results, (4) take action on the results to maintain strengths and improve on weaknesses, and (5) sustain improved engagement over time, including by readministering the survey. The model is shown as a circle because the process is continuous. Communication is at the center of the model—the core—because it is an essential ingredient of every aspect of the engagement strategy and is therefore critical to both short- and long-term success. Each step in the model is briefly summarized in this chapter and then described in more detail in Chapters 8–11.

It is important to emphasize that this is a *process* model. That is, the model outlines steps a public-sector organization, jurisdiction, or agency should take to assess engagement and act on the results. The model does not specify what actions to take—these are determined by analysis of engagement survey results and other supplemental data. These results and data should drive decisions on the actions the jurisdiction or agency should take to maintain areas of strength and improve areas of weakness.

Figure 7.1. Employee-engagement process model.

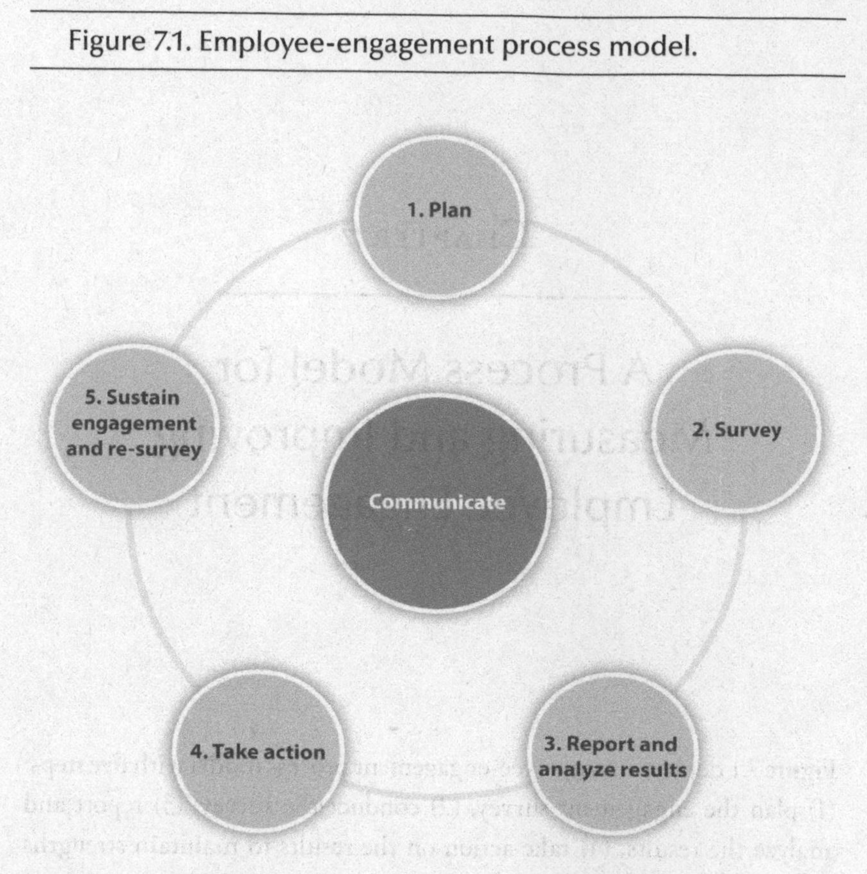

This five-step process model may appear simplistic. However, done right, implementing the engagement process model can produce powerful results in the form of improved employee and organization performance. As Herb Kelleher, the founder and former CEO of Southwest Airlines, has described the Southwest focus on talent, "The concept is simple, but the execution takes a lot of work and a lot of attention."[1]

STEP 1: PLAN

Advance planning is critically important not only for the employee-engagement survey itself but also for subsequent steps. As discussed in Chapter 8, planning includes deciding whether to survey, whom to survey, what questions to ask (e.g., develop a survey or use an existing survey), and when and how to administer the survey. The organization should select or develop a survey that is valid; in other words, the survey questions should accurately assess the level of employee engagement. Planning should also include decisions about how survey results will be analyzed and reported. This includes deciding what format the survey data will be reported in, whether an overall index of engagement will be computed, whether agency results can be benchmarked against comparable organizations, what the units of analysis will be (e.g., overall organization or agency, individual work units, specific managers, demographic groups), how the results will be reported, and who will receive the data.

Planning should also include deciding on the strategy and process for acting on the survey data, often by forming action teams of a cross-section of employees. The overall plan should include the long-term engagement strategy, including the schedule for regularly conducting follow-up surveys.

STEP 2: CONDUCT THE ENGAGEMENT SURVEY

The organization can develop the engagement survey itself or administer one of the many available surveys. Similarly, the agency can administer the survey by itself or hire an outside contractor to conduct it. While most agencies will conduct the survey online, it may also be necessary to provide a hard-copy option for employees who can't, or won't, be able to complete it online. Maximizing response rates means ensuring that individual employee survey responses will be held in confidence (e.g., not seen by anyone in the organization) and also following up to remind employees to complete the survey.

STEP 3: REPORT AND ANALYZE THE RESULTS

There are a wide variety of ways to report on and analyze the survey results. One important aspect to analyze is the survey response rate—the percentage of employees who complete the survey.

Many surveys can also generate an engagement index—a composite score that summarizes the overall level of engagement across the entire organization. Analysis should also include reporting and reviewing the results question by question to identify engagement areas of strength that should be maintained, as well as areas the agency needs to improve. This can be done for the organization overall, as well as by breaking down the survey results into smaller components such as work units and locations, individual managers, and demographic groups.

Analyzing survey results can also include more detailed and sophisticated analytics, such as comparing agency results against similar results from outside organizations (benchmarking), identifying the "drivers" of engagement (i.e., the items that statistical analysis reveals are most influential in determining the engagement levels of employees), and comparing the responses of managers/supervisors to the responses of frontline staff to identify any disconnects.

In addition to the quantitative survey results, most engagement surveys also allow respondents to provide narrative responses. Through these narratives, employees can expand on and explain their survey responses and offer additional insights. Analyzing the narrative comments can help the agency identify the root causes of engagement issues revealed by the survey.

STEP 4: TAKE ACTION

Surveying itself won't automatically improve the level of employee engagement or workplace conditions. Real change requires taking action on the data. In fact, surveying and then not taking action on the results can frustrate employees and actually decrease the level of engagement.

Many agencies have responded to engagement data by forming action teams that include employees from across the organization. These team members make a commitment to analyzing the survey data, developing recommendations to act on the data, and then putting together detailed action plans to implement approved recommendations.

The action team should develop a plan of action that includes maintaining strengths and improving on weaknesses. The plan should also identify who is responsible for specific actions and include milestones to assess progress. The team may also decide to collect additional information, often through focus groups, to add context to the survey data and help explore and identify root causes.

It's unlikely that any organization can respond to every issue an employee survey (and any additional data collected) reveals. Therefore, the organization (through the action team) needs to make decisions about priorities, including identifying short-term actions as well as longer-term solutions.

STEP 5: SUSTAIN ENGAGEMENT

A key aspect of sustaining engagement is regularly measuring it through surveys. That's the only sure way to really know if employees are engaged. Periodic surveying makes the entire organization—including leaders, managers, and supervisors—accountable for employee engagement. Agencies that conduct engagement surveys typically do them on a regularly scheduled basis (e.g., every one, two, or three years). Surveying less frequently can kill any momentum to improve engagement.

Sustaining engagement also requires continued support by leaders, managers, and supervisors. It also means that these leaders need to be held accountable for maintaining and/or improving engagement.

Agencies that have made the commitment to improving engagement also should identify performance metrics that make sense for their mission, strategy, and culture. Then, over time, the organization should track not only its level of employee engagement but also whether metrics important to the agency are trending in the right direction.

COMMUNICATE

This is at the center of the model because communication should be a unifying force in the journey to improved employee engagement.

Agencies must communicate frequently and candidly, before, during, and after the survey process, including throughout action planning and implementation.

The engagement survey model is not a one-size-fits-all approach. The steps in the model are intentionally broad to allow individual public-sector organizations to tailor it to their needs. Each jurisdiction and agency needs to adapt the model to its own mission, values, strategy, culture, and capabilities before adopting it.

Chapter 8

Steps 1 and 2: Planning and Conducting the Employee-Engagement Survey

Employee-engagement surveys are the most direct—and therefore, I believe, the best—way to assess engagement. However, since almost nothing is ever perfect, surveying has its advantages and disadvantages and must be approached and planned carefully, especially in government.

One obvious advantage is that well-designed and well-administered surveys quantify the level of employee engagement with a precision that other approaches can't match. For example, let's look at one of the "agree/disagree" statements suggested in the "diagnostic checklist" cited in Chapter 6 as a way to determine if employees are engaged: Employees are asked if "performance assessment and development often feel like transactional activities that are done to the employee as opposed to being driven by the employee."[1] An important question, but rather than try to answer it anecdotally or subjectively, a survey can answer this (and other important questions) quantitatively and therefore more precisely. In addition to identifying areas to focus on to improve engagement in the short term, survey results can also provide benchmarks to assess and improve engagement over time.

Another advantage is that good surveys deliver results that can be clear and actionable. For example, if survey results show that engagement is low because employees aren't receiving regular and useful feedback from their supervisors or aren't sure what their roles and responsibilities are, managers can act to address these shortcomings. In addition, surveys like the U.S. Merit Systems Protection Board (MSPB), U.S. Office of Personnel Management (OPM), and the U.K. questionnaires allow the surveying organization to develop an engagement index that summarizes the engagement level across the organization. This can be an important benchmark to assess overall engagement. One survey firm also provides a "change index," a summary number (on a 0–100 scale) that rates organizational readiness to make the kind of change needed to improve engagement.

But surveying can be a double-edged sword. A poorly planned survey, or a survey with no follow up, can create more problems than it solves. Therefore, planning requires considering a range of issues:

- Deciding on survey governance
- Deciding whom to survey
- Deciding how often and when to conduct the survey
- Locking in senior leadership support
- Communicating the survey purpose, process, and results
- Designing the survey
- Preparing for possible public visibility

PLANNING A SURVEY

Deciding on Survey Governance

An important starting point is for the agency to consider how the survey process will be "governed"—that is, who will be responsible for managing the process (e.g., a steering committee, human resources). The U.K. Ministry of Justice, which has 80,000 employees, formed an engagement steering group of high-level business sponsors, in large part to achieve executive buy-in across the organization. The ministry also created a working group, representing all sectors of its workforce, that dealt with practical issues such as how the survey would be coordinated, what questions to ask, and who should receive results reports.

Decisions about governance are particularly critical in public-sector organizations, which, as described earlier, operate in a fishbowl environment where decisions and operations are subject to intense scrutiny by multiple stakeholders with often-conflicting interests. Smart agencies will involve as many stakeholders as possible in some capacity, perhaps through a steering committee. Given that labor unions still have strong influence in the public sector, they can also play a key role in governance.

The U.S. Postal Service (USPS), which has had its share of employee problems, provides an example of what can happen if unions aren't involved. In 2010, the American Postal Workers Union, which represents more than 200,000 current and former USPS employees, called for its members to boycott the 2012 survey because, according to the union, "the Postal Service has misrepresented the results of employee opinion surveys in the past, when it used survey data to justify claims that employees supported its wage proposals."[2]

Often, HR manages the employee-engagement survey process, but this depends on several factors, including HR's reputation and credibility. Unfortunately, HR is not viewed as a credible business partner in some organizations. This is often true in government, where HR can be perceived as the "personnel police" because it is charged with enforcing the many personnel and civil-service rules that govern public-sector jurisdictions and agencies.

When we conducted an engagement survey at the University of Wisconsin, HR coordinated the survey process but we also worked hard to ensure that this was not perceived as "just another HR project." With the active support of our executive sponsor, we continually reminded our group of senior executives that they themselves developed the strategic goal that drove the engagement initiative—that is, the goal to "create an environment of respect and inclusiveness through opportunities for employee engagement." HR's intent was simply (or not so simply) to help implement that goal.

Deciding Whom to Survey

Does the agency want to survey all employees or just a sample? The postal service surveys 25 percent of its employees every three months. In 2012, the OPM transitioned from surveying a sample of all federal employees to surveying the entire workforce. The University of Wisconsin Hospital and Clinics surveys all employees who have been on board for at least three months, since newer employees would not have a solid basis on which to answer the survey questions.

Another issue is what types of employees to include: permanent full-time, part-time, temporary, or intermittent employees; contract employees; senior executives; employees in all locations; and so on.

Most government agencies that conduct surveys allow their employees to complete surveys while they are at work, on the clock. This decision needs to be communicated across the organization, particularly to supervisors.

There are several statistical issues related to surveying that may need to be considered, particularly if the agency decides to administer the survey to a sample (and not all) employees. A detailed discussion of these technical issues is beyond the scope of this book.

However, one example is a technique known as "weighting" the survey results to ensure they represent the true demographics of the entire workforce. For example, if an agency's workforce is 50 percent women and 50 percent men, but only 40 percent of the survey respondents are women, the results would have to be proportionately adjusted (weighted) in favor of women to ensure that the data represent that 50 percent of the workforce are women.

Another statistical technique is to calculate "confidence intervals" to estimate the extent that the results of a sample approximate the results that would occur if the entire workforce responded to the survey. This is the technique public-opinion polling organizations use to analyze and report their results (i.e., determine the extent that sampling errors may exist). We often see the results expressed with a "margin of error"—that is, if the sample percentage of positive responses to a question is 60 and the margin of error is plus or minus 3 percent, then the real percentage of positive responses for the entire population would be between 57 and 63 percent.

These types of statistical issues can best be considered and addressed by someone with statistics expertise. Consulting firms that conduct surveys and analyze the results should provide this expertise.

Deciding How Often and When to Conduct the Survey

Ideally, jurisdictions and agencies should conduct engagement surveys on a regular schedule. This means deciding how often to conduct the survey. In the United States, the federal government now conducts the Federal Employee Viewpoint Survey annually. (The survey was initially conducted every other year.) The Canadian federal government conducts its survey every three years. While annual surveys continually refresh the engagement database, the counterargument is that one year is not enough time to act on the survey results and produce real change. The city of Tamarac, Florida, conducts surveys every two years but supplements these with "minisurveys" it administers more often to make sure the city is on the right track. The decision about survey timing can also hinge on resources, particularly in staff- and cash-strapped government agencies, because conducting an engagement survey costs both time and money.

After making the decision on the survey cycle, the next step is to decide the specific time during the cycle to conduct the survey. Finding a time to conduct the survey that everyone involved agrees on is ideal may not be possible.

There may be times to avoid, like when the budget is being prepared or right before an election. The University of Wisconsin Hospital conducts its annual engagement survey in February or March, after the hospital budget process is completed but before the annual performance evaluation cycle begins. The city of Juneau conducts its annual engagement survey in May, when the city finally emerges from the long Alaska winter (and employees are presumably in a more positive frame of mind in general).

In 2012, the OPM conducted the Federal Employee Viewpoint Survey in March but waited until a few weeks after the presidential election to release the results, which showed a decline in both federal-employee satisfaction and engagement.

For a university, the beginning or end of the semester should be avoided. At the University of Wisconsin, we had lengthy conversations about finding the "right time" to survey our employees. Some executives were concerned that employees might still be reeling from actions taken by the state legislature and governor to drastically restrict public employees' collective bargaining rights and also increase employee contributions to retirement and health insurance. The fear was that employees would again voice their frustrations through the survey, even though the university did not have the authority to roll back these changes. Another concern was the "squeaky wheel" feeling that only disaffected employees would complete the survey and use it to vent their concerns.

After much back and forth with our division directors, we realized that there was no perfect time for us to conduct an employee-engagement survey. We also pointed out that the survey instrument we planned to use, developed by the MSPB, really focused on conditions in the workplace, not factors beyond our control (i.e., decisions made by the governor and legislature). Plus, we needed to establish a baseline and, if engagement was indeed low, it was important for us to know that empirically. Our solution was to conduct the survey in early spring—the time of year that seemed to present the fewest obstacles, in our case.

Locking in Senior Leadership Support

Government organizations that have conducted employee engagement surveys and then acted on the results consistently emphasize the absolutely essential need for executive support. This is particularly true in government where, as we have discussed, decision making is complex and often not transparent, and leadership can change rapidly. When I arrived at the University of Wisconsin, the strategic goal to focus on employee engagement was in place but not much work had been done on the goal. Therefore, the timing was right for us to make the case for moving forward using a survey to measure engagement.

We made this business case to our vice chancellor and, after he endorsed our approach, we made a similar case to our division directors. Despite what we thought was a compelling case for collecting survey data as a starting point and baseline, several directors were clearly uncomfortable with this approach. It took a strong statement from the vice chancellor reinforcing that (1) we were committed to employee engagement, (2) collecting empirical engagement data was consistent with our ranking as one of the top 20 research institutions in the world, and (3) we were therefore going ahead with a survey. To his credit, he also decided to administer the survey to his own direct reports. His commitment and leadership enabled us to proceed with the survey approach.

This was also true of the survey strategy of the Canadian province of Alberta. Without the ongoing support of the province's deputy ministers, Alberta would not have been able to sustain its survey programs for 16 years and counting.

Surveys will almost always reveal problems, so agency leadership has to also be prepared to take the results seriously and make a firm commitment to responding. In public-sector agencies, where politics can rule and change is hard, this can take real courage. With survey data, management can no longer plead ignorance about the problems its employees identified. These employees—who have invested time and effort to complete a survey—expect management to act on the results. Failure to act will lead to cynicism, jeopardize future attempts to obtain employee feedback, and perhaps even lead to employee disengagement.

Communicating the Survey Purpose, Process, and Results

The organization must communicate to employees, right from the start, about why the survey is being conducted, how the initiative relates to the agency mission and strategy, what the survey is intended to accomplish, why the results will matter, how the survey will be administered, and how the results will be used. Without a well-developed communication strategy, confusion (and rumor and speculation) can sabotage the initiative. The agency must also emphasize to employees that their responses will be anonymous. Otherwise, they may not respond or, if they do, may not provide candid answers.

After the survey, results should also be communicated promptly and completely. Juneau and Oregon Metro, for example, post all their survey results online so employees can access them. Then, when an agency takes action to improve engagement, it must describe these actions, explain how they link to the survey results, and then provide regular progress reports.

The University of Wisconsin Hospital prepares a standard PowerPoint presentation on the survey results for its 400 managers. Each manager then tailors this presentation to include his or her unit-specific results: response rate, engagement score, work-group key drivers, the five questions that showed the greatest positive percentage changes and the five with greatest negative percentage changes. In this way, the hospital-wide message is consistent but individual unit managers present their own survey results to their units.

The Chorley Borough Council (a local government jurisdiction in the United Kingdom) made presentations on its survey results to its staff, highlighting organizational strengths and weaknesses. At the end of the sessions, employees were asked, "What is the one thing that would improve your working day?" Participants were also asked to write answers on Post-its and stick them on the wall before leaving. This generated 200 Post-its and lots of ideas, which were then presented to a staff forum—made up of around 25 employee representatives—for consideration and implementation.

While communication is critical for organizations in any sector that want to improve employee engagement, it is particularly important in government, where low turnover and long tenures can created highly entrenched workforces that often resist change. Getting the rank-and-file employees on board is therefore essential, and communication is an important tool to make this happen.

Appendix 2 is a sample communication plan to support an employee-engagement initiative.

PREPARING FOR POSSIBLE PUBLIC VISIBILITY

In many government jurisdictions, employee-engagement surveys and results are subject to laws or ordinances regarding freedom of information and open records. This level of public access and transparency simply doesn't exist in private-sector organizations. While this shouldn't prevent the agency from conducting a survey, it is a planning consideration. How will the organization, including senior leaders and elected and appointed officials, react if the results reveal problems, as they inevitably will? What if a survey of law enforcement, emergency-services personnel, or fire fighters shows that these workforces are not fully engaged? Is the jurisdiction/agency prepared to deal not only with internal employee-engagement issues but also with potential political, media, and public scrutiny? This possibility, including how to respond, needs to be anticipated.

CONDUCTING THE ENGAGEMENT SURVEY

So how should a public agency proceed to administer the engagement survey, including deciding which questions to ask and how to administer the survey?

There are many reputable firms that conduct employee-engagement surveys. I've mentioned some, including consulting firms such as BlessingWhite, TowersWatson, Kenexa, and Gallup. Engagement surveys are also conducted by other organizations such as the Great Places to Work Institute (which produces *Fortune* magazine's "100 Best Companies to Work For" list) and the *Chronicle of Higher Education* (which produces the "Great Colleges to Work For" list). These firms and other organizations can provide invaluable support in reporting and analyzing the survey results and, most important, taking action to respond to them. Unfortunately, there are also organizations that may not be as reputable or experienced, especially working with government agencies.

With these issues in mind, there are several options when designing and administering an engagement survey:

- The organization can design and conduct the survey itself.
- The organization can hire an outside survey organization.
- The organization can hire an outside organization to conduct the initial survey(s) but then administer follow-up surveys itself.

DESIGNING AND CONDUCTING THE SURVEY BY THE ORGANIZATION ITSELF

One alternative is for the government organization or agency to handle the entire process itself, including designing the survey. Some government agencies have done this, but it takes time, expertise, and resources. The Canadian interjurisdictional survey, for example, was developed internally after extensive research on what other organizations have done. The MSPB engagement survey questions were developed based on a review of the literature on engagement and engagement surveys, as well as applying a series of statistical techniques that included factor analysis and measurements of reliability and validity to determine which group of questions could best measure employee engagement. In other words, some fairly sophisticated statistical work. Other widely used engagement surveys were developed in similar fashion.

Therefore, while it may seem attractive for a jurisdiction or agency to develop its own survey, there are existing surveys with proven statistical power and validity. Given the number of surveys that have already been tested and shown to quantify engagement, it may not make much sense to develop a new survey from scratch.

However, a viable alternative is for an agency to use an existing survey but manage the actual survey administration process itself. As we've described, there are surveys, like those used by MSPB and OPM, that are valid and accessible because they're in the public domain. These surveys can also generate engagement composite scores or indexes—a useful way to summarize survey results (e.g., overall and/or by work unit or manager).

Doing it yourself requires resources and technical expertise to do the following:

- Decide what survey questions to ask.
- Develop and implement the communication strategy, particularly internally for agency employees.
- Design and administer the survey (typically this is done online but also includes allowing employees to respond who can't

access the survey online and/or don't speak English as their first language).

- Follow up to maximize response rates.
- Summarize, analyze, and report the results.
- Act on the survey data to maintain strengths and improve areas of weakness.
- Follow up, including repeating the survey regularly to assess whether the needle of engagement is moving in the right direction.

If an agency doesn't have the expertise and horsepower to handle these steps itself, or can't commit to this level of effort, it probably shouldn't design and conduct the survey without help.

The U.K. Ministry of Justice—Developing and Implementing an Engagement Survey

One government agency that managed its own survey process is the Ministry of Justice, the third largest agency in the U.K. national government. The ministry surveyed its 80,000 employees and achieved a 65 percent response rate. The project framework included a high-level steering group to achieve an "executive buy-in" across the entire ministry. A working group that included representatives from all parts of the organization grappled with practical issues such as what questions to ask, what reports to produce, and who should receive them. "Employee-engagement champions" were selected to help bring the process to life in units throughout the ministry.

The Ministry of Justice also initiated a major internal marketing push, with the slogan "Start a chain reaction," which was part of a ministry communications campaign as well as a vehicle for local champions and advocates to build on.

What began as an engagement "project" ultimately became business as usual and was absorbed into the ministry's corporate university, the Justice Academy.[3]

USING AN OUTSIDE SURVEY ORGANIZATION

Another alternative is to contract with an organization that has employee survey experience and expertise (e.g., Kenexa, BlessingWhite, Towers-Watson, Gallup). This can be an effective strategy even though it can cost more, at least in direct expenses, than if the agency conducts the survey itself. The University of Wisconsin Hospital and Clinics, for example, has successfully used Kenexa for its surveys.

One variation on this approach is to hire an outside organization to conduct an agency-developed survey or one of the publicly available surveys. The province of Alberta used this approach, conducting research and working with an outside survey design expert to develop its own engagement survey and then contracting with an outside firm to administer it. Alberta did this largely to reassure its employees that no one internally would see their responses. This helped achieve a 71 percent response rate.

At the University of Wisconsin, we used the MSPB survey but hired a survey research firm to administer it. Like Alberta, a key reason for us to hire the outside firm was to help convince our employees that no one at the university would see their individual responses.

USING AN OUTSIDE SURVEY ORGANIZATION WITH AGENCY FOLLOW-UP

In this blended approach, the agency hires a consulting firm to conduct the initial survey (and maybe the first follow-up as well), but then the agency takes over. This is the approach used by the city of Juneau, Alaska. Juneau conducts an annual employee-engagement survey that was initially done by an outside contractor, but the city now administers it under a licensing agreement with the firm that owns the survey.

The advantage of this option is that the organization has outside help to do the initial survey planning, setup, communication, administration, and analysis. Then, after this development work is done, the agency can take over. This assumes that the agency has (or can acquire) permission to administer the survey, as Juneau did through a licensing agreement to use the consulting firm's proprietary survey.

Selecting and then working with an employee-engagement survey contractor can be a complex process in government. Most, if not all, public-sector organizations have procurement rules they must follow to contract with an outside firm. This usually involves issuing a request for proposal (RFP), evaluating the responses, and then selecting the contractor that submits the best proposal. The following are some questions a jurisdiction or agency may want to ask if it decides to select an outside firm to either provide and/or administer a survey. In fact, even if an agency decides to conduct the engagement survey itself, it should consider many of these issues:

- **Does the firm have public-sector experience?** While I agree that there are aspects of how government operates that should be more businesslike, this can be a slippery slope.

  That's why I think it's important to work with an outside organization that understands the environment and unique character of the public sector, including the challenges identified in Chapter 4. This includes how government operates, including the mission and culture of government, how decisions are made, the complexities of operating in a political environment, the role of labor unions, the public visibility of government activities, and so on. Acting on survey results almost always means change and, particularly in government, this usually means culture change. So those who are helping to create that change must understand the public-sector environment and culture.
- **Does the firm have a validated survey that includes benchmark data (preferably from the public sector) to compare results against?** Having a valid survey is critical to ensure that the results accurately reflect the level of engagement in the organization. Just because a set of questions looks like it can measure employee engagement doesn't mean the questions are truly valid. What evidence does the company have that its survey will validly measure the level of engagement? Has the survey been validated across a

large sample of employees and organizations? Does the company have benchmark data from other organizations and employees—preferably from the public sector—to compare results to? How will employees' narrative comments be analyzed and reported?

- **How will the firm administer the survey, including follow-up, to maximize the response rate?** Will the consultants test/pilot the survey before administering it across the organization? How will it reach employees who don't have access to computers and/or have limited or no English language skills? How and when will the contractor follow up to maximize the response rate? How will the anonymity of individual respondents be ensured? How long will it take employees to complete the survey? Can they complete it partially, save their responses, and then return later to finish it? Will the survey allow respondents to provide narrative comments in addition to answering the specific survey questions?

  To boost response rates, some agencies appoint employees to serve as "survey champions" to promote the survey and urge their colleagues to respond, including by sending reminders. In the city of Minneapolis, survey champions are trained and then responsible for (1) helping with the process of surveying and taking action (with an emphasis on "helping" since survey champions themselves are not responsible for conducting the survey or acting on the results), (2) providing expertise and helping managers/leaders interpret survey reports and create action plans, (3) driving leader/manager ownership and accountability to share results and create action plans, and (4) encouraging union buy-in to support solutions.

  The city of Juneau also relied on survey champions to help generate an exceptionally high 94 percent response rate. Likewise, survey champions appointed by the U.K. Department of Justice helped this 80,000-employee organization generate a 65 percent response rate.

- **How will the contractor help communicate across the agency?** Communication is critical—before, during, and after the survey. What is the communication plan to inform all staff about the survey, the results, and follow-up actions? How and when will the results be reported to management and employees (e.g., email, meetings, focus groups, online)?

- **How will the contractor analyze and report on the survey data (e.g., in what formats, and can it analyze and report the results by work units, managers, and demographic groups)?** After the survey is completed, how will the consultant deliver the results? How will data be tabulated, analyzed, and reported? What data "cuts" will the consultant deliver (e.g., by work units, demographic groups, job titles/occupational groups, tenure groups, work shifts, locations, managers compared to staff)? How will results be reported? Will reports include raw data (i.e., question-by-question results), a summary, or both? In what format (e.g., Word, Excel)?
- **Does the consultant have a proven methodology to calculate engagement indexes and drivers?** Will the firm calculate an index that summarizes the results across all the engagement questions? This index can be an important tool to compare an agency's scores against other similar organizations, compare units within the agency, or assess progress over time. Also, can the consulting firm do statistical analysis to identify the drivers of engagement (i.e., the survey questions that are most important to employees and therefore most directly influence their engagement levels)?
- **Will the contractor help you decide how to act on the data to maintain engagement strengths and shore up weaknesses?** Collecting employee-engagement data is the beginning, not the end, of the engagement process. Survey results often raise questions that the results alone won't answer. Conducting a survey and then not acting on the results can leave the organization in worse shape than if it hadn't even done a survey. After the survey, employees will be eager to not only see the data and results but learn about what's next. So the consultants should be prepared to help the agency move forward. Moving forward can mean helping create engagement teams and then working with the teams to identify and implement action plans, monitor progress, and measure results.

So Many Engagement Surveys to Choose From—What to Do?

The wide variety of available employee-engagement surveys can be confusing. The different surveys include different questions and can also produce different engagement indices and lists of engagement drivers.

Given my contention that solid engagement surveys have a lot in common, I believe that it's most important to make sure that the survey selected is valid and will truly measure engagement. Surveys developed by many consulting firms, as well as organizations such as the MSPB and the OPM, meet this standard. While each survey has its proponents, any of these (and others) can enable an agency to measure engagement with confidence. And the real payoff comes from acting on the results. The goal should not be to try to develop or find a perfect survey. Instead, the idea is to (1) select an instrument that will work for the agency, its strategy, and culture; (2) conduct the survey and analyze the results; and (3) act on the data to maintain areas of strength and improve areas of weakness.

CONDUCTING AN ENGAGEMENT SURVEY AT THE UNIVERSITY OF WISCONSIN

At the University of Wisconsin, we administered an employee-engagement survey to about 4,500 employees in the 13 units that provide administrative support to our campus. These units include HR, facilities planning and management, the police department, the student union, student health services, and student housing. These units represent a wide range of employees, occupations, and demographic groups, ranging from custodians to medical doctors. Our workforce also includes many employees who do not have computer access and/or do not speak English as their first language.

We started by piloting the survey first in the Office of Human Resources to work out any survey kinks and also show our campus colleagues that HR was willing to take this step ourselves before we asked other units to do it. We used the MSPB survey, plus the three questions from the OPM Federal Employee Viewpoint Survey that the Partnership for Public Service uses to calculate "Best Places to Work in the Federal Government" scores.

For the pilot, the university survey research center administered the survey to our 150-person HR staff (including student employees). The survey center provided us with overall summary results for the Office of Human Resources, plus summaries for the specific work units in HR. We did not see any individual employee responses, thus preserving employee anonymity.

Then, after the pilot, we expanded the survey to the other 12 units but used an outside contractor to administer the survey and report the results. This firm was selected through a competitive bidding process.

Our contractor conducted the survey largely online by providing each of the 4,500 employees surveyed with a customized web address to access the survey. Creating 4,500 employee-specific web addresses may seem overly complicated, but this was an important step to guarantee confidentiality—no university employee had access to these web addresses or any individual employee's responses. We supplemented the online survey with paper copies (with random identification numbers, not names) for employees who don't have easy access to computers, and we translated the survey into Spanish, Hmong, and Tibetan (that's right, Tibetan—the university has almost 100 employees who speak this as their native language).

Our contractor kept the survey open initially for three weeks and then extended it for another two weeks to boost the response rate. The firm sent three email reminders.

We also worked directly with the other 12 units to help them communicate with their employees about the survey and prepare to receive, and act on, the results. We spoke with each director to explain the initiative, including the business case for engagement; distributed talking points (see box) to each director; and worked with each division to identify the subunits in their divisions they wanted reports on. We also asked each division to appoint a "data director" who was responsible for receiving the survey results and understanding how to explain and use them.

Employee Engagement Communication Suggestions and Talking Points for University of Wisconsin Division Directors

The following is a list of suggested talking points we distributed to managers at the University of Wisconsin to help them explain the employee engagement initiative to their staff members.

Suggested Communication Process/Talking Points

1. Involve managers and supervisors on the front end in communication. They may be able to help design the process and/or anticipate questions from staff. Make sure they are prepared to explain the initiative when staff members follow up with questions.
2. Make a deliberate choice about how you communicate. This may be different for different divisions. Venues could include the following:
   - All-staff forums with time for questions
   - Unit forums in smaller groups
   - Emails to staff
   - Combinations of these approaches
3. Follow up your initial communication by discussing staff reactions with managers and supervisors. Identify questions that should be answered at the outset to avoid unnecessary confusion or concern.

Suggested Communication Messages

1. **Describe the employee engagement initiative.** One of the goals in the strategic plan for the Office of Vice Chancellor for Finance and Administration is to "create an environment of respect and inclusiveness through opportunities for employee engagement." To accomplish this goal, each division strives to engage

employees more effectively in both how work is accomplished and how decisions are made.

2. **Explain why we are doing this.** Greater employee engagement will not only improve how individual employees feel about their jobs and the unit but also produce better unit decisions and better organizational performance. Research in both the public and private sectors confirms the power of employee engagement to improve individual and organizational performance.

Anticipated Benefits and Desired Outcomes

1. Greater personal meaning in work
2. Heightened connection to work, the university and division mission, and coworkers
3. Increased involvement and collaboration in division decision making, resulting in better organizational performance
4. More informed decision making by each division to help use resources effectively
5. Stronger partnerships across the organization

Division Process

1. Division creates engagement team with a mix of employees and managers/supervisors.
2. Contractor conducts employee-engagement survey.
3. Contractor collects and analyzes survey data.
4. Division-engagement team reviews baseline survey data.
5. Team establishes work plans and timelines to sustain areas of strength and address areas for improvement.
6. Team works across division to implement plans, monitor progress, learn, and make adjustments.
7. Division resurveys employees after about one year.
8. Division reports on best practices and shares learning across divisions.

The Survey

- The survey includes 20–25 questions/statements that have been shown to assess employee-engagement levels.
- The survey is administered online with hard copies for employees who don't have access to computers.
- A third party administers the survey and analyzes the data. No one in the division or HR sees any employee's individual responses.
- The contractor administering the survey provides summaries of the results (but not individual responses) to the divisions for analysis and action.

After the survey, our contractor provided each division with a series of spreadsheets containing unit-specific data, broken down question by question for the division's work units and demographic groups. Each unit also received employee-engagement index scores based on the 16 MSPB engagement questions/statements. Because these questions were scaled from 1 to 5 (1 was "strongly disagree" and 5 was "strongly agree"), the index aggregated and summarized the unit's overall responses to these 16 questions into a single number between 1 and 5, reflecting the overall level of engagement.

Our contractor also provided question-by-question results, as follows:

- The average score for each survey question (on the 1–5 scale)
- The percentage of "favorable" (4–5 on the 5-point scale), "neutral" (3), and "unfavorable" (1–2) responses for each question

The contractor also delivered to each division a summary that aggregated the results (question by question and via the engagement index) from across all 13 divisions to serve as a benchmark; division leaders could then compare this benchmark against their division's results. Finally, each division received a summary of its employees' narrative, verbatim comments, summarized by themes.

* * *

While there are several different ways for a government jurisdiction/agency to assess employee engagement, conducting a well-designed employee-engagement survey is the best approach to generate actionable data on an agency's level of engagement.

Selecting and then administering an employee-engagement survey can seem like a daunting challenge. While there is no perfect solution, the key decision is to conduct the survey. Then it's about selecting a survey instrument that will work for the organization and its mission, values, strategy, and culture; conducting the survey; analyzing the survey data; communicating the results; and acting on the data.

Chapter 9

Step 3: Reporting and Analyzing Survey Results

So What Do All These Numbers Mean?

Conducting an employee-engagement survey is a solid first step on the road to improving engagement. The next step is to analyze the results, including breaking the data down to identify the best opportunities for improvement (the specific areas where engagement is low) as well as the engagement strengths that need to be maintained.

This analysis can start with a review of the summary results from the survey (i.e., an overall engagement index, if one was computed, or a question-by-question summary). Then more detailed analysis breaks the data down by key variables that can include agency work units, locations, individual managers/supervisors, demographic groups, occupations, employee tenure groups, salaried versus hourly employees, and union members compared to employees not in unions. In 2012, for the first time, the U.S. Office of Personnel Management provided federal agencies with the ability to design customized reports with their agency-specific employee survey data from the Federal Employee Viewpoint Survey.

Effective analysis of survey results depends on careful planning. If an agency decides to analyze data by work units, for example, the survey must include a question that asks each employee to identify his or her work unit. The same is true for analyses by demographic groups, manager by manager, managers compared to rank-and-file employees, and so on.

There are several approaches to reviewing and analyzing engagement survey results.

RESPONSE RATE

An often overlooked data point is the survey response rate. Without even looking at the actual survey results, the response rate itself can be revealing. A high response rate suggests a high level of employee interest (and perhaps even engagement) and indicates that the data are representative of the entire workforce and should be reviewed carefully. On the other hand, a low rate could suggest a lack of interest that, by itself, can indicate a problem and also mean that the results are not truly representative.

So the logical next question is, What is a good response rate? This isn't a statistics textbook, but the answer is "it depends." Usually, the more employees an organization has, the more difficult it is to achieve a high response rate.

In the U.S. federal government, the response rate for the 2012 Federal Employee Viewpoint Survey of 1.6 million federal employees was 46 percent (more than 687,000 responses), an impressive number given the size of the federal government workforce. Among the large federal agencies, response rates ranged from 31 percent (Department of Veterans Affairs) to more than 77 percent (Office of Management and Budget). In the small agencies, the response rate ranged up to 94 percent (Chemical Safety and Hazard Investigation Board) and down to 36 percent (Nuclear Waste Technical Review Board).[1]

The state of Washington, which conducts an employee survey every two years, achieved a 56 percent response (about 33,000 employees responded) in the most recent survey in 2011.

In local government, Oregon Metro achieved a 70 percent response rate, and the city of Juneau has achieved a 94 percent response rate.

In 2012, participants in the Canadian interjurisdictional engagement initiative reported survey response rates ranging from 45 to 72 percent.

At the University of Wisconsin Hospital, which has been conducting engagement surveys annually since 2005, the 2012 response rate was an impressive 83 percent of its almost 5,400 employees. One piece of advice the hospital offers is to consider setting a response rate goal and then working with management (and the survey contractor, if one is used) to achieve the goal. Setting the goal too low can undercut the value of the results, but setting it too high can also raise unrealistic expectations. The hospital typically strives for an 85 percent participation rate, which is very high for an organization of the hospital's size. Because the survey response rate has exceeded 83 percent, pushing for the extra 1 to 2 percent is probably not worth the time and effort and could even lead to employee resentment.

It can be much harder to generate a high response rate in a large, decentralized, and geographically dispersed organization such as a large federal agency. (Note that more than 85 percent of federal employees work outside the Washington, DC, area.)

Maximizing the Survey Response Rate at the U.S. Securities and Exchange Commission (SEC)

The SEC achieved a record high response rate of almost 70 percent in the 2012 Federal Employee Viewpoint Survey by building participation through a series of communications during the survey administration period. To kick the survey off, the SEC chairperson sent out a personal communication encouraging all employees to participate. The division directors also sent personal messages to their staff members urging them to complete the survey. The chairperson and division directors received weekly updates on participation rates. The SEC also collaborated with its union to encourage employees to complete the survey. HR also inserted periodic notices in *SEC Today*, the daily electronic newsletter that goes to all SEC staff.[2]

If the response rate is disappointing, it will be worthwhile to try to analyze why and perhaps collect additional data. For example, at the University of Wisconsin, response rates across the 13 units we surveyed ranged from 14 to 100 percent. When we looked deeper, we found that the low response rates were in the units with higher percentages of student employees and second- and third-shift workers, many of whom don't have strong English language skills or easy access to computers. Although we translated the survey into three languages, administered it in hard copy as well as online, and tried to time the survey to reach student employees during the academic year, we obviously missed large numbers of these populations. With students, this was not fatal, because even though student employees are important contributors to the university, they are temporary employees who are at the university for reasons other than their part-time jobs.

The low response in other employee groups, however, was more troubling and led us to reconsider how we administered the survey and also seek other ways to get their feedback, such as in focus groups.

QUESTION-BY-QUESTION ANALYSIS

The survey questions/statements themselves are the essence of an engagement survey, and that is logically where most organizations focus their analytical energy. The key here is to identify the questions that highlight the issues needing the most attention. To do this, the results should ideally be reported in several different ways, including the following:

- **Average (mean) scores for each question.** For example, using the U.S. Merit Systems Protection Board survey, in which employees respond to each statement by selecting responses that range from 1 (strongly disagree) to 5 (strongly agree), the mean response for each statement would be reported as a number between 1 and 5.
- **Percent favorable and unfavorable.** As we learned in statistics class, mean scores can be deceiving: If half the employees who respond to a specific question rate it a 5 and the other half rate it a 1, the average is 3, but that is deceiving. An alternative is to

calculate the percentage of favorable and unfavorable responses to each question. This requires deciding which scores fall into these ranges. In the 1–5 scale, 4–5 might be "favorable," 3 might be "neutral," and 1–2 could be "unfavorable." By sorting the data like this, it's fairly easy to see the positives and negatives: The favorable items are strengths to maintain and the unfavorable items are areas to improve.

COMPARISONS BY WORK UNIT AND BY DEMOGRAPHIC GROUP

In addition to reviewing organization-wide results, slicing and dicing the survey data into smaller chunks can also provide revealing insights. Work-unit-by-work-unit comparisons can identify the units that need to pay particular attention to improving engagement. In fact, one of the most valuable ways to analyze survey data is to break the data down into the smallest components possible and identify specific issues that units can act on.

At the Air Force Materiel Command, for example, which used the Gallup Q12 survey, every work unit that had at least five responses received unit-specific survey results. According to an official, these were the most powerful and actionable results because they enabled individual managers to understand how their employees were feeling about their individual work units. These comparisons can spotlight units that have high levels of engagement, enabling the agency to identify good practices to share, adapt, and adopt across the entire organization. The state of Washington urges state agencies to "celebrate" positive results that show up in agency-specific results from the statewide biennial employee survey.

The U.S. Department of Justice conducted "best practices sessions" to share employee-engagement lessons across the department from units that scored well in the "Best Places to Work in the Federal Government" rankings.

At the University of Wisconsin, our contractor provided individual summaries of survey results for each of the 13 units that participated in the survey. We also asked each of these units to identify the subunits they wanted reports on. One department director asked for the survey responses to be reported for each of his 26 operating units, as well as by demographic groups for each of these units. The data report spreadsheet for that unit was quite extensive, but it enabled this unit to conduct a series of deep dives with the results, including providing each operating manager with detailed data for his or her unit.

It can also be useful to review the data by demographic groups, including gender, age, race, and ethnicity. Different levels of engagement by group can reveal problem areas, particularly if some demographic groups seem less engaged than others. The city of Tamarac, Florida, segments results from its biennial survey by age group, including employees under the age of 35, to analyze concerns linked to age.

In 2012, the U.S. Office of Personnel Management added several demographic questions to the Federal Employee Viewpoint Survey that allowed it to assess the levels of engagement for additional groups of federal employees: part-time workers; veterans; employees with disabilities; and members of the lesbian, gay, bisexual, and transgender (LGBT) communities. For the latter category, "I prefer not to say" was added as a response choice.

The responses revealed that federal employees who self-identified as disabled or as members of the LGBT community reported substantially lower levels of engagement than employees who were not disabled or in the LGBT community, respectively.[3]

Most organizations promise their employees that their responses will remain confidential. To maintain this confidentiality, it is wise to set a minimum number of responses for reporting—that is, in order to report responses (e.g., by unit, demographic group), a minimum number of employees must complete the survey. At the University of Wisconsin, we agreed that we would not report responses for any unit or demographic group with fewer than five complete responses.

BENCHMARKS

Comparing engagement survey results to results from comparable organizations can shed light on an agency's employee-engagement level in ways that simply reviewing the agency's own data can't. Many consulting and other organizations that provide employee-engagement surveying and related services also offer a database of other organizations for client comparison. Gallup, for example, has an extensive database of Q12 data. In addition, many of the rankings for "best places," "best companies," and so on are based on organization-to-organization comparisons.

In the U.S. federal government, the Office of Personnel Management provides federal agencies with a set of benchmarks by computing government-wide satisfaction and engagement indices, as well as individual scores, for 37 separate departments and agencies.

The Partnership's "Best Places to Work in the Federal Government" rankings divide federal agencies into three categories based on the size of their workforces. Agencies can see where they stand against the government-wide benchmark and compare their scores against agencies with similar-size workforces.

The state of Washington also provides each if its 36 state agencies with benchmarks by publishing the following for each of the 16 questions in its biennial employee survey:

- Mean scores, agency by agency
- Statewide results
- Trend data, agency by agency, comparing current and previous survey results

The Canadian interjurisdictional engagement initiative uses a similar benchmarking approach but with an important twist: Each province provides its engagement survey results to a province that has agreed to summarize the data and then each province receives a report that aggregates the results from across all the participating jurisdictions (i.e., the benchmarks). The summary includes question-by-question results, as well as an engagement index. Each province can then compare its results against these cross-province benchmarks. The Canadian federal government also participates, thus providing each province—and the federal government—with benchmark data from public-sector organizations in different levels of government.

In general, the challenge in benchmarking is to find valid and logical comparisons. Comparing a government agency to a manufacturing company may not make much sense. Similarly, comparing engagement in a small public jurisdiction to engagement in a large federal agency probably doesn't wash either.

In government, it can be difficult to find comparable benchmark data. If government-specific benchmarks aren't available, an alternative is to benchmark internally. That can be done by comparing results work unit by work unit. At the University of Wisconsin Hospital, Kenexa, the firm that surveys hospital employees, provides unit-by-unit data and also calculates a "best in class" benchmark—the engagement index score that separates the top-scoring hospital work units from the rest. In this way, each unit can clearly see where it needs to be to become best in class. The hospital also analyzes the survey data to identify units that are in both the top and bottom 10 percent. The former are reviewed for best practices while the latter are analyzed to see how they can improve. Minneapolis uses a similar approach by identifying the "most engaged" city government units—those that score in the top 20 percent.

Another solution for a government jurisdiction or agency is to benchmark against itself, over time, by conducting regular engagement surveys. The initial survey becomes the baseline for future comparisons. This can be likened to a "golf score" approach. Most golfers try to improve their own scores, not compare themselves to the scores of professional golfers. The same strategy in engagement can enable an organization to identify areas it needs to address and then make steady progress over time in those areas. It's a marathon, not a sprint.

DRIVERS OF ENGAGEMENT

A more sophisticated but extremely valuable analysis uses statistical techniques to identify the "drivers" of engagement—that is, the survey responses (individual questions) that most influence the overall level of employee engagement (i.e., the engagement index). Identifying the drivers usually involves a statistical technique known as regression analysis that isolates the questions that "drive" employee engagement. This kind of analysis can more precisely identify the key areas that are either strengths to be maintained or weaknesses to be addressed.

Some organizations will include a specific question or statement, such as, "I intend to stay at this organization for at least the next two years," and then identify, through regression analysis, the other questions that most influence positive responses to the stay-or-leave question. These drivers therefore highlight the issues that the organization should focus on to maximize retention. In "Best Places to Work in the Federal Government," the drivers of employee satisfaction are computed by identifying the questions that correlate with respondents' answer to this one question: "Are you considering leaving your organization within the next year?" In each of the six iterations of "Best Places," "leadership" has been the number one driver of employee satisfaction.

At the University of Wisconsin, we used regression analysis to identify which of the 16 engagement statements most significantly influenced our overall employee-engagement score. This analysis identified the following five statements as the most important in predicting the overall engagement index score. The driver statements are shown in order of importance, highest first. The numbers represent the percentage of positive responses:

1. My opinion counts (67 percent).
2. I am given the opportunity to improve my skills (54 percent).
3. I am satisfied with my supervisor (65 percent).
4. I have the resources to do my job well (68 percent).
5. The work I do is meaningful to me (73 percent).

This driver analysis revealed the priority areas we needed to focus on (i.e., statements that are most important but had relatively low scores), such as the opportunity to improve skills. On the other hand, the driver analysis showed us that our employees find meaning in their work, a very positive result even though there was room for improvement. In other words, this is an area we needed to maintain.

In addition to computing the overall drivers across all units surveyed, our contractor also calculated the individual engagement drivers for each of the 13 units surveyed. These unit-specific drivers, which varied from division to division, were highly actionable because they identified the key engagement areas each division needed to focus on.

COMPARING ENGAGEMENT DRIVERS WITH ENGAGEMENT QUESTION/STATEMENT SCORES

At the university, we then took this analysis a step further by constructing a matrix that shows the relationship between the scores (the percentage of positive responses) for each of the 16 engagement questions/statements and the extent that each was a driver of engagement. Figure 9.1 shows how these relationships can be plotted.

In the chart, the horizontal axis—"question importance"—shows the extent to which each question was a driver of the overall engagement

Figure 9.1. Engagement survey question score-importance comparison.

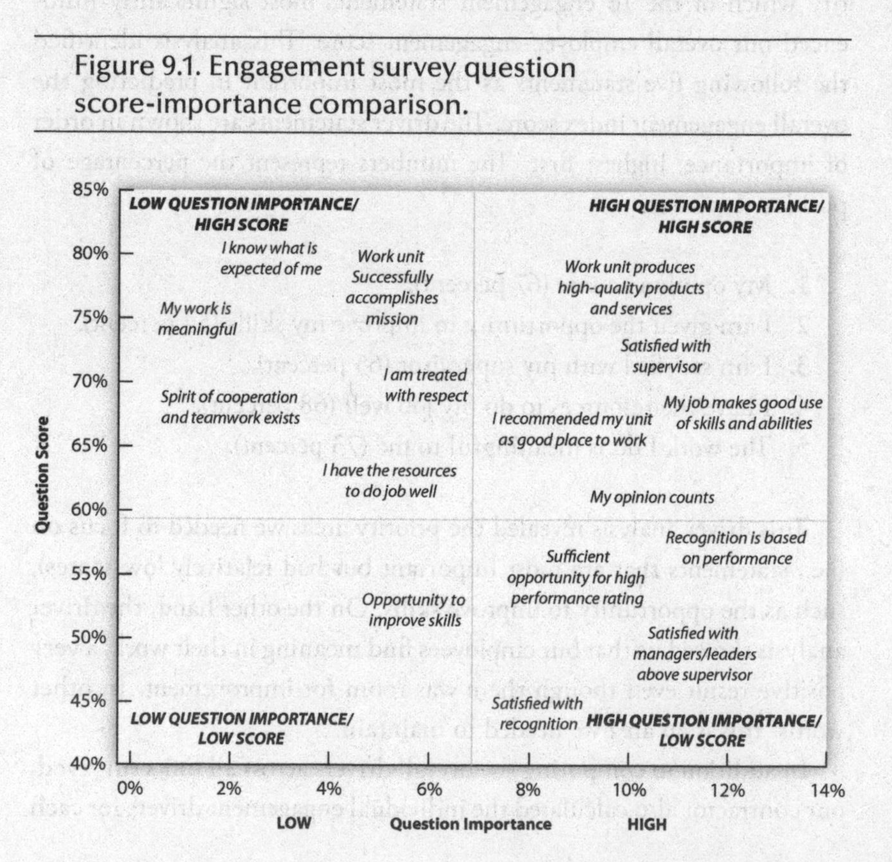

score, from low to high. The percentages reflect how much each question influenced the overall engagement score (e.g., a question rated at 10 percent is statistically twice as important to engagement as a question rated at 5 percent). The vertical axis—"question score"—shows the overall employee rating (percentage of responses that were favorable) for each question.

The four quadrants represent the interactions between the two factors: the importance of each question to employee engagement and the engagement score (percent positive response) for each question. Each question was then plotted into where it belongs (one of the four quadrants):

- Low question importance, high engagement score (northwest)
- High question importance, high engagement score (northeast)
- Low question importance, low engagement score (southwest quadrant)
- High question importance, low engagement score (southeast)

Most organizations should strive for high scores in the high-importance engagement questions—the questions that fall into the "high question importance, high engagement score" (northeast) quadrant. These are areas of strength to maintain. On the other hand, the engagement questions (and corresponding issues) that require the most attention (for improvement) are in the "high question importance, low engagement score" (southeast) quadrant. These questions most influence the level of engagement but are the lowest-scoring; thus improvement in these areas will yield the greatest employee-engagement benefit to the organization.

COMPARING ENGAGEMENT SCORES OF MANAGERS/ SUPERVISORS TO RANK-AND-FILE EMPLOYEES

Another analysis compares the overall survey responses of managers and supervisors to the responses of frontline employees. As noted earlier, higher-level employees are generally more engaged than rank-and-file employees. In most organizations, including in government, employees further up in the hierarchy earn more and have more control and influence—a set of circumstances that usually translates into higher engagement.

However, larger-than-expected gaps between management and front-line employees can reveal systemic problems, particularly if managers/supervisors have much rosier views about the state of employee engagement. This disconnect can make dealing with engagement issues especially difficult. That is, if higher-level employees don't agree with the rank and file that improving engagement is necessary (or vice versa), improvement will be harder to achieve. Both groups need to agree that action is needed.

In fact, change is more likely (even if an agency's engagement scores are low) if the scores of managers and rank-and-file employees are close. In other words, there needs to be agreement across the organization that engagement is low and improvement is therefore necessary. Given that achieving change in most government agencies is challenging, this type of agreement can be a big advantage for an agency committed to improving engagement.

At the Partnership for Public Service, we analyzed these gaps for federal government agencies by calculating staff/manager "alignment scores." The scores assessed the degree of alignment (or misalignment) between agency managers and staff based on 50 questions from the Federal Employee Viewpoint Survey.[4]

The alignment scores ranged from +50 to –50. Agencies received one point (+1) for questions from the employee survey showing that managers and staff were "aligned" (i.e., the gap was smaller than the government-wide average), received no points (0) for questions that were close to the government-wide average, and lost one point (–1) for questions showing that managers and staff were "disconnected" (i.e., the gap was larger than the government-wide average). A negative score can signal disconnects between staff and managers.

Just as the engagement key drivers and the engagement scores were graphed in Figure 9.1, the Partnership graphed each federal agency's staff/manager alignment score against the agency's "Best Places to Work" index score. This graph, shown in Figure 9.2, also has four quadrants:

Figure 9.2. Manager/employee alignment matrix.

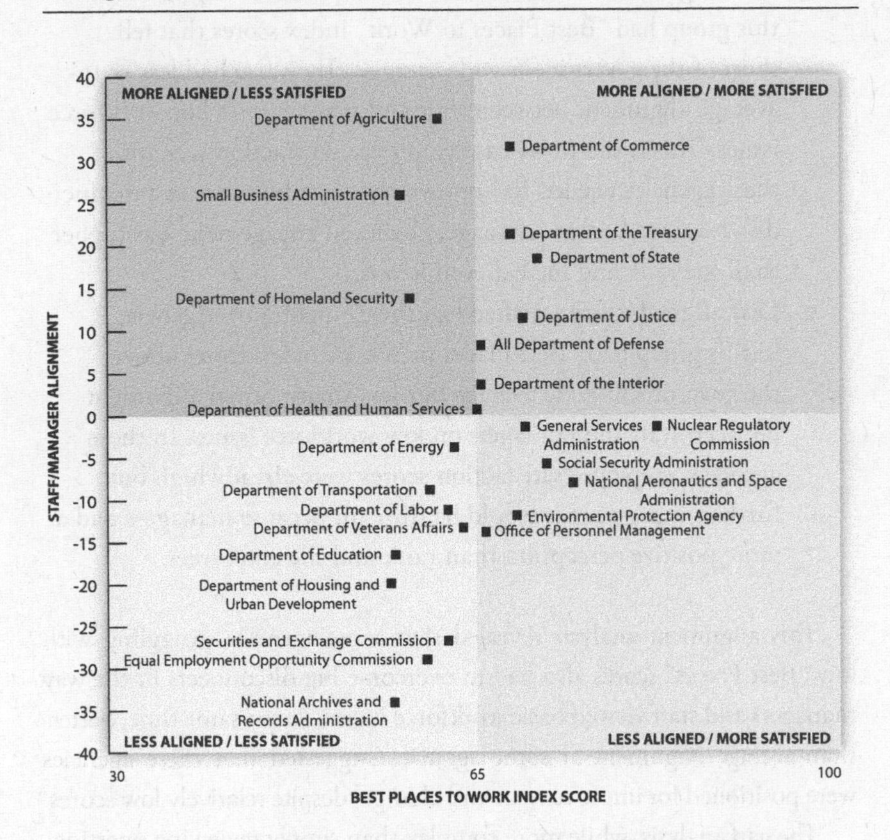

1. **More aligned/less satisfied** (northwest quadrant). Agencies in this group had "Best Places to Work" satisfaction index scores below the government-wide average but also had greater-than-normal alignment between managers and staff on key workforce issues. These agencies needed to improve and were poised for improvement because managers and employees agreed that workplace conditions needed to get better.
2. **More aligned/more satisfied** (northeast quadrant). Agencies in this group had "Best Places to Work" satisfaction index scores higher than the government-wide average and also had greater-than-average alignment between staff and managers on key workforce issues. This is the quadrant where an agency should want to be, with high scores and high alignment.

3. **Less aligned/less satisfied** (southwest quadrant). Agencies in this group had "Best Places to Work" index scores that fell short of the government-wide average. They also had less-than-average alignment between staff and managers on key workforce issues. This is the worst-case employee satisfaction scenario; these agencies needed to improve the most but were at a distinct disadvantage because managers believed engagement was higher than the rank and file believed it was.
4. **Less aligned/more satisfied** (southeast quadrant). Agencies in this group had "Best Places to Work" index scores above the government-wide average but less-than-normal alignment between staff and managers on key workforce issues. In these agencies, employee satisfaction scores were already high but further improvement would be difficult because managers had a more positive perception than rank-and-file employees.

This alignment analysis revealed that some agencies struggling with low "Best Places" scores also had to overcome big disconnects in the way managers and staff viewed basic workforce issues. At the same time, better-than-average alignment at some agencies suggested that these agencies were positioned for improvement and change, despite relatively low scores.

The gap analysis, while more complex than simply reviewing question-by-question responses, can be a useful way to more deeply analyze engagement survey results, including for a jurisdiction or agency that surveys multiple work units and/or employee groups.

VERBATIM RESPONSES

Well-constructed surveys allow employees to not only answer survey questions but also add narrative responses. These responses, known as *verbatims*, can provide richness that complements the quantitative results, including helping to reveal why employees answered the way they did. While agencies need to be careful not to overgeneralize based on individual verbatim responses, these narratives provide data that the survey questions by themselves can't.

In some cases, when large numbers of employees are being surveyed, there may simply be too many narrative responses to absorb or analyze. Even in a small organization like the Partnership for Public Service, we had fewer than 100 employees, yet we'd receive hundreds of verbatim responses. Drawing conclusions from all this information was a challenge.

One approach to solving this problem involves categorizing the narratives—that is, developing specific categories and then sorting the narratives into these categories. This takes some additional time but can help the agency process a large volume of narrative responses. At the University of Wisconsin, for example, our survey of 4,500 employees generated thousands of verbatims. We worked with our contractor to identify response categories for each question, and then the firm sorted the narratives into these categories. If we hadn't done this, our divisions would have been overwhelmed with narrative responses.

For example, we sorted the narrative responses into both positive and negative categories in order to compare and analyze both the positive and negative comments:

- Good communication, poor communication
- Trust, distrust
- Expectations clear, expectations unclear
- Trust leadership, distrust leadership

Our contractor summarized the percentages of all narrative responses that fell into each category. In effect, this was a shorthand way of summarizing a large number of verbatim responses in a useful and usable way.

The key take-aways about analyzing engagement survey data are that there are different ways to look at survey results, ranging from simply reviewing responses question by question to more sophisticated assessments of engagement drivers and disconnects between managers and frontline staff. Before conducting a survey, an agency needs to plan how it wants to analyze the results and then construct or modify the survey to ensure the data it needs are collected.

Chapter 10

Step 4: Taking Action to Improve Employee Engagement

Before this book, I'd written a series of articles on employee engagement, including one subtitled "Free Pizza and Coke on a Friday Afternoon Is Not an Engagement Strategy."[1]

My point was that an agency truly committed to improving engagement needs to take real and sustained action to improve engagement. This means going beyond just conducting an employee survey, which is merely the starting point to improve engagement. We can't improve individual or organizational performance with surveys and data unless we use the results wisely. The city of Minneapolis analyzed survey results, and, according to Charles Bernardy, city HR manager, in the departments where action was taken—and employees knew about it—engagement scores were significantly higher. According to Bernardy, "Employees who say their department leadership took action on the results of the 2009 employee survey are 45 percentage points more engaged."[2] In addition, the following is also true:

- City employees who said they were given an opportunity to see/hear about the employee survey results were 26 percentage

points more engaged than those who did to have this opportunity.
- Employees who reported they had the opportunity to discuss their ideas about the results of the survey results were 34 percentage points more engaged than those who did not.[3]

The Norfolk City Council in the United Kingdom has turned its commitment to act on engagement survey results into a catchy motto: "You said, we did."[4]

At the University of Wisconsin Hospital, work units that acted on the engagement survey results improved over time and the units that didn't act didn't improve. While this makes intuitive sense, the hospital did the math, made the comparisons, and proved it empirically—a powerful message for an organization with a culture that highly values data.

No matter how an agency approaches taking action, it's important to understand that improving employee engagement is a long-term proposition. Conducting an engagement survey and then analyzing the results is the beginning, not the end. As a jurisdiction or agency analyzes engagement survey data, it may decide to put in place long-term changes or target specific engagement issues immediately—or both.

Even organizations that have good employee-engagement results/scores can strive to go from *good* to *great*. In the "Best Places to Work in the Federal Government" rankings I've been citing, 71 percent of federal agencies improved their initial employee satisfaction scores when their employees were resurveyed.

The Partnership for Public Service developed an action planning guide to help agencies take action on satisfaction/engagement survey results. The guide includes specific steps a jurisdiction or agency can take to act on survey data:

- Identify focus areas/priorities.
- Find an executive champion and engage key stakeholders.
- Communicate, communicate, communicate.
- Form action teams and create action plans.
- Collect additional data.

- Set measurable goals and milestones.
- Develop recommendations.
- Obtain executive sponsor approval.
- Put the plan into action.[5]

IDENTIFY FOCUS AREAS/PRIORITIES

It is unlikely that any organization, public or private, could immediately respond to all issues identified in an engagement survey. That's why it's important to focus on the survey responses that identify the greatest opportunities to improve. There may be low-hanging fruit where short-term improvement is possible—and may even be necessary. In Chapter 9, I outlined some approaches to analyzing survey data that can help identify the areas that have the greatest potential to improve engagement. The engagement survey questions that are low-scoring but have high importance (the engagement drivers) are a logical place to start. Given that government resources are constrained (and becoming even more constrained), identifying the priority areas of focus is a critical step.

It's important to emphasize again that acting on survey results isn't just about shoring up weaknesses. It's also about focusing on the strengths identified in the survey and then maintaining them.

At the Air Force Materiel Command, action teams were formed to work on issues identified in the engagement survey. These teams were asked to identify two areas of focus in order to maximize the probability of success. The University of Wisconsin Hospital used the same approach—individual departments were asked to identify and then work on two high-priority items.

FIND AN EXECUTIVE CHAMPION AND ENGAGE KEY STAKEHOLDERS

Improving employee engagement requires a shared vision for change that starts with senior leadership, extends to managers and supervisors, and then reaches other employees and stakeholders across the organization, at all levels.

Any organization-wide effort such as improving engagement requires executive-level support. This is a particularly true in government where, as we have discussed, decision making is often diffused and subject to external forces. An executive champion can generate buy-in from internal and external stakeholders and also provide resources. Plus, employees who are energized by their executives' commitment to improving the agency workplace can themselves become ambassadors for change.

The commitment of managers and supervisors is also a key to improving engagement, regardless of which survey is used. Strong leadership is almost always critical to improving employee engagement, especially in government, where (as we described in Chapter 4) agencies committed to improving engagement face a set of particular challenges, including entrenched workforces.

Unions can also be powerful allies for change, especially since they are still very influential in many government jurisdictions and agencies. Agencies that involve unions in the development and administration of employee surveys—like the city of Minneapolis, Oregon Metro, and the Air Force Materiel Command—have an advantage when they are ready to take action on survey results. In the long run, improving union members' level of engagement should resonate with organized labor, particularly if unions have been involved in the process from the beginning.

COMMUNICATE, COMMUNICATE, COMMUNICATE

In the words of George Bernard Shaw, "The single biggest problem in communication is the illusion that it has taken place."[6] This echoes what organizations that have surveyed their workforces and then successfully acted on the survey results advise—communicate early and often.

As described in Chapter 8, communication should begin even before the survey is conducted. The agency should broadly announce the initiative, including how it supports the organization's strategy and why engagement matters (i.e., the business case for engagement), and emphasize the agency's commitment to improving the working environment.

Chapter 8 includes the communication guide we used at the University of Wisconsin.

Communication continues after the engagement survey is conducted. Employees who complete the survey will be eager to learn about the results. Not providing this feedback promptly will create a perception that the organization is not serious about improving engagement or, even worse, has something to hide. The U.S. Merit Systems Protection Board (MSPB) recommends sharing survey results with employees no later than one month after the jurisdiction or agency receives them.

That's one reason Oregon Metro posts comprehensive survey data on its intranet so all employees (and labor unions) can see the results. Metro also provides all employees with a written summary of the results. In the city of Juneau, every city employee receives citywide results as well as the data for his or her department. The state of Washington posts the complete results of its biennial employee survey, agency by agency, on the state HR website.

In most organizations, the survey results will be a combination of good news and bad news, and it's important to share both messages, publicizing areas of strength as well as areas for improvement. For example, when the city of Minneapolis did its first engagement survey, the results identified some clear areas of strength (Table 10.1).

Table 10.1.

Statement	% Who agree
I believe the quality of my work is important to the overall success of the city.	89
My work unit provides quality services to customers.	88
The people in my work unit are committed to doing quality work.	84
I understand how my work contributes to the overall goals of the city.	83
I understand how my job helps fulfill my department's mission and goals.	83

These positive results were impressive and worthy of publicizing. On the other hand, the survey identified areas for improvement that city employees (and elected officials) also needed to know about (Table 10.2).

In the federal government, the "Best Places to Work in the Federal Government" results are widely publicized by the Partnership for Public Service through a high-profile release event that includes award presentations to the top-ranking agencies, press releases, and posting of agency-by-agency scores and rankings on the Partnership's public website. This generates press and other media coverage.

The transparency and publicity generated by the Partnership puts pressure on each ranked agency to also communicate internally with its staff—sharing not just the survey results but also what the results mean to the agency and, more important, what the organization intends to do about them. Shortly after the Partnership released one set of "Best Places" rankings, a federal department secretary announced to his senior managers that his goal was to be ranked in the top 10 the following year. The leadership team got the message directly from the top—that they needed to get serious about employee engagement; this filtered down to frontline employees. While the agency did not make it into the top 10 the following year, it did improve.

Absent the kind of public announcement that the Partnership makes, it is up to each agency to not only share results but also communicate what the organization intends to do about the survey data,

Table 10.2.

Statement	% Who agree
My work is valued by elected officials (mayor and city council).	32
A spirit of cooperation and teamwork exists among departments in the city.	35
The morale in my department is positive.	39
My department manager informs me about how decisions are made and how they affect me.	41
I believe my department is valued by elected officials.	44

including forming action teams, if that's how the agency plans to proceed.

As the agency moves forward to act on the survey results, it becomes important to regularly report on progress. At the University of Wisconsin Office of Human Resources, we did this through regular all-staff meetings, a monthly newsletter written and produced by our employee-engagement team, and a series of coffee breaks with the director (me). To keep the number of coffee break attendees down to a number that facilitates a real conversation, we invite specific employees to attend each session. We designed the rotation to ensure that during the year every one of our staff members would be invited (but not required to attend). Government agencies have also used the following methods of communication:

- **Individual in-person meetings.** Meeting with key internal stakeholders (e.g., key managers, union leaders) individually may facilitate a candid exchange that can help the agency understand and anticipate potential concerns. Similarly, meetings with external stakeholders (e.g., legislators, board members, citizens' groups) can help create momentum for change, or at least forestall potential opposition, which in government can crop up from many different sources. The city of Minneapolis, for example, briefed the city council on its engagement work to be as transparent as possible and also build council support for the city's engagement strategy.
- **Symposiums and town-hall meetings.** When agency leaders and managers participate in organization-wide town-hall meetings to describe and discuss the engagement initiative, employees will see the agency's commitment and better understand the results and what the agency plans to do about them. Employees also appreciate the opportunity to ask questions and receive immediate answers from senior leaders.
- **Electronic communication.** Email newsletters, downloadable videos, social media postings, intranet and website announcements, or agencywide blogs can quickly and efficiently share information with large groups of employees.

- **Printed memos and posters.** The old-fashioned way to communicate can reach employees who don't have regular access to computers at work.
- **Public announcements.** Messages can educate external stakeholders, job seekers, and the general public about how the agency values engagement and what it is doing to enhance it. Press releases can generate positive news stories about the agency's commitment to engagement and improving the workplace.

FORM ACTION TEAMS AND CREATE ACTION PLANS

Many agencies have successfully responded to and acted on employee survey results by forming action teams. These teams analyze the survey data to identify key issues (as described in Chapter 9), conduct further research to diagnose the root causes of these issues, set priorities for action, develop recommendations—and then help implement them.

A common approach to creating these teams is to ask for volunteers. Employees who are personally committed to, and invested in, workplace improvement can be powerful forces for changes grounded in engagement survey data. Bringing this kind of energy to an action team is essential. Selecting committed volunteers also helps reduce the risk of convincing employees to handle the responsibility of serving on these teams in addition to their day jobs. Action teams should be carefully assembled to include employees who represent a cross-section of the agency workforce and who have the right skills to help lead change.

Each team should appoint a team leader—ideally someone who has successfully led a group like this in the past. Agencies may also find it useful to assign a trained facilitator to help the team make decisions and progress. At the university, we made this resource available to each of the engagement teams in the 13 divisions we surveyed. Our facilitators helped the teams get started, analyze survey data, formulate plans, and make decisions. In some cases, the facilitators dropped off after the teams made key decisions and formulated their strategies and plans.

An approach that may seem appealing but is risky in the long term involves empowering managers and supervisors, by themselves, to take action on the survey data. This can seem like an efficient strategy, since managers have the authority and power to make changes that a team of rank-and-file employees typically doesn't. But this can be fool's gold. A managers-only approach probably won't have credibility with frontline employees, particularly if the engagement survey shows that the managers and supervisors themselves are at the root of the engagement problems. Credibility issues like these could damage the ability of the agency to implement real change that is accepted across the entire organization.

At the University of Wisconsin, a few of our units initially decided to have their management teams lead the survey-based change efforts. However, this approach was eventually shelved in favor of teams that represented a cross-section of employees, including labor representatives. At the University of Wisconsin Hospital, each department created its own team to analyze its department-specific survey results, identify two priority issues to focus on, and then come up with approaches to address the two issues.

COLLECT ADDITIONAL DATA

While action teams should rely on engagement survey data as the basis for identifying the key issues, it is also useful to collect additional data, often through focus groups. These discussions can add richness and detail to the survey data, including insights on engagement nuances, as well as the root causes of barriers to engagement. Ideally, these focused discussions will involve open-ended questions and be conducted by a trained facilitator who does not have a stake in the process or outcomes.

The U.S. Bureau of Engraving and Printing (BEP), for example, was the third most improved agency subcomponent in the 2011 "Best Places to Work" rankings and improved again in 2012. The BEP prints all the folding money we have in our wallets—billions of dollars a year in U.S. currency. In response to a low ranking in 2010, BEP created a "best places to work committee" that held focus groups that included white-collar workers, employees who do manual labor, midlevel managers, and entry-level employees. The focus groups were designed to take the pulse of the workforce and identify the reasons for the low employee ratings.

The number one concern voiced by employees was lack of communication. To respond, the bureau developed an action plan that focused on letting employees know what was happening in the organization and the rationales for bureau decisions. BEP put mechanisms in place to regularly obtain feedback, act on employee concerns, and let employees know they were being heard.

BEP supervisors, as part of their own performance expectations, began meeting regularly with employees to discuss and address workplace issues, understand what motivates employees, and actively engage them. Bureau leaders also worked closely with union leaders and held offsite meetings to find areas to work together to improve the work environment.[7]

At the University of Wisconsin, after we surveyed the Office of Human Resources staff, we hosted a series of facilitated focus groups in which we discussed the survey results and also asked participants to respond to the following:

- Recall a time when you worked in a place that had a highly engaging workplace culture. Share an experience from that time that illustrates what made it a "culture of engagement" in your mind. As you talk together, find the key elements that emerge from your stories.
- Have a brief conversation about the "key elements of engagement" that emerged from your anecdotes. What are those key elements? Are there some that especially resonate? Also, describe behaviors associated with each element (e.g., "respect" might also include "respect is shown by listening really carefully to everyone's ideas").
- Come up with two to three key elements that should apply to our organization, either because they are already present and should be strengthened or because they are currently lacking and are needed.

The focus group discussions allowed our staff to explain, in detail, how they responded to the survey questions and why. In turn, this allowed us to better understand what our staff's concerns were and then identify priorities for action.

SET MEASURABLE GOALS AND MILESTONES

Engagement survey data will likely identify important improvement areas (e.g., key drivers of engagement), such as quality of supervision, role clarity, and rewards/recognition. These areas can be the basis for short-term, midterm, and long-term goals, and all should include timelines.

It's important to confirm what the employee-engagement team is expected to deliver. Here are some clarifying questions:

- What format will the recommendations and action plan take (e.g., memo, report, presentation, some combination)?
- How often will the team check in with its executive sponsor (e.g., regular interim check-ins, one final briefing)?
- Who is the primary audience for any deliverables (e.g., senior leaders, managers, staff)?
- When are deliverables due?
- How will the team's results be communicated across the agency?
- Who will be responsible for implementing recommendations (e.g., the action planning team, a separate implementation team, senior staff, supervisors)?
- Will there be follow-up deliverables (e.g., to evaluate results)?

Effective action planning also requires accountability. At the University of Wisconsin Hospital, each department is required to publicly post its action plan, and HR makes sure they are all posted. The hospital does not centrally monitor the specific execution of each plan but instead monitors unit engagement scores from year to year.

Table 10.3. A Sample Action Plan for Improving Supervision (Adapted From the Partnership for Public Service Model)

Action plan step	Champion	Milestone	Measures
Post action plan: • Use intranet. • Share in multiple places.	John Smith	Upon receipt and approval	Action plan posted, number of views
Implement internal communication strategy.	Jane Doe	January	Employee feedback
Hold all-hands strategic meetings twice a year to discuss priorities, goals, and objectives.	John Smith	Every six months, beginning October 1	Attendance; accomplishment of organizational priorities
Hold quarterly department briefings on program priorities, metrics, and projects with all employees.	Jane Doe	Begin January, monthly	Feedback from employees
Offer brown-bag listening sessions.	Jane Doe	Begin January, monthly	Session turnout
Implement senior leader walkabouts once a month.	John Smith	Begin January, monthly	Completion; feedback from employees
Set expectations for supervision; new and existing supervisors will be required to have an individual development plan (IDP) that includes a developmental plan for supervisory skills.	John Smith	Set expectations by January; review every six months.	Develop supervisory score cards and gather employee feedback.
Leverage current and upcoming leadership programs and training.	John Smith	Ongoing	Participation rates; employee feedback

Table 10.3. (*continued*)

Action plan step	Champion	Milestone	Measures
Set up physical and digital anonymous question boxes: • Post questions asked. • Respond to questions at all-staff events.	Jane Doe	Quarter 1	Physical and digital boxes are available; questions at town halls.
Include training needs as part of the employee/supervisor reviews and encourage the development of IDPs.	John Smith	Quarter 1	Publish guidance on training needs and performance reviews, percentage of employees with IDPs, and percentage completion.
Establish and implement outcome-based performance measures.	Jane Doe	Quarter 1	Enterprise-wide measurement system will be used to assess the organization's effectiveness.
Require managers and supervisors to discuss their 360-degree assessment report results (areas of strength and areas of improvement) with staff.	John Smith	Quarter 1	Assessment shared with staff on schedule; received feedback.
Communicate consistently on the performance review policy and process with staff; address perceptions and myths around performance ratings.	Jane Doe	Quarter 1	Better scores in fairness and performance-based rewards and advancement.

DETERMINE BUDGET AND RESOURCES

Action teams should also project costs and review them with the executive sponsor. For example, what are the anticipated costs for the team to analyze the survey results and develop recommendations; what will implementation of the recommendations cost; what other resources are needed; and how will the team coordinate with managers across the organization?

DEFINE METRICS FOR SUCCESS

The team should identify measures of success for both its work (e.g., developing recommendations) and the implementation of priority recommendations. Specifically, how will the teams collect and analyze data to measure outcomes and success; how will the team track the progress of its action plan; how will the team measure the impact of implemented recommendations; and over what time period?

Establishing Action Team Ground Rules

Action planning teams should set ground rules for how they will operate. These may include principles such as respect and striving for equal participation. Teams should also clarify and assign basic roles and responsibilities, such as the following:

- Should the team develop a charter to outline goals, roles and responsibilities, deliverables, milestones, and so on?
- How and how often will the team meet (i.e., in person only, teleconference, videoconference, weekly) and for how long?
- What is the attendance policy (i.e., principals only or substitutes when necessary)?
- Who will serve as team lead?
- If there is an assigned facilitator, what will his or her role be?

- What are the roles and responsibilities of the team members?
- What is the confidentiality policy about team discussions?
- Will the team keep meeting minutes and, if so, who will take notes?
- Who will communicate with the executive sponsor and senior leaders?
- How will the team make decisions?

Sample Template: Action Team Charter

Project name ______________________________

Executive sponsor ______________________________

Project manager ______________________________

Primary stakeholder(s) ______________________________

Project description / statement of work

____

Business case / statement of need
(Why is this project important now?)

____

Customers ______________________________

Customer needs / requirements ______________________________

Project definition

Goals ______________________________

Scope ______________________________

Deliverables ______________________________

Project constraints / risks *(Elements that may restrict or place control over a project, project team, or project action)*

____

Implementation plan / milestones *(Due dates and durations)*

____

Communication plan *(What needs to be communicated? When is communication needed? To whom? How?)*

____

Change management / issue management *(How will decisions be made? How will changes be implemented?)*

____

Project team roles and responsibilities

Team member	Role	Responsibilities

Stakeholder roles and responsibilities

Stakeholder	Role	Responsibilities

DEVELOP RECOMMENDATIONS

Once the team understands the agency's engagement challenges, based on the survey results and any additional data (e.g., focus group discussions) and identifies priority areas, the team should develop concrete recommendations to improve engagement. One approach is to begin by brainstorming potential solutions. During this initial brainstorming phase, team members should offer any solution that might address the agency's engagement challenges. If the team has a facilitator, he or she can lead these discussions.

Another approach is to reach out to agency staff for solutions, perhaps using in-person or online forums where employees can share their ideas to improve engagement and the workplace environment. Employees could even be asked to vote on the ideas submitted, as Oregon Metro asked its employees to do.

Usually, the engagement team will identify a set of recommendations that must be put in priority order. One way to do this is to map the recommendations to the driver analysis (or matrix, described in Chapter 9) that identified the issues that agency employees feel are most critical to engagement and therefore drive their engagement levels. Recommendations that respond to statements/questions in the low-scoring, high-impact quadrant have the most potential to improve engagement. For example, improving the capabilities of supervisors is almost always a high-impact activity (and often a low-scoring area). However, the team should not limit itself just to long-term solutions. Small changes can also be meaningful and demonstrate to employees that the agency *is* taking action on the survey results.

The team should also evaluate the cost of, and barriers to, possible recommendations. The MSPB suggests creating recommendations that are "SMART":

- Specific—Clear and concrete, stating in behavioral terms what will happen
- Measurable—Measured and can be evaluated
- Achievable—Practical, giving the organization the capability to actually accomplish the objective
- Relevant—Will make a significant positive difference for the organization
- Time bound—Has specific time parameters[8]

OBTAIN EXECUTIVE SPONSOR APPROVAL

After the team has identified its priority recommendations, the next step is usually to pitch the recommendations to the executive sponsor for approval and commitment of resources. The team should make a well-organized presentation that summarizes the following:

- What the work team did, including analyzing the survey data and any additional data it collected
- The results of its analysis, including priority areas
- The high-priority recommendations and why the team feels they are most important
- How implementing the recommendations will improve employee engagement and the workplace climate
- A specific plan to implement the recommendations, including a change management strategy
- Resource needs (i.e., money, staff, outside assistance) to implement changes
- How results and progress will be evaluated
- A cycle/schedule for resurveying the workforce

Appendix 1 provides a checklist for evaluating the content and completeness of employee-engagement action plans.

PUT THE PLAN INTO ACTION

After receiving approval and a commitment of resources, the truly hard work begins: implementing the high-priority recommendations. The implementation approach will depend on the specific actions the organization decides to take. The action team could be commissioned to work on implementation, or this responsibility can be assigned to another team, the HR office, individual managers, or another unit.

It's important for the agency to understand that improving engagement is not just about new policies, programs, or practices. It is often just as much about driving cultural change. This is especially true in government, where workforces and organization culture are usually well entrenched. That's why FDIC created a "cultural change council" and appointed a "director of cultural change" to help improve its "Best Places to Work" rankings. The result was a number one ranking in 2011 and again in 2012.

The importance of cultural change as a lever to improve engagement becomes clear when reviewing the drivers of engagement. For example, the dimensions of engagement the MSPB identified are as follows:

- Pride in the work or workplace
- Satisfaction with leadership
- Opportunity to perform well at work
- Satisfaction with recognition received
- Prospect for future personal and professional growth
- Positive work environment with some focus on teamwork

Certainly, some of these dimensions, such as satisfaction with recognition received, can be improved by implementing new reward and recognition policies and practices. The same is true for the opportunity to perform well at work, which can be addressed by more robust performance management and employee development. Communication, which underlies much of the engagement model, can also be improved with new policies and practices. However, truly ingraining a culture of engagement often involves an intentional change-management strategy to transform the agency culture.

Effective implementation also requires continual and candid communication. This should include an explicit statement from the executive sponsor reiterating and reemphasizing why actions are being taken, as well as describing the specific actions and milestones. Throughout the implementation process, communication should be regular and widespread across the agency, including progress on deliverables.

Training Managers on Employee Engagement

The University of Wisconsin Hospital depends heavily on its 400 or so managers to take action on its employee-engagement survey results. But the hospital also realized that to make this happen it needed to equip its managers with the knowledge and skills to improve engagement. A key piece of the strategy is a training program for managers, titled "Understanding, Interpreting, and Responding to Employee Survey Results." The hospital trains all new managers and provides refresher training for managers who have already gone through the full program. The training was originally delivered by the hospital's employee-engagement contractor, Kenexa, but then the hospital decided to deliver the training itself. The program covers the following:

- Understanding employee engagement and why the hospital measures it
- The engagement survey process
- Survey results, engagement drivers, and priority areas
- Expectations of managers around employee engagement
- Understanding and interpreting work-group engagement scores
- Effectively sharing survey results with employees
- Facilitating an effective action planning session
- Following up

Chapter 11

Step 5: Sustaining Higher Levels of Engagement

Improving employee engagement should make intuitive sense to managers, particularly in today's government environment, where they face intense pressure to perform more efficiently and effectively.

However, maintaining and improving employee engagement requires a systematic approach and a long-term commitment. Taking action on employee-engagement survey results can produce some solutions that work and others that don't. Creating permanent change requires assessing what worked and what didn't by measuring, analyzing, and communicating the impacts of these actions. Specific areas of focus should include the following:

- Which solutions improved engagement with acceptable investments in time, money, effort, and other resources?
- Which actions cost too much for too little benefit?
- Which changes already in place will require continued support and/or resources?
- Did improved employee engagement drive improved organizational outcomes in a measurable way?

As I've emphasized throughout, it's important to regularly communicate about progress and results to reinforce buy-in for future actions. Sustained improvement requires continued support not just from the top but from across the entire jurisdiction or agency. Generating this support and momentum means regularly reporting on results and communicating with key stakeholders about how the organization is responding, including specific actions to maintain areas of strength and improve areas of weakness. This includes internal stakeholders—agency executives, managers, supervisors, and rank-and-file employees—as well as union and employee-association leaders. In government, this can include external stakeholders such as legislators and even the citizens government serves. This approach should be incorporated into the communications strategy.

One important way to maintain engagement momentum is by spotlighting successes. This means recognizing units and employees who have been instrumental in improving the workplace environment (e.g., the Federal Aviation Administration's annual "Making the Difference" award). Recognition can inspire others to act. That's the rationale behind the University of Wisconsin Hospital's "Best-in-Class Library of Action Steps," which publicizes the good ideas implemented by hospital units in response to employee-engagement survey results.

Immediate results can be immediately satisfying. But, in the long run, maintaining or improving employee engagement requires a culture of improvement. Employees across the organization and at all levels (especially agency leaders/managers and in the HR department) must model sound employee-engagement practices. This can be tough in government, particularly in agencies that come under public criticism and/or where leaders and budgets can change from year to year. However, if commitment to improvement becomes part of the agency's DNA, improved engagement can endure.

Managers and supervisors are critical to moving the needle of engagement. In other words, it's about leadership. This means that leaders should be held accountable for maintaining and improving engagement. Oregon Metro did this by explicitly incorporating improved employee engagement into the organization's vision and strategic plan and then developing a set of competencies based on employee-engagement survey results (i.e., by answering the question, What makes Metro a great place to work?).

In the Canadian province of Alberta, the engagement strategy really took hold when two actions were taken:

1. An engagement index was created that summarized survey results in a way that was far more understandable, transparent, and comparable across units than reporting only the results of individual questions.
2. Employee engagement was included in the performance standards/contracts of the deputy ministers in each department. This focused leaders' attention on engagement issues.

But sometimes it just takes patience and persistence. Gary Johnson, director of HR at the University of Wisconsin Hospital, says he is now peppered with questions from senior-level colleagues and key operational directors about how to improve engagement. They all want to talk about it, including at Gary's 6:00 a.m. spinning class. When the hospital first started on the road to improved engagement, however, the questions were at times negative, focused on why the hospital decided to take this on and whether it was truly needed. Despite this pressure, the hospital persisted, and a culture of engagement has emerged.

Consider again the Federal Deposit Insurance Corporation (FDIC), which initiated a multiyear culture-change program focusing on engagement that started in 2008 and continues. This program helped FDIC ascend to the number one spot among large agencies in both the 2011 and 2012 "Best Places to Work" rankings.

How Oregon Metro Sustains Employee Engagement

Oregon Metro, the regional government for the greater Portland area, has been conducting employee-engagement surveys since 2008. In addition to reviewing and acting on specific survey results, Metro has worked hard to incorporate engagement into the agency's strategy and culture. To do this, Metro took the following steps:

- Directly reference engagement in the Metro statement of purpose: "We inspire, *engage*, teach, and invite people to preserve and enhance the quality of life and the environment for current and future generations."
- Include engagement as a component of one of Metro's key values (teamwork): "We *engage* others in ways that foster respect and trust. Teamwork forms the essence of our work environment. Through collaboration and commitment to common goals, we achieve greater outcomes. We value positive relationships and nurture them with cooperation and honest communication. Individually, we contribute to the greater whole by being dependable and accountable for our actions."
- Identify engagement as a key aspect of the HR department's vision and strategy, as follows:
  - Vision: Create a great workplace with diverse, *engaged*, productive, and well-trained employees.
  - Strategic goal: Increase the level of *employee engagement* in order to maintain a productive workforce to meet the agency mission.
- Include employee engagement as a key management competency—"*People—engage and develop*"—and then linked this competency to training and manager accountability. This competency is further defined as follows:
  - Create an environment of trust and respect; model and reinforce Metro values.
  - Manage individual and team performance.
  - Clarify expectations and provide timely feedback.
  - Recognize the contributions of others.
  - Address performance issues and resolve conflict.
  - Develop self and others.
  - Create development plans with employees.
  - Delegate to help employees expand their skills.[1]

MAKE MANAGERS ACCOUNTABLE FOR ENGAGEMENT

Leadership is a key to improving and maintaining engagement because leaders have influence over the conditions that drive engagement. Accountability can help convert an engagement "project" into a way of doing business, day in and day out. Accountability can be achieved by incorporating engagement into the agency vision and strategy (as Oregon Metro does), including it in managers' contract standards or performance expectations (as Alberta does), or widely and publicly disseminating the results of satisfaction/engagement surveys (as the Partnership for Public Service does for the "Best Places to Work in the Federal Government" rankings).

In the federal government, the Office of Management and Budget, a powerful central agency that drafts the federal budget, announced that it would consider agency "Best Places to Work" scores and rankings in deciding on agencies' funding.[2] Not surprisingly, this focused the attention of many agencies on the rankings (even though more than a few also complained that employee satisfaction scores shouldn't be incorporated into budget decisions).

At the University of Wisconsin Hospital, managers' performance bonuses now depend, in part, on hospital-wide engagement scores. According to hospital HR staff, this has helped maintain the long-term focus on engagement. In my organization, we made senior managers accountable, as part of their annual performance expectations, for analyzing and responding to their units' engagement issues, as identified in the survey.

MEASURE RESULTS

A substantial stream of research has demonstrated that higher levels of employee engagement result in better organizational performance. While much of this research has been in the private sector and focuses on financial outcomes such as revenue and profit, there is also solid and growing evidence about public-sector outcomes.

Government organizations, jurisdictions, and agencies that take action to improve engagement also need to put in place a process to measure the impacts of a more highly engaged workforce, including linking improved engagement to important agency outcomes. Despite the compelling private-sector results linking engagement with organizational outcomes, public-sector organizations committed to improving employee engagement need to make this commitment to measuring their own results.

Demonstrating outcomes is a key to sustaining engagement momentum and high levels of engagement. Whether it is better employee retention, improved quality or timeliness, faster response times, fewer on-the-job accidents, a higher level of customer service, improved performance as measured by employee performance evaluations, or success achieving the agency's strategic goals, metrics enable the organization to link improved engagement to agency outcomes. While this can be particularly challenging for government programs that don't have readily measurable goals, connecting the dots between engagement and performance is important and possible.

Results at the U.S. Patent and Trademark Office (PTO) show how improved employee satisfaction/engagement can drive key agency outcomes. The PTO issues patents and registers trademarks. In 2007, the PTO ranked 172 out of 222 federal government subcomponents in "Best Places to Work in the Federal Government." After steady progress in 2009 and 2010, PTO moved into fifth place in 2012. This improvement occurred when agency leaders made workforce improvement a priority. Changes included reengineering the patent-examination system by (1) revising the milestones for reviewing patent applications, (2) giving patent examiners more flexibility, and (3) allowing them to have more direct contact with applicants. PTO management did not impose these changes unilaterally or confrontationally. Instead, management collaborated with employees, union representatives, and other stakeholders to understand their concerns and find common ground.

According to a PTO executive, this process created "a sense of teamwork between managers and employees" and "helped employees feel empowered." As a result, examiners now have "more time to do their examinations correctly" while being more productive and feeling "more in control of their work."

The PTO also implemented employee and manager award programs and gave employees the opportunity to provide feedback to management on workplace issues. In addition, it is among the federal agency leaders in percentage of employees who telecommute.

The results are measurable. At the end of fiscal year 2011, the PTO backlog of unexamined patent applications was reduced to 669,625—the lowest total in five years. While still a huge caseload, this was a 10 percent decrease in the backlog from fiscal 2009, even with an average 5 percent annual increase in patent application filings. The PTO's trademarks operation also met or exceeded all fiscal 2011 goals for quality, timeliness, and expanding online service through e-government. PTO officials attribute these measurable improvements in large part to improving workplace conditions.[3]

READMINISTER THE SURVEY

Sustaining improved engagement also means continuing to regularly measure it through surveys. The initial engagement survey establishes the baseline, and subsequent surveys enable the agency to compare improvements against this baseline. This is the only sure way to really know if employees are engaged. Surveying also makes the entire organization—including leaders, managers, supervisors, and rank-and-file employees—accountable for employee engagement. Agencies that conduct engagement surveys typically do them annually or biennially. Surveying less frequently can put a brake on momentum to improve engagement. That's why the province of Alberta has surveyed its employees every year but one since 1996. Measuring and then improving employee engagement requires this kind of a long-term commitment.

Chapter 12

What Public-Sector Organizations Have Actually Done to Improve Engagement

As I've cited, many government jurisdictions and agencies have already taken action to collect data on, analyze, and improve employee engagement. While I have referred to examples of how agencies have acted on survey data, my emphasis has been on how these agencies have approached the *process* of surveying and acting on the results.

In this chapter, I highlight examples that focus on what these agencies have done in response to engagement data, including steps they've taken to improve the level of engagement. As I've noted, employee engagement is a hot topic. While the lion's share of attention focuses on the private sector, there is also growing recognition in government that engagement matters. This attention is particularly timely for government organizations, which, as I described in Chapter 4, face unique challenges in improving engagement and also face pressure to do more with less. In government, the chief and sometimes only resource an agency has is its workforce. That's why, in the public sector, success depends on a talented and fully engaged workforce.

What have public-sector agencies actually done to act on employee-engagement survey results, to maintain strengths and improve areas of weakness? The responses include a range of steps detailed throughout this chapter. This list of actions is not intended to be an exhaustive inventory of every action an agency can take to improve engagement. However, the list and the descriptions that follow highlight what individual government jurisdictions and agencies that have surveyed their employees have done to maintain or improve engagement. I've emphasized that there is no one-size-fits-all solution to improving employee engagement. However, I also think it's useful to understand what public-sector organizations have done. The examples that follow can serve as a partial menu of proven approaches to improving employee engagement. The challenge for individual jurisdictions, agencies, and work units is to select the approaches, based on survey results and data analysis, that will support their mission, values, goals, and culture.

Here are some specific approaches that public-sector organizations have used to drive higher levels of employee engagement:

- Provide senior-level and enterprise-wide leadership on employee engagement.
- Improve agency communication.
- Build leadership and management competencies.
- Improve the management of employee performance.
- Ensure that employees believe that their opinions count.
- Create a more a positive work environment.
- Incorporate engagement into assessment of job applicants.
- Implement a new employee onboarding process.
- Help employees improve their well-being.
- Clarify the line of sight between employees' work and the organization mission.
- Enhance employee prospects for career growth.
- Recognize employee contributions.

PROVIDE SENIOR-LEVEL AND ENTERPRISE-WIDE LEADERSHIP ON EMPLOYEE ENGAGEMENT

Virtually all analyses and lists of employee-engagement drivers conclude that leadership as critically important. For example, all the engagement dimensions identified by the U.S. Merit System Protection Board (MSPB) suggest that leaders can impact, negatively or positively, almost every aspect of employee engagement. (That's in addition to the dimension specifically titled "satisfaction with leadership.")

The leadership challenge in the public sector includes focusing on engagement despite the distinctive aspects of government, discussed in Chapter 4, that include frequent leadership changes, diffused decision making, and hard-to-measure goals. Part of the leadership solution to improve engagement is for senior-level and enterprise-wide leadership to make engagement an organizational priority and also model sound engagement practices. This includes explicitly integrating engagement into the strategic direction of the organization.

In both the United States and United Kingdom, the central HR departments in the national government have taken this to heart. The U.K. Civil Service annually conducts the People Survey of 500,000 civil servants. The U.K. Civil Service office instituted the national survey to replace more than 100 separate surveys previously conducted by individual agencies. The U.K. Civil Service also created a government-wide "employee engagement program team" in the prime minister's cabinet. The team was charged with the following tasks:

- Provide a consistent set of measures for employee engagement across the entire U.K. Civil Service.
- Reduce the cost of engagement surveys across departments.
- Support government departments to successfully deliver the annual government-wide survey.
- Identify areas of employee-engagement best practices in the public and private sectors.
- Embed the concept and practice of proactive employee engagement across all levels of civil-service leadership and management.
- Encourage departments to focus on the four enablers of engagement that the U.K. Civil Service office identified:
    1. **Strong strategic narrative.** Explain where the organization is going and why, which helps employees understand how their role contributes.

2. **Engaging managers.** Motivate, challenge, and support people, treating employees as individuals and seeking and responding to their views.
3. **Effective employee voice.** Ensure that employees in all areas are involved in decision making.
4. **Organizational integrity.** Align stated values and actual behaviors.[1]

The engagement team's activities include encouraging U.K. agencies to integrate engagement into existing organizational strategies—that is, to help agencies view engagement as a key dimension of their strategies and make engagement business as usual and not just a program or an extra burden. The team has also matched organizations across government that face similar issues to help them support each other, share ideas and solutions, and avoid duplication of effort; developed "Civil Pages," an online collaborative tool (described as the "the Facebook of the civil service") that helps agencies share information and learn about best practices in engagement in civil service and other public- and private-sector organizations; and put on monthly engagement workshops to share best practices, enable agencies to share case studies, and provide examples from the wider public sector. These workshops include training on how to use engagement survey data, conduct enterprise-wide action planning, and create successful plans for fostering and communicating about employee engagement.

The U.K. Home Civil Service has also created a network of engagement practitioners that includes representatives from each government organization that participates in the People Survey. These practitioners take a lead role in using the survey results to drive improvements through communication and action planning. The network serves as a virtual team that tries to embed the principles of employee engagement across government departments as well as within them. Network members also provide feedback to the central employee-engagement team on the survey and data analysis and how to get the most value from the People Survey.

In the United States, the Office of Personnel Management (OPM), the federal government's central HR agency, administers, analyzes, and reports on the annual Federal Employee Viewpoint Survey. OPM not only provides government-wide leadership on the survey but also strives to be a model employer, with a workforce of more than 5,000 employees. In the 2011 "Best Places to Work" rankings, OPM cracked the top 10 for the first time and maintained its place there again in 2012.

Improving engagement within OPM became a priority in 2009. At that time, the newly appointed OPM director, John Berry, made it clear to OPM senior executives and other leaders and supervisors across the agency that they would be held accountable for analyzing the OPM employee survey results and coming up with plans and strategies to address problem areas. Berry challenged his agency executives to be proactive and "drive change" by communicating, implementing workplace flexibilities, delivering training, and dealing with wellness issues.

One OPM strategy focused on improving the competencies of supervisors to help build employee trust. This commitment included the following:

- Targeting supervisory training to focus on specific competencies linked to the engagement survey results
- Creating supervisors' forums to bring together leaders from across OPM to discuss common challenges
- Expanding performance-management training to improve communication with employees about performance expectations

Also in the U.S. federal government, the Department of Transportation registered the largest improvement in the 2012 "Best Places to Work" rankings for large agencies, repeating what it also accomplished in 2010. In 2009, the department was ranked last among large federal agencies. The agency's improvement since then has been driven by department secretary Ray LaHood, who said, "When I found out that DOT was last I was stunned. I made a commitment that day to do everything I could to engage people and really change morale and opinions at the department."[2] LaHood made a personal commitment to improving the agency's score, using the ratings as a tool for change.

This philosophy was communicated through listening sessions and in emails from the secretary and other Department of Transportation senior leaders. Most importantly, the changes resulting from employee feedback have been communicated to frontline employees.

After improving its "Best Places to Work" score by 8.2 points in 2010, the department added its own agency-specific questions to the OPM survey. From those questions, the agency realized that employees wanted to improve work processes. The secretary then asked senior leaders to let employees know that management heard this message and also encourage more feedback. The secretary's office then solicited input from each operating unit and made changes to meet employee needs.

In local government, the city of Minneapolis and Oregon Metro Government both have made the commitment to employee engagement that includes incorporating engagement into strategic goals and then acting to achieve these goals. In Minneapolis, the strategic goal ("A city that works") includes "city employees are high-performing, empowered, and engaged."[3] This focus on engagement also starts at the top with Mayor R. T. Rybak. He reviews survey results himself and meets with department heads. If there are areas where a department can improve, Rybak will discuss with department leaders. Oregon Metro's commitment to engagement includes the following:

- The HR department's vision is defined as "increase level of employee engagement in order to maintain a productive workforce to meet agency mission."
- In its list of employee values, Metro encourages "teamwork—we engage others in ways that foster respect and trust."
- A strategic goal in the HR department's five-year plan is to "create a great workplace with diverse, engaged, productive, and well-trained employees."[4]

Driving Improved Engagement Through Strong Leadership at the Chorley Borough Council

Chorley Borough is a public-sector jurisdiction in the United Kingdom, akin to a U.S. county government. In 2006, Donna Hall took over as council chief executive, bringing a different style of leadership, including focusing on the customer. In 2008, the council was rated as excellent by the national government Audit Commission and was ranked number 2 and named "best improver" in *The Times*' list of "Best Councils to Work For."[5]

Hall communicated a "customer first" vision. Her changes included "listening days" every six to eight weeks that run for 60 to 90 minutes, where all staff contributed ideas; "back-to-the-floor exercises" to keep managers in touch with staff and residents; a well-being program; and a focus on reducing sickness absence.

According to Hall,

> I don't have the monopoly on good ideas. The people who do the job are now being asked and because we're a small council we need everyone to play their part. We simply needed to remind ourselves what we are here to do—serve the public—and put that at the heart of the way we work.[6]

IMPROVE COMMUNICATION ABOUT ENGAGEMENT, THE ORGANIZATION, AND THE WORKPLACE

Communication is the glue that holds employee-engagement initiatives together and is particularly critical for government. As discussed in Chapter 4, public-sector organizations face engagement challenges that include persistent attacks on government, hard-to-measure goals, complex decision making, and frequent leadership changes. Effective communication can help overcome these obstacles to improved engagement

Public-sector organizations must communicate throughout the entire cycle of planning, conducting, and acting on engagement surveys. In addition, however, agencies have learned through their engagement surveys that they need to improve communication in general. Communication helps put employees in the best position to perform well—one of the key drivers of engagement.

In the city of Juneau, the survey results showed that a department leader wasn't clearly communicating his vision to department employees. In response, HR facilitated a series of structured meetings between the director and key department supervisors. The result was a dramatic increase in this department's engagement scores in the next survey. According to Mila Cosgrove, the Juneau HR director, communication in this department (and in the entire city) requires managers to "look every employee in the eye and tell them they're part of the solution."

Oregon Metro learned from its engagement survey data that employees wanted more—and more accurate information. The survey data also showed that managers were "removed from their employees." In addition, first-line supervisors were not viewing themselves as management but instead as labor-union allies. Metro also realized that simply asking managers to communicate more or better was not the real solution. Managers had to be equipped with the information they needed to communicate effectively.

The solution was "intentional communication," an approach to push information to employees by engaging first-line supervisors. The goals were to deliver accurate information to employees in a timely manner and also strengthen first-line supervisors' connections to management.

Metro started by developing a more purposeful way to communicate about the organization's budget—a critical area of concern for employees. Metro began this process with an all-managers meeting where managers were encouraged to ask questions about the status of the budget. These answers were then converted into talking points, and managers were asked to share this information in conversations with their staff. This approach departed from the usual practice of discussing a topic with the senior leadership team and then assuming that leaders would communicate down and across the organization. Instead of this hit-or-miss approach, Metro's intentional communication approach organized both the message and the way it was communicated. After developing the budget talking points, Metro applied this tactic to other issues its employees said were important.

In the federal government, the Federal Deposit Insurance Corporation (FDIC) faced enormous pressures and increased workloads stemming from the 2008 financial crisis. FDIC rose to the top of the "Best Places to Work in the Federal Government" rankings (after being near the bottom) in part because of improved internal communication with employees. This included creating an internal ombudsman position, reporting directly to the FDIC chairperson, to handle employee problems and grievances. FDIC also launched an internal website for employees to submit questions and get answers on workplace issues and held town-hall meetings and conference calls with the chairman that enabled all employees to have their questions answered and also provide direct input to FDIC leaders.

FDIC also created a "cultural-change council" that included employees from all divisions and levels. Council members were charged with developing ideas to better communicate with, and empower, employees. This council served as conduit for employees to generate ideas. The FDIC "director of cultural change" said that a key emphasis has been to demonstrate to employees that management "values their opinions and that their voices are being heard."

The Federal Aviation Administration: "From Worst to First"

The leadership of the Federal Aviation Administration (FAA) was not pleased when the 2009 "Best Places to Work in the Federal Government" rankings placed FAA third from the bottom for agency subcomponents. (FAA is part of the U.S. Department of Transportation.) The response to this low ranking was a concerted effort to improve workplace conditions, resulting in the FAA boosting its score by 19.2 percent in the 2010 rankings. Again in 2012, FAA was one of the most improved federal agencies.

The improvement began when the FAA administrator adopted the slogan "worst to first" and formed a steering committee that focused on employee engagement. The administrator held regular brown-bag lunches and town-hall meetings with employees to encourage them to voice concerns. Agency leaders made a commitment to get back to employees and answer questions they could not answer immediately.

Senior FAA leaders also became more involved in helping newly hired employees adjust to the workplace and also placed a new focus on providing positive feedback and better professional development opportunities.

FAA launched IdeaHub, a website that received 500 suggestions for improvement from FAA employees in just its first week and was eventually expanded to serve the entire Department of Transportation. Even the small step of instituting agencywide casual Fridays helped improve satisfaction and engagement.

Another creative solution was creating a "Making the Difference" award, presented by the administrator each January to an agency employee who made an important contribution to improving employee engagement.

The University of Wisconsin Hospital also made communication a priority. For example, the hospital launched an online "Best-in-Class Library of Action Steps" to communicate and publicize (and replicate, the hospital hopes) the good ideas implemented by units as the result of employee-engagement surveys. The library, which the HR department continually updates and makes available to all employees through the hospital intranet, lists and describes specific activities units have designed and implemented in categories such as communication, recognition and rewards, involvement and belonging, growth and development, future vision, trust, performance excellence, and diversity.

Other initiatives to improve communication in government driven by employee satisfaction/engagement survey data include the following:

- The Federal Labor Relations Authority (FLRA), after being ranked last in "Best Places to Work in the Federal Government," began publishing a weekly newsletter that covered important information about mission performance. The publication included updates on legislation, meetings, and budget information. The FLRA chairwoman also held all-employee town meetings that used videoconferencing to involve employees outside the headquarters.

- The state of Washington's Information Services System Division responded to employee survey results by establishing the expectation that each manager/supervisor should have routine (i.e., at least monthly) one-on-one and unit staff meetings to promote communication within and between units and give priority to sharing conversations from management discussions.
- The director of the federal OPM implemented several new ways to communicate in response to low "Best Places" scores. His initiatives included conducting "free-flowing" monthly town-hall meetings to solicit employee feedback and implementing "IdeaFactory," where workers are encouraged to submit innovative ideas for workplace improvements.
- At the British Department of Work and Pensions (DWP), once a year all DWP senior managers are asked to participate in "back to the floor," where they spend a week working with staff who directly serve customers. More than 200 senior managers did this in 2009–10. This frontline experience provided leaders with ideas on what works well for delivering customer service and allowed employees to speak directly with managers about service improvements. One department secretary personally went back to the floor four years running and then shared his experiences through a published personal diary. Employees reported that it was valuable to see senior colleagues experiencing their world firsthand.[7]
- A U.S. regulatory agency, the Federal Maritime Commission (FMC), was one of the most improved agencies in the 2009 "Best Places in the Federal Government" rankings in part because of enhanced internal communications. Specifically, the FMC opened meetings of the full commission to all employees

and encouraged them to attend to improve their understanding of how important decisions are made by FMC management and the five commission members. The commission also sought to better educate staff about issues in the industry they regulate by inviting representatives from the maritime industry to speak directly with staff. Unfortunately for FMC, its engagement momentum stalled, and it plummeted in the 2012 rankings.

- At an air force civilian unit, engagement survey data and follow-up discussions revealed that employees were frustrated with some meetings that were being held in a long hallway. This was not only uncomfortable; it was also inefficient. The simple solution was to move the meeting to a conference room. The lesson here is to never underestimate the value of taking small steps.

BUILD MANAGERIAL AND LEADERSHIP COMPETENCE TO IMPROVE ENGAGEMENT

As the U.S. OPM does, other government agencies that have focused on assessing and then improving engagement understand the connection between strong leadership and employee engagement. These organizations have taken action to build and upgrade leadership competence, which underlies virtually every driver of employee engagement.

The Air Force Materiel Command, which conducted the Gallup Q12 engagement survey, has made its supervisory staff a critical part of its engagement strategy. In analyzing its survey results, the command realized that when supervisors are engaged, their employees are also more likely to be engaged. The survey results helped the command understand where supervisory training had been successful and where it needed to focus more on the needs of supervisors. In response, the command developed and implemented a more robust training and development program for managers and supervisors.

The results have been encouraging—employee turnover has decreased, particularly for newly hired staff: use of sick leave and workplace accidents are down; the ratio of engaged to disengaged employees is up;

and according to Minnott Gaillard of the command, "Engagement is becoming a mindset, not just a buzzword."

The California Department of Motor Vehicles (DMV) Communication Programs Division conducts biennial employee satisfaction surveys. In response to the survey results, the DMV collaborated with the University of California–Davis on a leadership development program that focuses on the different levels of management and includes a component on empowering employees, management styles, and how styles need to align with employees.

According to Oregon Metro, one of the core management competencies involves fostering employee engagement. Metro has linked training and development programs to these competencies, including engagement.

In the United Kingdom, the city of Sussex's police force, which conducts employee surveys, has developed a leadership-capability framework to describe the types of leaders the force needs and also help ensure that leaders behave in ways that reflect the force's stated values. The framework includes components such as "moving from checker to coach," "putting *we* before *me*," and "standing in the shoes of the public," to clearly communicate what the police force means by *leadership*. A new leadership-development program based on these values, for leaders at all levels, is being rolled out. According to the force's HR director, it will take time to change the management culture because many officers still expect HR to "do the people-management bit." Police-force leaders recognize that too many sergeants and inspectors and even some chief inspectors still seem to think they are one of the team; they don't really accept that they are managers. The force's next step is to ensure that the new leadership-capability framework is incorporated into how staff are recruited and assessed for management positions and how they are appraised and developed.[8]

In the U.S. federal government, FDIC focused on leadership by creating a set of core values that directly relate to engagement: integrity, teamwork, accountability, fairness, and effectiveness. The FDIC chair (the corporation's chief executive) and other top FDIC leaders then delivered clear and repeated messages that they were dedicated to creating a high-functioning workforce and improving workplace conditions. The result was ascension to the number one spot in the 2011 and 2012 "Best Places" rankings.

In Canada, the province of Alberta's response to engagement survey results included making senior executives accountable for improving employee engagement by including engagement as an element in the executives' performance goals/contracts.

The U.S. General Services Administration (GSA) Federal Technology Service (FTS) southwest region, which serves civilian and military agencies and the Native American community, administered the Gallup Q12 engagement survey. FTS acted on the survey results in several ways, including by incorporating the Q12 questions into an outline for supervisors to use in their performance appraisal discussions with subordinates. According to the GSA regional administrator, "We discussed the (survey) results during staff meetings, during associate meetings, and any other opportunity we had. Each group developed action plans. We discussed these actions during our leadership sessions. Managers discussed these action plans during meetings with their associates."

As a result, FTS engagement scores increased by 10 percent overall, with one FTS group raising its score by 90 percent. The overall engagement scores for the southwest region were in the 99th percentile in the Gallup database. According to Gallup, this is world-class engagement.[9]

Improved employee engagement in FTS also improved customer-satisfaction scores—a key metric. The region's goal is at least an average 4.0 rating (on a 5-point scale) on customer satisfaction surveys. Actual satisfaction scores were about 4.8. In addition, although FTS's business volume increased by more than 112 percent, operating costs only increased by 4 percent.[10]

Leadership Competencies: The Office of Personnel Management

In the U.S. federal government, OPM has developed five executive core qualifications, which embody the competencies senior leaders are expected to master and demonstrate. Each of the five competencies includes a set of specific behaviors, many of which link to employee engagement:

1. **Leading change.** Bring about strategic change, both within and outside the organization, to meet organizational goals. Inherent is the ability to establish an organizational vision and to implement it in a continuously changing environment. This competency includes these specific behaviors:
   - Creativity and innovation
   - External awareness
   - Flexibility
   - Resilience
   - Strategic thinking
   - Vision
2. **Leading people.** Lead people toward meeting the organization's vision, mission, and goals. Inherent is the ability to provide an inclusive workplace that fosters the development of others, facilitates cooperation and teamwork, and supports constructive resolution of conflicts:
   - Conflict management
   - Leveraging diversity
   - Developing others
   - Team building
3. **Results driven.** Meet organizational goals and customer expectations. Inherent is the ability to make decisions that produce high-quality results by applying technical knowledge, analyzing problems, and calculating risks:
   - Accountability
   - Customer service

- Decisiveness
- Entrepreneurship
- Problem solving
- Technical credibility

4. **Business acumen.** Manage human, financial, and information resources strategically:
   - Financial management
   - Human-capital management
   - Technology management
5. **Building coalitions.** Build coalitions internally and with other agencies, state and local governments, nonprofit and private-sector organizations, foreign governments, or international organizations to achieve common goals:
   - Partnering
   - Political savvy
   - Influencing/negotiating[11]

DRIVE ENGAGEMENT THROUGH IMPROVED MANAGEMENT OF EMPLOYEE PERFORMANCE

To be fully engaged, employees need to understand what their roles, responsibilities, and expectations are and receive feedback on their performance. In the world of HR, this is known as performance management and is fundamental to the driver that the MSPB identified as the "opportunity to perform well at work."

Performance management is especially critical to employee engagement in government because, as described in Chapter 4, managers are constrained by frequent leadership changes, complicated decision making, hard-to-measure goals, and restrictive civil-service rules, and they also lack the financial incentives that private-sector managers have.

What Is Performance Management?

The University of Wisconsin has defined *performance management* as follows: "A continual process of establishing relevant and reasonable expectations, measuring outcomes, and providing appropriate follow through in the form of coaching, training, rewarding, and taking corrective action and/or discipline. A primary purpose of performance management is to create a climate and environment for employee development and success."

Employee-engagement research conducted by the U.S. Merit Systems Protection Board has revealed the power of effective performance-management practices to improve employee engagement. The board compared the practices of the four federal agencies with the highest levels of employee engagement to the four bottom-scoring agencies. The most significant factor that differentiated the high-engagement agencies from the low-engagement agencies was effective performance-management practices. According to the MSPB report, "Every positive performance-management practice we reviewed (e.g., senior leaders communicating openly and honestly with employees, employees having written performance goals) is employed more widely in high engagement agencies than in low engagement agencies." Based on these findings, MSPB made a series of recommendations to executives, managers, and supervisors to ensure that performance-management practices drive high employee engagement (see box).[12]

U.S. Merit Systems Protection Board Recommendations for Effective Performance Management

For All Leaders (Executives, Managers, and Supervisors)

- Hire with care and use the probationary period as part of the selection process, particularly in government. The best way to avoid performance problems is to hire candidates who have high potential for success. Provide job applicants with an accurate job description and a realistic preview of the pros and cons of the position. Use a multiple-hurdle approach in which only the best qualified candidates move on to the next step in the selection process. Use the probationary period as the final step in the selection process, and remove employees who do not perform well.

- Develop a strong working relationship with each employee by talking informally and frequently (e.g., two or three times per week). Get to know employees as people, provide informal feedback, and learn about individuals' concerns and goals.
- Meet regularly with each employee to review progress and provide feedback. Schedule regular meetings (at least monthly) with each employee to discuss progress and any obstacles to success, provide feedback and recognition, explain new assignments, communicate high performance expectations, provide information about the work unit or organization, respond to questions or concerns, and review progress on development plans.
- Model how to request and use feedback. Set an example by requesting feedback on your performance as a supervisor and by sharing feedback you receive from your manager. Discuss with employees how you plan to use the feedback you receive.
- Conduct annual or semiannual assessments of each employee's strengths and development needs. Provide development opportunities for all employees, including both specific training needed for the current job and broader skill development.
- Manage poor performance promptly and assertively. Hold all employees accountable for their performance:
  - Provide recognition and other positive consequences for good work.

    - Take prompt corrective action when employees are not performing well, making it clear that continuing poor performance will not be tolerated and following up with consequences if the poor performance continues.
- Avoid transferring poor performers' work (or the poor performers themselves) to other units.

For Managers and Executives in Particular

- Involve employees in building a high-performance organization. Use the results of agency engagement surveys, plus additional employee input, to identify organizational strengths and weaknesses. Work with employees to create and implement an action plan to build a high-performing organization.
- Build employee trust and confidence through frequent, open communication. Invest effort in gaining the respect and trust of your employees by openly sharing information about the organization, both positive and negative; aligning words and actions; and making it safe for employees to express their perspectives. Develop personal connections with employees through meetings, visits to work sites, exchanges of ideas, and other forms of in-person communication.
- Engage new employees and nurture your investment in new employees by providing a yearlong onboarding program.
- Develop and communicate with employees about a recognition program that tightly links recognition to performance. Use pay raises as a recognition tool, giving raises only to employees who are performing at "fully successful" or better levels. Let employees know they are receiving the increases because of their successful performance. Develop nonmonetary recognition practices.
- Select supervisors who will effectively manage performance and then hold them accountable for

effective performance management. Make it clear that they are personally responsible for effectively managing their employees' performance to produce results. Regularly review management strategies with each supervisor.

- Provide supervisors with the support they need to successfully manage their work groups, including training, resources, and support. In particular, remove organizational obstacles to taking action against poor performers, and back supervisors up when they do this.
- Evaluate the effectiveness of the agency's current performance appraisal system. Assess how it contributes to or detracts from accountability, communication, and recognition of good performers. Involve employees and solicit their ideas for alternative approaches.

ENSURE THAT EMPLOYEES BELIEVE THEIR OPINIONS COUNT

As described in Chapter 4, decision making in government is often influenced by outside events and actors, including political forces, that can make decisions seem irrational. This is at odds not only with engagement drivers ("my opinion counts") but also with the public-service motivation that attracts many public servants to government. In response, agencies striving to improve engagement have reached out to their employees to involve them more directly in decision making.

In the previous section on communication, I wrote about ways in which agencies have communicated the rationales for their organizational decisions. Agencies have also implemented approaches to solicit opinions and innovative ideas from employees and then adopt the best ones.

One example is the IdeaFactory at the U.S. Transportation Security Administration (TSA) in the Department of Homeland Security. TSA has a difficult mission that requires its employees to strike the difficult balance between airport security and customer service. TSA therefore also has a particularly tough employee-engagement challenge. It is a large agency, with its 60,000+ employees scattered across more than 450 airports not only in the continental United States but also in remote locations in Alaska and places like Pago Pago and Guam. In addition to this workforce challenge, TSA employees are also regularly criticized by the public, the media, and politicians. Not surprisingly, TSA is a high-turnover organization for government, with annual attrition among screeners as high as 20 percent.

It's not a huge surprise, therefore, that TSA has been near the bottom of the federal "Best Places" rankings, but it has improved since it was first ranked in 2005. One approach to improve engagement by soliciting employee opinions is the IdeaFactory, dubbed a "21st-century suggestion box." IdeaFactory is an online system similar to a blog that applies a social-media approach to create an online community that gathers and shares employee suggestions. This program, created after an employee survey revealed that TSA employees believed their voices were not being heard by the agency's leaders, sets out three main goals, all directly or indirectly linked to employee engagement:

1. Engage employees and ensure that every member of the large and dispersed TSA workforce has a voice in the way the agency and its operations evolve.
2. Collect constant, fresh input and perspectives on improvements to keep the agency flexible and effectively mitigate security threats.
3. Disseminate information about new and existing programs, initiatives, and policies to frontline employees and provide a forum for communication.

Employees post their ideas online, and then other employees rate and comment on the posted ideas. In this way, employees communicate with agency leaders, TSA offices, and each other. These employee ratings for each idea are also posted. The IdeaFactory team reads each idea and evaluates those that are popular or that fit especially well with specific strategic agency goals. Senior leaders and program managers react to the posted ideas by debunking myths and responding to suggestions, including explaining why some suggestions are not going to be implemented.

Ideas that receive the most support from other employees may ultimately be implemented across the agency. Winning ideas net the suggesting employees a trip to TSA headquarters to help implement their ideas. Employees who submit accepted ideas are rewarded with a certificate of recognition and a TSA coin, which is highly valued across the agency.

IdeaFactory suggestions that have been implemented range from small procedural changes in baggage inspection to more strategic approaches, such as establishing separate family and road-warrior passenger lanes. Other implemented ideas include the following:

- A nationwide employee referral bonus program to help recruit transportation security officers
- A job-swap website that allows officers to post their interest in swapping job locations
- "Mourning bands" that allow officers to place special markings on their badges to recognize employees who have passed away
- Clarifying on the TSA public website that the "children" listed as being allowed to bring liquids through the checkpoint actually means "infants/toddlers"
- Updated training programs based on employee suggestions

In its first two years, more than 25,000 employees visited the IdeaFactory site and posted almost 9,000 ideas. This led to the implementation of 85 innovative ideas.

The FAA also implemented a similar online program, "IdeaHub." In its first year, IdeaHub engaged 25 percent of the FAA workforce, generated more than 4,000 ideas, and received 55,000 ratings on these ideas plus more than 12,500 employee comments. FAA officials point to this innovation as one reason employee satisfaction improved by 19 percent in the 2010 "Best Places" rankings.

The National Health Service "Engagement Tool Kit"

The publicly funded National Health Service (NHS) in Great Britain takes engagement seriously. The service has produced a 75-page engagement tool kit that includes "practical advice for increasing staff engagement" as well as links to other resources. The tool kit covers the following:

- Benefits of engagement
- Business case for engagement
- Financial benefits
- The staff engagement star (employee-engagement model)
- Top tips on improving engagement
- What to include in the engagement strategy
- Tool for continuous assessment of engagement
- Communicating and involving staff
- Advice for line managers
- Tips for induction (onboarding) to support engagement
- Using NHS staff survey scores[13]

CREATE A POSITIVE WORK ENVIRONMENT

Public-sector organizations that have measured employee satisfaction/ engagement and then acted on the results have also taken specific steps to create more positive work environments, including helping their employees balance their work and personal lives. Given what I described in Chapter 4 about the challenges that government jurisdictions and agencies face as they attempt to improve employee engagement—including attacks on government, frequent leadership changes, influence of external forces on decisions, and limited financial tools to influence behavior—creating a positive work environment is critical.

As discussed previously, effective performance management by supervisors is fundamental to creating a positive work environment. In addition, so is implementing more flexible work arrangements.

In the Partnership for Public Service report, "On Demand Government: Deploying Flexibilities to Ensure Service Continuity," we documented that flexible work arrangements (e.g., compressed work weeks, flextime, part-time work, job sharing, and telework) were underutilized in the federal government. The Partnership found that many managers resist adopting flexibilities because they view them primarily as employee perks. In state and local governments, a key flexibility—telework—is also underutilized for essentially the same reason.[14]

This attitude ignores research that has proven the value of workplace flexibilities. Benefits include expanding service hours and reducing costs through downsized physical office space, fewer staff relocations, reduced employee travel, and expanded use of online training. Workplace flexibility also enables agencies to maintain operations during times when facilities are closed unexpectedly.

Ironically, even agencies that have not implemented flexibilities like telework report that they believe that increased use of flexibilities will improve employee satisfaction and engagement and allow agencies to better adapt to changing workforce expectations.[15] For example, in the federal government, employees who telework scored seven percentage points higher on the 2012 federal government engagement scale (based on the Federal Employee Viewpoint Survey) than employees who did not telework.

During the historic series of major snowstorms that pounded the Washington, DC, area in 2010 ("snowmaggedon"), the federal government was officially closed for almost a week. However, several agencies continued operating via telework. The Patent and Trademark Office, for example, reported that about 4,400 of its patent examiners, trademark attorneys, and other employees—about 46 percent of PTO staff in the DC suburbs of northern Virginia—teleworked even though the federal government was officially closed. About 30 percent of the employees in the U.S. GSA and OPM also teleworked during the storms.[16]

Other federal agencies also understand the need to implement workplace flexibilities, often in response to employee survey results.

In addition to the Patent and Trademark Office (a federal leader in the percentage of employees who telework in general, not just during snowstorms) and OPM, the Government Accountability Office (which consistently ranks high in "Best Places") has adopted "flexiplace" and telecommuting to help employees better balance the demands of work and home. The GSA has made a commitment to accelerate the pace of telework for federal government employees and is leading by example. According to GSA, its telework activities have helped reduce highway traffic congestion and associated vehicle emissions. GSA's senior leadership actively communicates the value of telecommuting, advocating for the technology needed to support a mobile workforce. GSA also launched mandatory training to educate employees on the changing culture at GSA and emphasize the benefits of telework—that is, to help employees find greater balance between their work and personal lives.

At another agency, the FAA, even the small step of instituting agencywide casual Fridays helped create a more positive work environment that improved employee satisfaction.

Despite these examples, the Partnership for Public Service's "On Demand Government" reported that one of the major barriers to greater use of workplace flexibilities is resistance by managers who said they need to see their employees face to face to make sure they are actually being productive. As pointed out in the report, however, managers who can only be sure that their employees are working by seeing them sitting at their desks are not doing their own jobs; they should have other ways to "measure" productivity.[17]

The city leadership in Minneapolis, which has been conducting engagement surveys since 2004, understands the value of flexible work arrangements. In the city's 2009 survey, 71 percent of employees who responded agreed that having flexible work arrangements was important to them. In 2010, in response to these results, the city council approved an alternative work arrangement policy.

This new policy was designed specifically to "increase employee commitment, engagement, morale and productivity" and includes the following alternative work arrangements:

- **Compressed workweeks.** Full-time employees work 40 hours each week (or 80 hours every 2 weeks) but have the flexibility to work fewer than 5 (or 10) days (e.g., they can work four 10-hour days).
- **Flextime.** Employees can deviate from standard starting and ending times.
- **Job sharing.** More than one employee can share the work of one full-time budgeted position.
- **Gradual retirement.** Employees nearing retirement can modify their schedules to retire gradually instead of transitioning from full time to fully retired overnight.
- **Telework.** Employees can work remotely, from their homes, mobile worksites, customer sites, or other locations.

Although not all alternative arrangements are right for all positions (or employees), the city HR department believed it was important to provide departments with a set of work flexibility policies and tools. Since Minneapolis has a heavily unionized workforce, HR has also worked with unions and city departments to expand coverage to bargaining units interested in extending coverage to their members. Several have done so.

City of Minneapolis

Alternative Work Arrangement Agreement for Telework

Employee name________________________________

Employee ID ________________________________

Department/division____________________________

Employee home address
(include city and state) ________________________

Home or cell phone number______________________

Remote work location
(specify home or other) ________________________

Schedule (in city office) Monday Tuesday Wednesday Thursday Friday

____

I (employee), have read, understand, and agree to adhere to the city of Minneapolis AWA policy, the AWA procedures, my department's telework procedures, and the terms as described in this agreement. I will request any deviation from the approved AWA as soon as possible with my supervisor. Special circumstances (special division rules, conditions, etc.) are listed separately in an attachment to this agreement. I have discussed the telework agreement, including scheduling days and hours of work, communications, employee/supervisory responsibility for work progress and monitoring work, the use of the city's equipment, data security, and data privacy with my supervisor. Teleworkers are responsible for damage to city-owned equipment and for filing a police report with their local police department for stolen city-owned equipment. I understand that I must notify my supervisor in the event of any damage to or loss of city property. I understand that I need to have proper insurance coverage in place at the remote work location. I understand that either the city or I may terminate the telework agreement with reasonable notice to the other party. Upon termination, I will return all city-owned equipment to the city immediately or facilitate the city's access to such equipment for retrieval. (**Note:** Additional sheets may be attached to this agreement to document other important aspects of the AWA.)

Other Important Information

Employee signature__________________________ Date _______

For the City

Supervisor signature __________________________ Date _______

Department head or
designee signature__________________________ Date _______

INCORPORATE EMPLOYEE ENGAGEMENT INTO ASSESSMENTS OF JOB CANDIDATES

Engaged employees are made, not born, but one innovative way to "bake in" engagement is how the U.K. Department for International Development (DFID) incorporates engagement into how it assesses candidates for senior civil-service positions. The DFID candidate evaluation process includes a session during which candidates interact with a group of staff from across the department. The candidates are asked to analyze a set of U.K. Civil Service People Survey engagement-survey results to identify key issues and then discuss their ideas about how to deal with these issues. This discussion assesses each candidate's ability to do the following:

- Engage with staff in analyzing issues and developing responses.
- Weigh the costs, benefits, and impact of possible solutions.
- Apply knowledge of how to manage people.
- Gain commitment for the proposed actions.
- Reflect upon his or her own behavior and evaluate its impact.

Each candidate's performance is scored along with other job dimensions to determine if he or she has the leadership competence needed for senior civil-service positions. All candidates receive feedback on their performance in the selection process. DFID management believes that this exercise has helped identify well-qualified candidates who have strong engagement, management, and leadership skills. The process shows DFID's commitment to engagement as well as using People Survey results to improve the department.[18]

Incorporating engagement into job candidate assessment doesn't have to be limited only to leadership positions. Research by the consulting firm Development Dimensions International (DDI) on almost 4,000 employees in a variety of jobs has revealed six personal characteristics that predict the likelihood of becoming an engaged employee:

- Adaptability
- Passion for work

- Emotional maturity
- Positive disposition
- Self-efficacy
- Achievement orientation

Job applicant questionnaires, sometimes referred to as "career batteries," can help hiring organizations, and managers identify candidates with these characteristics who therefore have the highest probability of performing effectively, while also being satisfied and engaged. The questionnaires cover how candidates would handle certain situations and how they would rate the effectiveness of various actions to achieve goals. These tools can be particularly useful in public-sector agencies, given the importance of identifying candidates who have the public-service motivation that is critical to success in government.[19]

IMPLEMENT A NEW EMPLOYEE ONBOARDING PROCESS

The following anecdote appeared in "Getting Onboard: A Model for Integrating and Engaging New Employees," a Partnership for Public Service report:

> Two dollars and 85 cents. That's what a new government employee found in his desk when he reported for his first day of work. We know this because this civil servant showed up for his first day with no computer and nothing better to do than count the loose change and throw away the chewing gum wrappers he also found in his desk. Maybe the $2.85 was his hiring bonus.[20]

In "Getting Onboard," we catalogued the often sad state of onboarding new employees in the federal government. More important, we laid out a comprehensive model for how government can ensure that new employees are onboarded effectively. This is critical because effective onboarding and employee engagement are directly related.

Most of us have our stories of reporting for a new job when we were ready for the job but the job wasn't ready for us. My personal "favorite" is when my family and I, including our two young daughters, moved halfway across the country for a job in Wisconsin state government. When I arrived for my first day at work, eager to get started, I was greeted with the news that our family wouldn't be eligible for employer-paid health insurance until I had worked there for six months. That definitely took the edge off my excitement about the new job—and also made for a tough conversation at home that night.

As emphasized in "Getting Onboard," perhaps no aspect of human-resources management has been more overlooked by government than *onboarding*—integrating new employees into their agency work environments and equipping them to become successful, productive, and engaged.

Onboarding is particularly critical in government for at least two reasons. First, as we noted in Chapter 4, strong civil-service requirements can make hiring in government slow and laborious. Therefore, agencies should be especially committed to making sure that new hires get off to a good start and don't quickly become disillusioned and leave. There's no excuse for wasting the time, money, and effort spent on recruiting and hiring by following it up with an ineffectual onboarding process.

Second, as noted earlier, it is unfailingly difficult to remove poor performers in government after they pass probation. Poor performers who pass probation therefore become the "gift" that keeps on giving. It's critical to weed out poor fits during the onboarding process.

Good onboarding is not just the right thing to do; it also pays dividends. Research by the consulting firm Hewitt Associates revealed that organizations that invest the most time and resources on onboarding are rewarded with high levels of employee engagement. The Recruiting Roundtable found that effective onboarding can improve employee performance by up to 11.3 percent.[21]

Despite this evidence, the Partnership's research on onboarding in government revealed that newly hired public servants often have disappointing experiences on their new jobs. Here are more quotes from focus groups with brand-new federal employees:

- "My first week was terrible. I didn't have any equipment, I wasn't given any assignments, there was nothing on my desk, and my supervisor did not even come see me for the first three days I was there."
- "When I showed up for work on my first day, my manager had no idea I was coming. Apparently HR had not informed her of my start date."
- "I was sent to a conference room where someone from HR helped me complete a bunch of forms. I was not introduced to anyone, I had no one to go to lunch with, and no one had set up my computer access so I sat there and stared at the wall. By the end of the day, I felt I had made a terrible mistake in leaving my old job."
- "I couldn't receive my ID on the first day so it was hard for me to go anywhere and my manager did not give me any work to do . . . my manager was not very welcoming. By the end of the day, I was terrified that I had left a great job for this."[22]

In many cases, problems like these result from small, easily avoidable mistakes. While minor, these mishaps can have a major impact on a new employee's view of government, as well as his or her level of engagement. After all, you only get one chance to make a first impression.

To address this often underappreciated issue in government, the Partnership for Public Service, in cooperation with Booz Allen Hamilton, developed a comprehensive model for strategic onboarding designed specifically for government, although it can also be applied in other sectors too. The model has been adopted by public-sector organizations, including the University of Wisconsin.

The model onboarding process starts with a set of onboarding principles:

- Align onboarding to agency mission and vision.
- Connect to culture, strategic goals, and priorities.

- Integrate across process owners (e.g., HR, information technology, new hire's supervisor).
- Apply to all employees (i.e., in all jobs, at all levels, and at all locations).

As shown in Figure 12.1, the onboarding process itself has five phases, beginning when the new employee accepts the job offer and continuing through the entire first year of employment. The five phases vary in length but represent critical steps during the new employee's first year.

The five steps are as follows:

1. **Before the first day.** Good onboarding begins when a new hire accepts the job offer, not just when he or she shows up on the first day. This first phase of onboarding occurs after the employee accepts the job but before his or her first day of employment. During this time, HR staff notify other key "process owners" such as IT (to make sure the new employee has a working computer as well as a valid ID and password) and space management (to set up a work station); send hiring and benefits paperwork to the new hire (so he or she doesn't have to waste time completing these forms on the very first day—a surefire way to dampen enthusiasm for the new job); and communicate logistical information. This is also when a "peer partner" should be designated to help the new employee become adjusted to the agency's norms and culture.
2. **The first day.** The second phase, first day/orientation, occurs when the new employee reports to work and continues with orientation activities in the first few days. Formal orientation is critical because it's usually the first substantive encounter a new employee has with the agency. Generally, HR welcomes the new employee and ensures that orientation covers the basics.
3. **The first week.** New employees shouldn't have a letdown after orientation. Colleagues in the new employee's office—manager, peers, sponsors, and executives—play key roles motivating and acculturating new employees. The new employee should spend

Figure 12.1. Strategic onboarding model.[23]

PRINCIPLES

Align to mission and vision | **Connect** to culture, strategic goals and priorities | **Integrate** across process owners | **Apply** to all employees

ROLES

PROCESS OWNERS | PROCESS CHAMPIONS | EMPLOYEE

PROCESS PHASES AND KEY ACTIVITIES

BEFORE FIRST DAY	FIRST DAY/ORIENTATION	FIRST WEEK	FIRST 90 DAYS	FIRST YEAR
• Extended personal welcome to employee • Communicate first day logistics to employee • Send paperwork in advance and/or online portal access • Prepare for employee	• Focus on sharing the mission and values • Incorporate senior leadership • Orient employee to organization and office norms • Introduce employee sponsor • Meet immediate requirements for employment	• Ensure direct managerial involvement • Set performance expectations and job scope • Assign meaningful work • Communicate resources or networks required for work	• Provide essential training • Monitor performance and provide feedback • Obtain feedback through new hire survey and other means	• Recognize positive employee contributions • Provide formal and informal feedback on performance • Create employee development plan

OUTCOMES

High employee **job satisfaction** level | **Retention** of high-performing employees | Continued **employee engagement** and commitment | Faster time-to-**productivity** some or all of this week doing purposeful work, obtaining the resources he or she needs, and becoming acclimated to the job and the surroundings.

4. **The first 90 days.** The fourth phase covers the time between the new employee's first week and the end of the first three months of employment. This is when the new employee should complete new employee training. During this time, new employees should begin to take on a full workload while managers/supervisors monitor performance and provide early feedback. Lack of attention to this phase can result in new employees not feeling fully engaged by the end of their first 90 days.
5. **The rest of the first year.** The last phase is the time between the end of the new employee's first three months and the end of his or her first year. For most agencies, formal onboarding activities do not extend into this period. But for the employee, the feeling of newness—and the accompanying learning curve—linger. Continued support during this time can help speed employees to full performance. Managers and supervisors should provide formal performance reviews at least at the six-month and one-year marks.

IMPROVE EMPLOYEE WELL-BEING

Forward-thinking government agencies are also beginning to understand that employee well-being and employee engagement are related and that both drive fewer health-related absences and improved productivity and performance.

At the U.K. Driver and Vehicle Licensing Agency (DVLA), rates of sick-related absences were cut in half after the agency introduced a preventative strategy that focuses on health and well-being. At the same time, DVLA's engagement score, measured by the U.K. Civil Service People Survey, increased from 51 to 55 percent. In 2010, DVLA won the Civil Service Human Resource Award, recognizing the agency's success improving engagement and well-being in support of organizational efficiency.

DVLA has more than 6,000 employees, the majority of whom perform administrative tasks (think Department of Motor Vehicles in the United

States). About 75 percent earn less than $35,000 annually. In 2005, DVLA employees averaged 14 sick days per year, costing more than $16 million and leading to a National Audit Office report criticizing the agency.

The DVLA approach to reducing sickness absence focused on three factors: health, well-being, and attendance. Specific goals were to improve well-being and the working environment; move from a culture of "illness" to "wellness"; and develop an engaged, inclusive workforce.

The initial focus involved intervening in ways that would produce short-term results. This involved generating more detailed data about sick absences, reviewing and updating policies and procedures, and developing guides to support staff and managers. DVLA set agencywide attendance objectives and began more intensively managing long-term absence cases by keeping in closer touch with employees during absences and encouraging more proactive rehabilitation. The agency also launched a new training course to help line managers deal with sick-related absences.

In addition to these short-term tactics, DVLA put in place strategies to improve employees' long-term health and well-being:

- A quality-of-working-life survey, with an action plan to address the issues employees identified
- A health promotion program that focused on wellness rather than illness, including a pedometer challenge, weight management program, and smoking cessation classes
- Proactive occupational health and well-being services that included earlier support for stress-related absences and access to a physiotherapist for musculoskeletal disorders
- Closer links with local doctors to provide employees with better access to rehabilitation assistance
- Employee assistance for staff and their immediate families including a 24-hour telephone counseling service that also provides debt and legal counseling
- Support to improve lifestyles, including a fitness center, marked walking trails around the DVLA building, and bicycling support

- Monthly health promotion events and a focus on mental health in response to increased absences caused by stress and mental-health issues

The agency also regularly analyzes absence data to enable HR to identify attendance trends and take early action to respond. Directors meet monthly to discuss the data and flag any emerging issues in their units.

This DVLA research revealed a direct relationship between employee engagement and overall average working days lost and the proportion of staff without sickness absences. A 10 percent increase in the engagement index correlates with a 1.1 day reduction per employee in average days lost. Similarly, a 10 percent increase in engagement would lead to an 8 percent increase in the proportion of staff with no sickness absence in the preceding 12 months. A unit of 100 employees would have nine fewer absences per year.[24]

Another U.K. jurisdiction, the Chorley Borough Council, also focused on health and wellness. In 2001, Chorley averaged about 16 sick days per employee, which left it languishing in the bottom 25 percent of all similar U.K. jurisdictions, for sickness and absence. To respond, Chorley created a coordinator position to manage its new health program, "Active at Work," which included the following:

- Daytime activities such as Pilates, tai chi, and aerobics
- Health-promotion events measuring body-mass index, weight, and blood pressure
- A pedometer challenge, with more than 200 employees taking part in teams during a four-week competition (all participating employees received a free pedometer)
- Screening and support sessions that cover smoking cessation, osteoporosis, free eyesight tests, office ergonomics, and annual flu vaccinations
- A men's health week, with information on smoking cessation, cycling to work, and health checks

The council also revamped its stress-management program and established a support group called "workplace listeners" to provide employees with trained colleagues who will listen to their problems. Monthly holistic therapies such as massage and reflexology are provided on site at heavily discounted rates.

The result of all this activity was a reduction from an average of 16 sick days annually to less than 8 days lost. The well-being program also translated into improved engagement, including Chorley being ranked number 2 and most-improved in the *Times* "Best Councils to Work For in 2008" (with a first place in the health and well-being category). The council also received an award for customer service excellence.[25]

CLARIFYING THE LINE OF SIGHT BETWEEN THE JOB AND THE ORGANIZATION MISSION

I have described how public-service motivation is a strong influence on public servants' interest in, and commitment to, government. To nurture this commitment, however, public servants must have a line of sight between their work and the mission and achievements of their agency.

The Porirua, New Zealand, City Council (PCC) analyzed the results of its employee-engagement survey and realized that its engagement issues involved leadership, common purpose, direction setting, and internal planning. These line-of-sight issues revealed that what was missing was full staff buy-in to the council's vision and the new way of working achieving this vision would require.

To help bridge this gap, the council formed a cross-functional team whose charter was to clarify the line of sight between individual employee effort and the PCC's vision, mission, values, and community outcomes. The team included representatives from each business unit who were close to the frontline and was supported by senior subject-matter experts in communication and marketing, HR, and business excellence. This project was championed by PCC's CEO, who facilitated the team's meetings himself. The team was assembled to include employees who were close to the frontline, forthright, creative, and uninhibited by authority.

The team worked on initiatives that included modifying the council's vision statement, which at 65 words was too long and lacked appeal. The result was a more succinct and compelling message: "Together, we're making Porirua amazing!"

The team's next challenge was to come up with ways to excite and engage staff around this new vision and create alignment between staff roles, business-unit purpose, and the newly articulated vision.

The team decided on a series of interactive vision and values workshops that included discussions to help participants understand how they and their teams contribute to the big picture.

Out of 290 eligible council staff, 205 attended one of the workshops. The majority reported that they gained a greater understanding of how their job fits with the goals of their business group; how their job contributes to community outcomes; what inspires them in their work; and how the council's vision, mission, and values relate to them personally. After the workshops, the number of "engaged" employees increased by 5 percent. Results for specific engagement statements also improved, as shown in Table 12.1.[26]

In the United States, the University of Wisconsin Hospital and Clinics also strives to help employees see the connection between their work and the results the hospital is committed to. In one best hospital practice,

Table 12.1.

Engagement survey statement	Positive responses before program (%)	Positive responses after program (%)
PCC has a clear vision of where it's going and how it's going to get there.	66	70
The CEO and executive team help staff understand the council's vision.	62	67
Staff believe in what PCC is trying to accomplish.	73	77
There is a sense of common purpose in PCC.	62	69
Cooperation between teams is encouraged.	63	71

this connection begins with employee orientation, where new hospital employees in one unit are shown some of the letters and positive comments from patients about department employees. This enables the new hire to see, right from the start, how his or her role can directly affect the hospital's primary customers—its patients.

I think it's worth repeating a quote from a public servant (cited in Chapter 5) about connecting with the people that government serves: "When I found myself getting down, I would head to the frontline. Being among the citizens we served reminded me why I was there and why it was important to keep fighting."[27]

ENHANCING EMPLOYEE PROSPECTS FOR CAREER GROWTH

Another important driver of engagement is providing employees with opportunities to develop and grow. This is critical to government-engagement efforts to overcome barriers identified in Chapter 4 that include frequent leadership changes, complicated and inefficient decision making, few financial incentives to affect behavior, and strong civil-service rules that limit the flexibility of both managers and employees.

At the National Science Foundation (NSF), one pillar of the foundation's consistently strong "Best Places to Work in the Federal Government" score is encouraging staff members to actively engage with their research communities by delivering presentations, attending conferences, and making on-site visits to NSF grant recipients. These connections to the scientific community enhance the NSF work environment by broadening the reach and impact of employees' work.

Oregon Metro has developed a series of training and development programs and identified those that map directly to the leadership competency "engage and develop":

- Clarifying performance expectations
- Correcting performance problems
- Conducting difficult conversations

- Providing feedback and coaching
- Managing at metro

In the state of Washington, the Information Systems Services Division implemented a series of actions to improve survey scores on the statement "I have opportunities at work to learn and grow." The division did the following:

- Implemented employee training plans to maintain/advance skills and education
- Created more cross-training and internal-training opportunities within the division, most notably through developmental job assignments
- Encouraged and supported technical certification
- Offered self-paced online training resources
- Closely linked employee training to the agency road map and strategic and tactical plans

Outside the United States, the Careers New Zealand agency took aggressive action to improve employee engagement by creatively expanding career-development opportunities. "Careers" is the national agency that provides New Zealanders with information, advice, and support to help them make career decisions.

Determined to practice what it preaches, Careers decided to extend its use of internal assignments. Despite its success achieving finalist status in the JRA "Best Places to Work in New Zealand" surveys in 2007 and 2008, the survey results also showed that staff wanted better development opportunities and that learning and development was a high priority for staff. These results became the catalyst for a concerted effort to find creative ways to expose staff to new challenges that would utilize and develop their skills.

The Careers approach went beyond just advertising internal transfers and promotions. Instead, staff were encouraged to volunteer for assignments that could mean transferring to a different work group, job, region, or even moving outside the organization temporarily.

The idea was to link people, their skills, their aspirations, and their circumstances to the many and varied opportunities available across the organization. HR publicized the available opportunities and then encouraged employees to take advantage of them.

The program ensured that Careers employees were considered first for opportunities—whether these opportunities were created through new projects, staff movement, or staff taking extended leave. Assignments ranged in length from six weeks to two years.

Specific results linked to the program included the following:

- Recruitment costs decreased by two-thirds.
- Staff turnover decreased from 21 percent to 11 percent.
- Satisfaction with learning and development opportunities rose from 71 to 78 percent.
- Percent of staff who said they feel encouraged to develop knowledge skills and abilities increased from 79 to 85 percent.[28]

RECOGNIZING EMPLOYEE CONTRIBUTIONS

Recognizing employee contributions and linking this recognition to performance are also keys to improved employee engagement. While this linkage is important in all organizations, it is particularly important in government today, to help counteract the negative images of the public service and public servants.

In many private-sector organizations, superior performance is recognized by pay raises and/or bonuses. But with today's tight public-sector budgets, government agencies need to find other ways to recognize outstanding performance.

One way to do this is to ask employees how they want to be recognized, as the University of Wisconsin Hospital has done. One hospital director responded to survey data showing that employees were dissatisfied with their recognition opportunities by surveying that unit's employees to find out how they wanted to be recognized. The hospital took this a step further by developing a "Thanks for Caring Recognition Tool Kit" that describes ways that managers and supervisors can provide on-the-spot recognition to their employees. The tool kit includes the catch phrase, "Reward small. Reward big. Reward the best of the best. Reward today." The tool kit lists rewards that managers and supervisors can purchase but also includes suggestions on how to thank employees "without spending a dime" that include the following:

- Mail a handwritten note to the employee's home.
- Offer verbal recognition at a staff meeting.
- Surprise the employee with a Post-it note of thanks.
- Put a thank-you note on the department bulletin board.
- Compliment the employee within earshot of others, and the word will spread.
- Send a department-wide email praising an individual employee or team.
- Start every meeting by recognizing an employee; ask employees to recognize each other.
- Pull an employee aside and ask for his or her opinion.

At the FAA, the administrator implemented an annual "Making the Difference Award," presented to an agency employee who made an important contribution to improving employee engagement.

Some jurisdictions and agencies have implemented peer-recognition programs in response to employee survey data. The city of Coral Springs, Florida, which has been conducting satisfaction/engagement surveys for 18 years, has what it calls a "layered approach" to employee recognition:

- A peer recognition "applause card" program, in which nominations are submitted online. Nominated employees are placed into a quarterly drawing and can win gift cards. Each month, 400–500 employees are nominated.
- An instant recognition program, which encourages employees or supervisors to nominate colleagues who exhibit the core values of the organization (customer service, empowered leadership, and continuous improvement) or who take on additional

responsibilities. Awards are mainly gift cards. The city budgets about $25,000 for this program each year.

- An annual "Employee Excellence Award" program, which also relies on peer nominations. Employees can nominate colleagues or themselves in any of the city's core value categories or for contributions to improve their organization. All submissions are done electronically and vetted by a committee of prior winners.

As a result of its employee-engagement surveys, the Air Force Materiel Command realized that it needed to do a better job recognizing employees. In response, the command implemented peer recognition programs—including an employee of the month and a "top-dog" employee.

While pay raises are usually not feasible during tough budget times, some public-sector agencies are trying to better link performance and pay. For example, the Government Accountability Office, a perennial leader at the top of the "Best Places to Work" rankings, implemented a performance-based compensation system in 2004. Similarly, according to HR director Dale Pazdra, the city of Coral Springs, Florida, has a "performance-based pay culture" that helps account for its exceptionally high scores on employee-engagement survey questions. Scores on these questions range from 84 to 97 percent positive. Even with tight budgets, the city is continuing its incentive pay program.

Sometimes it's also about helping employees understand what their total compensation includes—not just what their base pay is. In the city of Minneapolis, for example, employee perceptions about pay and benefits were not favorable. In response, the city developed and distributed to all employees a summary of the full dollar value of their compensation packages so that employees would better understand the total value of their pay plus benefits. As a result, in 2009, 82 percent of responding employees answered positively to the survey statement, "I understand my total compensation (pay and benefits) package." This was an increase of more than 40 percentage points on this question from the previous survey.

I began this chapter by emphasizing that there is no one-size-fits-all method of improving employee engagement. It's important to reemphasize that government jurisdictions and agencies have to tailor their approaches and actions based on their data—ideally employee-engagement survey results, as well as the organization's mission, values, strategy, and culture. However, it is useful and instructive to learn about what some other public-sector organizations (not just in the United States but also around the globe) have done to respond to engagement-survey data.

Chapter 13

The Role of Human Resources

As I've tried to emphasize, measuring and improving employee engagement in government is not "HR stuff." Instead, employee engagement should be a fundamental responsibility of the entire organization, including leaders, managers, supervisors, and rank-and-file employees.

But as an HR guy myself, I would be remiss if this book didn't also address the role of human resources in helping government jurisdictions and agencies achieve higher levels of employee engagement.

Helping the jurisdiction/agency improve employee engagement is an opportunity for HR to make a highly visible and highly significant impact. Human resources departments often complain about not having a "seat at the table" where key decisions are being made. Improving employee engagement is this kind of opportunity, but HR must bring something to that table.

This means playing an influential role in improving employee engagement, including serving as the catalyst to help improve engagement across the entire jurisdiction or agency. In public-sector organizations that have conducted engagement surveys, human resources has been a champion and guiding force, by advocating for collecting engagement survey data, putting in place the survey process, and then driving (or at least facilitating) strategies to act on the data.

First, HR needs to champion the value of employee engagement. This means understanding what engagement is, why it matters, and how to improve it and then advocating for taking action. Advocacy includes broadly and aggressively communicating the business case for engagement and also building momentum for surveying employees and then acting on the data. HR should also provide (or help find) the resources and tools to conduct engagement surveys and help work units analyze and take action on the results.

For many HR units in government, providing this kind of leadership and support will mean moving out of the comfort zone (developing policies, handling personnel transactions, and regulating agency personnel activities) into new and perhaps unfamiliar territories (delivering service and developing new and more strategic capabilities as a true business partner) and then delivering measurable results. This can be a real opportunity for HR to step up and help the organization meet the challenge of attracting, developing, and retaining talent. Making this transition also means developing new competencies, as described by the International Public Management Association for Human Resources (see box).

Human Resources Competency Model

The International Public Management Association for Human Resources (IPMA-HR) is the professional association for government human resources leaders and professionals. IPMA-HR has developed an HR "competency model" that goes well beyond the traditional technical and transactional orientation of HR. A *competency* is a set of behaviors (skills, knowledge, abilities, and personal attributes) that, taken together, are critical to achieving the organization's strategy.[1]

The IPMA-HR model includes 20 specific competencies in three broad areas—business partner, change agent, and leader. The competencies focus on transitioning HR from its role as a regulator and transaction processor to a strategic business partner. HR's ability to help public-sector agencies measure and improve engagement is directly linked to mastering these competencies. The specific skills and behaviors associated with the competencies are as follows:

Business Partner

- Understand the organization's mission, vision, and values and the business plan for execution.
- Be innovative, creating and sustaining a positive environment that supports calculated risk taking.
- Apply organizational development principles.
- Link specific human-resource initiatives to the larger organization's mission and service deliverables.

Change Agent

- Design and implement change by altering systems and procedures.
- Use return-on-investment and information-technology strategies in the practice of human-resource management.
- Effectively design, develop, and implement HR and organizational processes for all customers, including in the context of organizational and/or political resistance.
- Design and deliver marketing programs related to sourcing and selection of human capital (i.e., aggressively market career opportunities).

Leader

- Understand and effectively utilize the current and potential contributions of a workforce that is maximized in terms of all aspects of diversity.
- Practice integrity and ongoing ethics-based leadership behavior in all circumstances, including those that may jeopardize the professional future of the human resources leader.

Shared Competencies That Cut Across Roles

- Understand business process and how to change to improve efficiency and effectiveness.
- Have knowledge of human-resource laws and policies.
- Understand the public-service environment.
- Understand team behavior and lead teams toward high performance.
- Successfully communicate, verbally and in writing, including using persuasive public presentations on behalf of the human resources function.
- Assess and balance the competing values found within the organization (i.e., the larger mission and vision, various department values, values as demonstrated by executive and midmanagement leadership).
- Use business-systems skills, including thinking strategically and creatively.
- Analyze issues, recognizing the needs of all stakeholders for collaborative solutions.
- Use negotiating skills, including consensus building, coalition building, and dispute resolution.
- Build and sustain trust-based relationships, both individually and collectively over time.[2]

Human resources departments should also model how to measure and improve engagement in their own units. While HR should make this commitment for all aspects of talent management, this leadership is particularly critical for employee engagement and particularly in government, where lasting change usually requires cultural change. It is difficult for HR to tell the rest of the organization to focus on improving engagement if HR itself has not made this commitment.

At the University of Wisconsin, we piloted the engagement survey first in HR for several reasons: first, to work out any kinks in the design and administration of the survey. But, just as important, we took this on first in HR to show the campus that we were not just telling them to focus on engagement; we were doing it first ourselves. We also shared our initial survey results with the other divisions. Given that not all our survey results were positive, this transparency was a bit risky—and also a bit uncomfortable for us—but we believed it was important for the credibility of the engagement process and for the credibility of HR itself.

HR should also provide technical assistance to plan, develop, and administer the survey; report and analyze the data; and act on the results. Operationally, this can mean the central HR office actually conducts the survey, like the central HR offices in the U.S. and U.K. national governments already do. Or, if the agency uses a contractor, this can mean that HR manages the contractor's work. What follows is a summary of HR's specific roles and responsibilities in the employee-engagement process.

PLANNING THE SURVEY

HR's role includes facilitating key decisions such as who will manage the survey process, what survey will be used (i.e., if the organization will make it or buy it), when and how to survey, how results will be reported and analyzed, and how to communicate about the initiative.

HR should lead conversations about planning issues such as whether reports will include an overall engagement index score, a question-by-question summary with mean scores, favorable versus unfavorable percentages, narrative comments, and so on. Will engagement drivers be calculated? Will results be reported in spreadsheets, a narrative report, a PowerPoint summary, or something else? HR needs to understand these issues and recommend answers to these questions.

HR can also help individual work units decide what formats and data reports they want (e.g., results by work units, individual managers, demographic groups). At the University of Wisconsin, while we used standard reporting formats (Excel spreadsheets), we also consulted with each unit to determine the level of detail the units wanted. One division director wanted the data broken down into his 26 individual work units. Even though assembling all these data was complicated, we made sure he got what he wanted.

CONDUCTING THE SURVEY

Typically, HR will either conduct or coordinate the survey (if an outside organization administers the survey). HR must have or develop enough expertise to understand, explain, and implement the survey methodology. This includes the survey questions as well as how the survey will be administered (e.g., online only or with paper surveys for employees who can't access computers at work). Does the agency need to translate the survey for employees who don't speak English as their native language? How will the agency follow up to maximize the response rate?

SUMMARIZING, DISTRIBUTING, AND ANALYZING RESULTS

Human resources should help design the analytical approach and reporting format and then coordinate the distribution of the results. For example, in the province of Alberta, the engagement-survey contractors provide the survey results first to HR and the province's deputy ministers, who then distribute the results across their organizations.

At the Air Force Materiel Command, which used the Gallup Q12 survey, HR receives the results first, reviews, and then distributes them, initially to senior leadership and then to all employees. In Minneapolis, after each survey, HR meets with the head of each department and the department survey champion to discuss survey results, areas that have been identified for improvements, and potential initiatives to increase scores.

The state of Washington HR department manages the biennial employee survey process, including posting the agency-by-agency results on the state HR website for all employees to view.

If the survey results show that specific units have high levels of engagement, HR should identify what these units are doing well and serve as a clearinghouse to share the information across the entire jurisdiction/agency. That's what the University of Wisconsin Hospital "Best-in-Class Library of Action Steps" (developed and managed by HR) is designed to do—publicize good ideas that units have implemented in response to employee-engagement survey results.

Human resources can also help units analyze their individual results and act on them. At the university, HR assembled a "data manager" group that included representatives from each of 13 divisions that participated in the survey. This group helped design the survey reports and was also tasked with explaining the results to division leaders and the rank-and-file employees. We also provided support to action teams in the individual units, including providing team facilitators and consulting on how to analyze and act on the survey data.

IDENTIFYING AND ADDRESSING ENGAGEMENT ISSUES IN THE HR ORGANIZATION ITSELF

Human resources should also analyze and take action on the engagement survey results for its own employees. This is not only essential for the employees who work in HR but also important for the credibility of the overall engagement initiative. This helps dispel the "do as we say, not as we do" perception that often plagues HR.

The city of Juneau, Alaska, for example, took the engagement survey results to heart in part because the results had implications for HR's own operations. The data showed that HR itself needed to step up its own communications: HR staff members now continually ask themselves these questions: Who needs to know? Why? How can we inform them?

At the University of Wisconsin, we piloted the engagement survey first in HR and then shared our results with the other 12 divisions who would be surveyed once we rolled it out full scale. By showing these executives the results from our pilot survey, we made it clear that we too were committed to putting our house in order.

IDENTIFYING AND IMPLEMENTING ENTERPRISE-WIDE CHANGES

As the coordinator of the engagement survey and the recipient of the results, HR is in the best position to analyze the survey results and look across the agency to understand where organization-specific changes are needed—that is, where the data reveal issues and problems that are not isolated to specific units but cut across the entire organization and therefore call for enterprise-wide solutions. I've identified several of these approaches: incorporating engagement into organizational values and strategy, building managerial competencies linked to employee engagement, developing and delivering training on engagement, mounting a cultural change campaign to focus on engagement, instituting new employee recognition programs, and holding managers accountable for improving engagement. HR is uniquely positioned to see across the organization and, if HR itself has the right competencies, to design and lead enterprise-wide solutions.

In the city of Minneapolis, for example, the citywide alternate work arrangement policy and program were spearheaded by HR in response to engagement survey results. The most recent Minneapolis employee-engagement survey revealed that a major employee concern was not feeling valued, including being dissatisfied with recognition programs. As I have detailed, this is a common issue in the public sector where financial rewards are severely limited. As a result, in Minneapolis, HR is considering ways to implement citywide strategies to improve employee recognition.

The HR department can play a key role in designing, implementing, and acting on an employee-engagement survey. This can require HR to develop new capabilities. However, improving engagement should not be an "HR project." Instead, measuring and improving the initiative should be a shared responsibility across the organization, jurisdiction, or agency, with HR providing leadership, expertise, coordination, and support.

Chapter 14

Getting Started on the Journey to Improved Employee Engagement

I have tried to make a convincing argument that improving employee engagement in government is a goal worth pursuing. I began this book by emphasizing that this is a difficult time to be working in the public sector. I also emphasized, however, that this is also a critical moment in time for government as the nation deals with enormous challenges, ranging from economic and national security issues to challenges that we all face every day in our local communities.

There is an important role for government, and the public servants who *are* government, to help our nation and communities successfully meet these challenges.

But the public sector can only do this if it operates at peak performance. Unfortunately, employee-engagement surveys show that in government, like in the private sector, there is room for dramatic improvement in the level of engagement. On top of this, as I also described, government faces unique barriers to improving engagement.

Therein lies the challenge for government: to identify and then overcome these barriers and harness the power of employee engagement to improve individual and organizational performance. The research on employee engagement clearly shows that this potential exists, and nowhere is it greater than in government, where our most important resource is our talent.

I have also suggested a relatively simple but potentially powerful model for the process of measuring and improving engagement that focuses on the need to collect real, jurisdiction- and agency-specific data on the level of employee engagement:

1. Plan the engagement survey.
2. Conduct the survey.
3. Report and analyze the results.
4. Take action on the results to maintain strengths and improve on weaknesses.
5. Sustain improved engagement over time and resurvey.

I have also described several different methodologies to survey employees to measure the level of employee engagement, including the survey developed by the U.S. Merit Systems Protection Board (MSPB), which includes questions that fall into six areas that drive employee engagement:

1. Pride in the work or workplace
2. Satisfaction with leadership
3. Opportunity to perform well at work
4. Satisfaction with recognition received
5. Prospect for future personal and professional growth
6. Positive work environment with some focus on teamwork

The MSPB engagement dimensions (and the questions in the survey itself), like other engagement surveys, can serve as a checklist for managers. Generally speaking, if these conditions exist in a jurisdiction or agency, that organization should have a high level of employee engagement. Conducting an employee-engagement survey is the most effective and accurate way to determine if these conditions truly exist.

I also highlighted the approaches that government organizations have taken to measure engagement and then take action to improve it. These jurisdictions and agencies have implemented changes to improve engagement that include the following:

- Providing senior-level and enterprise-wide leadership on employee engagement
- Improving communication
- Building leaders' competencies
- Improving the management of employee performance
- Ensuring that employees believe their opinions count
- Creating a more a positive work environment
- Incorporating engagement into assessment of job applicants
- Implementing a structured and comprehensive new employee onboarding process
- Helping employees improve their well-being
- Clarifying the line of sight between employees' work and the agency mission
- Enhancing employee prospects for career growth
- Recognizing employee contributions

As this list suggests, there are a range of strategies to improve engagement. But I've also emphasized that there isn't a one-size-fits-all approach to improving engagement. Each government jurisdiction and agency should measure its own level of engagement, analyze the results, identify priority areas to focus on, and then take action. These actions to improve engagement also must fit the agency's mission, values, strategy, and culture.

Technical considerations aside, improving engagement in government requires the fundamental organizational commitment and will to first identify improving engagement as a strategic goal, then measure engagement, take action to improve it, and sustain this momentum over time.

As I also emphasized, there is no silver bullet to achieve superior organizational performance in government, and there is no silver bullet to achieve high levels of employee engagement. Instead, what's needed is silver buckshot—an integrated series of actions to measure and then improve engagement.

Improving engagement is a journey just as much as it is a destination. But it is a journey worth embarking on to help government—the nation's largest and perhaps most important employer—achieve its potential.

Appendix 1

Action Plan Evaluation Worksheet[1]

Note: This worksheet will help the organization assess the quality of its employee engagement action plan by scoring the plan in seven criteria areas: leadership and accountability, stakeholder engagement, robustness of plan, measures for progress and impact, communication plan, implementation, and feedback and review of plan.

LEADERSHIP AND ACCOUNTABILITY

Is there an executive champion for the improvement effort, and are senior leaders and implementing managers held accountable for implementation and progress?

Excellent (2 points)	Satisfactory (1 point)	Poor (0 points)	Score
Agency has identified an executive champion for the improvement effort.	Agency has identified an executive champion for the improvement effort.	Agency has not identified an executive champion for the improvement effort.	
Senior leaders and implementing managers are clearly held accountable for implementation and progress (e.g., performance plans, incentives).	No clear system of accountability for senior leaders or implementing managers.	No clear system of accountability for senior leaders or implementing managers.	

STAKEHOLDER ENGAGEMENT

Has the agency solicited or will the agency solicit feedback and ideas for improvement from stakeholder groups including senior leaders, supervisors, staff, and unions?

Excellent (2 points)	Satisfactory (1 point)	Poor (0 points)	Score
Well-defined plans to solicit feedback, support, and ideas for improvement from all stakeholder groups	Some plans to solicit feedback, support, and ideas from some stakeholder groups; may be vague, weakly defined	No plans to solicit feedback, support, or ideas from any stakeholder groups	

ROBUSTNESS OF PLAN

Has the agency identified or will the agency identify key priority areas for improvement? Do action items reflect challenge areas as identified by survey data?

Excellent (2 points)	Satisfactory (1 point)	Poor (0 points)	Score
Agency has clearly identified or will identify key priority areas for improvement. Agency has used or intends to use survey data to drive actions. Action items reflect challenge areas as identified by survey data.	Action items appear unfocused. Unclear whether agency has used or plans to use survey data. Action items may or may not reflect challenge areas as identified by survey data.	Agency has not defined or will not define key priority areas. It is unclear whether agency has used or plans to use survey data. There are few or no action items.	

MEASURES FOR PROGRESS AND IMPACT

Has the agency defined or will the agency define measurable indicators of progress and impact in both the short and long term? Does the agency plan for quick wins as well as long-term improvements?

Excellent (2 points)	Satisfactory (1 point)	Poor (0 points)	Score
Agency has defined or will define both qualitative and quantitative measurable indicators of progress and impact in both the short and long term. Agency plans for quick wins as well as long-term improvements.	Agency has defined some indicators of progress but may not be well defined. Plan may focus heavily on either short-term or long-term solutions but not necessarily both.	Plan does not contain any measures to gauge progress/ impact. Agency has not clearly defined its short-term or long-term objectives.	

COMMUNICATION PLAN

Has the agency shared or will the agency share employee survey results with all staff? Has the agency shared/will the agency share plans for improvement with all staff? Does the agency intend to share measures of progress and impact?

Excellent (2 points)	Satisfactory (1 point)	Poor (0 points)	Score
Agency has already shared and addressed employee survey results with all staff members. OR Agency has a clear plan to share survey results with staff. OR Agency has already shared this plan for improvement with staff. OR Agency intends to share plan in the near future. Agency describes how it plans to share measures of progress and impact with staff, preferably at regular intervals.	Agency has shared employee survey results with only a limited number of staff members. OR Agency does not intend to share plans for improvement with staff. OR Agency does not intend to or does not indicate plans to share measures of progress with all staff. OR Agency makes no mention of periodic updates for all staff.	Agency has not shared employee survey results with staff nor does it intend to address the results in any way.	

IMPLEMENTATION

Has the agency allocated financial resources and staff time to the improvement effort? Does the plan specify milestones and clearly assign responsibilities for implementation?

Excellent (2 points)	Satisfactory (1 point)	Poor (0 points)	Score
Agency clearly describes the financial resources and staff time allocated to the improvement effort. Resources adequately match requirements. Plan specifies milestones and clearly assigns responsibilities for implementation.	Agency indicates that it has allocated financial resources and staff time to the improvement effort, but actual amounts and sufficiency are unclear. Plan specifies some vague or high-level milestones and responsibilities.	Agency has not indicated any allocation of resources or staff time to the improvement effort. Plan specifies few or no milestones, nor does it assign responsibilities for implementation.	

FEEDBACK AND REVIEW OF PLAN

Has the agency made provisions to continuously review progress? Is there a defined mechanism to periodically assess progress and adjust plans accordingly?

Excellent (2 points)	Satisfactory (1 point)	Poor (0 points)	Score
Agency clearly intends to monitor and control its plan over time. Plan includes periodic, scheduled reviews and times for adjustment.	Agency suggests that it will monitor its plan over time but has not described specific plans to do so. Plan suggests flexibility for changes over time.	Agency does not indicate that it plans to review progress or adjust plans over time.	

Appendix 2

Sample Communication Plan[1]

Timeline	Audience	Objective	Content	Media/Forum
7/29/13	Managers	• Share survey results • Obtain commitment to action	• Review and discuss survey results • Identify review team members	Meeting
8/9/13	All employees	• Executive shares survey results • Solicit volunteers	• Review survey highlights • Identify focus areas • Explain next steps • Employees break into small groups to discuss • Q & A • Request volunteers	• All-hands meeting • Printed summary of results
8/16/13	All employees	Disseminate team action plans	• Explain action teams • Share each team plan • Explain role of each employee	Division meetings

Timeline	Audience	Objective	Content	Media/Forum
8/23/13–9/13/13	All employees	Report team progress	Describe progress, changes to plans, and impacts on employees	Email
9/20/13	All employees	Announce implementation of plans	• Announce plan implementation • Explain how plan will be implemented and what it means for employees • Recognize team members and others • Celebrate success	All-hands meeting
10/18/13	Supervisors and managers	Executive reminds supervisors and managers of their roles in supporting the change	• Emphasize value of the change • Review supervisors' and managers' roles • Discuss any obstacles and how to resolve them	Meeting
Each quarter	All employees	• Progress report • Encouragement	Inform employees of continued progress and encourage continued support	• E-mail bulletin • Posters

Notes

CHAPTER 1

1. The Bush School of Government and Public Service, Texas A&M University. 2011. "Mission and Vision." http://bush.tamu.edu/about/mission.
2. Tabar, Susan. 2010. "Should a Pay Raise Be Given to Michigan Government Employees in the Dismal Economy?" *Examiner*, March 9.
3. Pattakos, Alex. 2009. "The Search for Meaning in Government Service." *Huffington Post Blog.* January 28. http://www.huffingtonpost.com/alex-pattakos/the-search-for-meaning-in_b_161394.html.
4. U.S. Merit Systems Protection Board. 2008. "The Power of Federal Employee Engagement." http://www.mspb.gov/netsearch/viewdocs.aspx?docnumber=379024&version=379721.
5. BlesssingWhite Research. 2011. "Employee Engagement Report 2011." http://www.blessingwhite.com/eee__report.asp.
6. Harter, James K., Frank L. Schmidt, Emily A. Killham, and James W. Asplund. 2006. "Q12 Meta-Analysis." *Gallup Consulting.* http://strengths.gallup.com/private/Resources/Q12Meta-Analysis_Flyer_GEN_08%2008_BP.pdf.
7. U.S. Merit Systems Protection Board. 2008. "The Power of Federal Employee Engagement." http://www.mspb.gov/netsearch/viewdocs.aspx?docnumber=379024&version=379721.
8. TowersWatson Consulting. 2006. "Engaging the Employee: What 17,000+ Public Sector Employees Say About the Work Experience." Presented at the International Public Management Association for Human Resources Southern Region Conference, Chattanooga, Tennessee.
9. Kaplan, David. 2010. "Best Companies to Work for; SAS: A New No. 1 Best Employer." *CNNMoney*, January 21. http://strengths.gallup.com/private/Resources/Q12Meta-Analysis_Flyer_GEN_08%2008_BP.pdf.

CHAPTER 2

1. Clarke, Nita, and David MacLeod. 2009. "Engaging for Success: Enhancing Performance Through Employee Engagement. A Report to Government." http://www.bis.gov.uk/files/file52215.pdf.
2. Heintzman, Ralph, and Brian Marson. December 2005. "People, Service and Trust: Is There a Public Sector Service Value Chain?" *International Review of Administrative Sciences* 71(4).
3. Smith, Kevin. 2009. "I Can't Define It, but I Know It When I See It." Duke University Libraries. http://blogs.library.duke.edu/scholcomm/2009/10/13/i-cant-defi ne-2.
4. Clarke, Nita, and David MacLeod. 2009. "Engaging for Success: Enhancing Performance Through Employee Engagement. A Report to Government." http://www.bis.gov.uk/files/file52215.pdf.
5. U.S. Merit Systems Protection Board. 2008. "The Power of Federal Employee Engagement." http://www.mspb.gov/netsearch/viewdocs.aspx?docnumber=379024&version=379721.
6. U.S. Office of Personnel Management. 2012. "Federal Employee Viewpoint Survey Results. Employees Influencing Change, Governmentwide Management Report." Washington, DC. http://www.fedview.opm.gov/2012files/2012_Government_Management_Report.PDF.
7. Rothwell, William. 2007. "Beyond Rules of Engagement: How Can Organizational Leaders Build a Culture That Supports High Engagement?" Dale Carnegie White Paper.
8. Treasury Board Secretariat, Canada. 2009. "Public Servants on the Public Service of Canada: Summary of the Results of the 2008 Public Service Employee Survey." http://www.tbs-sct.gc.ca/pses-saff/2008/report-rapport-eng.asp.
9. BlesssingWhite Research. 2011. "Employee Engagement Report 2011." http://www.blessingwhite.com/eee__report.asp.
10. Csikszentmihalyi, Mihaly. 2004. *Good Business: Leadership, Flow, and the Making of Meaning*. New York: Penguin Books.
11. Visser, Coert. 2003. "Good Business: Leadership, Flow, and the Making of Meaning." http://articlescoertvisser.blogspot.com/2007/11/good-business-leadership-flow-and.html.
12. Zukav, Gary. 1990. *The Seat of the Soul*. New York: Free Press.
13. *Gallup Business Journal*. 2012. "Gallup Study: Engaged Employees Inspire Company Innovation." http://businessjournal.gallup.com/content/24880/gallup-study-engaged-employees-inspire-company.aspx.

14. Masarech, Mary. 2011. "Impacting Engagement: The Leader's Role." Presented at the IPMA-HR International Conference, Chicago, Illinois.
15. Palguta, John, vice president of policy, Partnership for Public Service. 2010. Personal communication.
16. University of Wisconsin Hospital and Clinics. 2012. "Engagement Surveys: How We Build Health Care's Best, Manager Refresher Training: Understanding, Interpreting and Responding to Employee Survey Results." PowerPoint presentation.
17. Harter, James K., Frank L. Schmidt, Emily A. Killham, and James W. Asplund. 2006. "Q12 Meta-Analysis." *Gallup Consulting.* http://strengths.gallup.com/private/Resources/Q12Meta-Analysis_Flyer_GEN_08%2008_BP.pdf.
18. Rath, Tom, and John Harter. 2011. "The Economics of Wellbeing." http://www.ofyp.umn.edu/ofypmedia/focusfy/The_Economics_of_Wellbeing.pdf.
19. U.S. Merit Systems Protection Board. 2008. "The Power of Federal Employee Engagement." http://www.mspb.gov/netsearch/viewdocs.aspx?docnumber=379024&version=379721.
20. TowersWatson Consulting. 2006. "Engaging the Employee: What 17,000+ Public Sector Employees Say About the Work Experience." Presented at the International Public Management Association for Human Resources Southern Region Conference, Chattanooga, Tennessee.
21. Taylor, Jessica. 2009. "Employee Engagement and Labor Relations." *Gallup Business Journal.* http://businessjournal.gallup.com/content/.122849/Employee-Engagement-Labor-Relations.aspx#1.

CHAPTER 3

1. Gallup Consulting. 2011. "Employee Engagement: A Leading Indicator of Financial Performance." http://www.gallup.com/consulting/52/employee-engagement.aspx.
2. Gallup Consulting. 2010. "Employee Engagement: What's Your Engagement Ratio?" http://www.gallup.com/strategicconsulting/main.aspx. Reprinted with the permission of Gallup Inc.
3. TowersWatson Consulting. 2009. "Employee Engagement Underpins Business Transformation." http://www.towersperrin.com/tp/getwebcachedoc?country=gbr&webc=GBR/2008/200807/TP_ISR_July08.pdf.

4. Clarke, Nita, and David MacLeod. 2009. "Engaging for Success: Enhancing Performance Through Employee Engagement. A Report to Government." http://www.bis.gov.uk/files/file52215.pdf.
5. Corporate Leadership Council. 2004. "Driving Performance and Retention Through Employee Engagement—Executive Summary." http://www.usc.edu/programs/cwfl/assets/pdf/Employee%20engagement.pdf.
6. Watson Wyatt Worldwide. 2009. "Continuous Engagement: The Key to Unlocking the Value of Your People During Tough Times." *Work Europe Survey Report 2008–2009.* http://www.watsonwyatt.com/research/pdfs/2008-EU-0617.pdf.
7. Clarke, Nita, and David MacLeod. 2009. "Engaging for Success: Enhancing Performance Through Employee Engagement. A Report to Government." http://www.bis.gov.uk/files/file52215.pdf.
8. Kenexa, an IBM company. 2008. "Employee Engagement: Stories of Success." New Zealand. http://www.jra.co.nz/storiesofsuccess.aspx.
9. Gallup Business Journal. 2009. "Gallup Study: Engaged Employees Inspire Company Innovation." http://businessjournal.gallup.com/content/24880/gallup-study-engaged-employees-inspire-company.aspx.
10. Gallup Consulting. 2007. "Public Sector." http://eu.gallup.com/consulting/118489/public-sector.aspx.
11. Krueger, Jerry, and Emily Killham. 2007. "The Innovation Equation." *Gallup Management Journal.* http://businessjournal.gallup.com/content/27145/innovation-equation.aspx.
12. Clarke, Nita, and David MacLeod. 2009. "Engaging for Success: Enhancing Performance Through Employee Engagement. A Report to Government." http://www.bis.gov.uk/files/file52215.pdf.
13. Truss, Catherine. Charted Institute of Personnel and Development. 2006. *Working Life: Employee Attitudes and Engagement 2006 Research Report.* London.
14. Launched in 2005, the Capability Review Programme (U.K. Civil Service, Capability Review Programme, http://www.civilservice.gov.uk/about/improving/capability) is part of the wider civil-service reform agenda, designed to lead to a civil service that is better at delivering public services. The reviews are designed to (1) improve the capability of the civil service to meet today's delivery objectives and be ready for the challenges of tomorrow, (2) assure the public and ministers that the civil-service leadership is equipped to develop and deliver departmental strategies, and (3) help departments act on long-term key development areas and therefore provide assurance on future delivery.

15. Clarke, Nita, and David MacLeod. 2009. "Engaging for Success: Enhancing Performance Through Employee Engagement. A Report to Government." http://www.bis.gov.uk/files/file52215.pdf.
16. Ibid.
17. Heintzman, Ralph, and Brian Marson. December 2005. "People, Service and Trust: Is There a Public Sector Service Value Chain?" *International Review of Administrative Sciences* 71(4): 549–75.
18. Kernaghan, Kenneth. March 2011. "Getting Engaged: Public-Service Merit and Motivation Revisited, Canada." *Canadian Public Administration* 54(1): 1–21.
19. Ibid.
20. Province of Alberta. 2012. *The Alberta Public Service: Proudly Working Together—Our Focus for the Future, 2012–2032.* Alberta: Province of Alberta.
21. U.S. Merit Systems Protection Board. 2008. "The Power of Federal Employee Engagement." http://www.mspb.gov/netsearch/viewdocs.aspx?docnumber=379024&version=379721.
22. Governing Institute, ADP, and International Public Management Association for Human Resources. 2012. "Employee Engagement." Presented at the 2012 IPMA-HR annual conference, Nashville, Tennessee.
23. Deloitte Development LLC. 2011. "Performance in a Cost-Constrained Federal Environment: Improving Employee Engagement to Do More with Less." http://www.deloitte.com/view/en_US/us/Industries/US-federal-government/afd23182cc1b3310VgnVCM3000001c56f00aRCRD.htm.
24. United Kingdom Department of Health. 2011. "Engaging Your Staff: The NHS Staff Engagement Resource—Supporting You to Increase Staff Engagement in Your Organization." http://www.nhsemployers.org/SiteCollectionDocuments/Staff%20engagement%20toolkit.pdf.
25. University of Wisconsin Hospital and Clinics. 2012. "Health Care's Best Work Environment: 2012 Engagement Survey Results." May 23, 2012.
26. Kranz, Gary. 2011. "Special Report on Employee Engagement Losing Lifeblood." *Workforce*, July 21; updated September 7.
27. Gallup Consulting. 2009. "Building Engaged Schools: A Scientific Method for Improving School Performance." Omaha, NE: Gallup.
28. Coldren, Mark. 2012. "Emerging Issues for Higher Education: Engaged Employees Are Critical for the Future." *The Higher Education Workplace* 4(1): 19.
29. Clarke, Nita, and David MacLeod. 2009. "Engaging for Success: Enhancing Performance Through Employee Engagement. A Report to Government." http://www.bis.gov.uk/files/file52215.pdf.

30. Government of Scotland. 2007. "Employee Engagement in the Public Sector: A Review of Literature." http://scotland.gov.uk/Publications/2007/05/09111348/6.
31. Kelly, N. 2010. "Employee Engagement Is Down." *Noreen Kelly Communications*. http://trustmattersgroup.com/spiritoftrust/?p=441.
32. BlesssingWhite Research. 2011. "Employee Engagement Report 2011: Beyond the Numbers—A Practical Approach for Individuals, Managers and Executives." http://www.blessingwhite.com/eee__report.asp.
33. Masarech, Mary Anne. 2011. "Impacting Engagement: The Leader's Role." Presented at the International Public Management Association for Human Resources 2011 International Conference, Chicago, Illinois.
34. TowersWatson Consulting. 2006. "Engaging the Employee: What 17,000+ Public Sector Employees Say About the Work Experience." Presented at the International Public Management Association for Human Resources Southern Region Conference, Chattanooga, Tennessee.
35. Clarke, Nita, and David MacLeod. 2009. "Engaging for Success: Enhancing Performance Through Employee Engagement. A Report to Government." http://www.bis.gov.uk/files/file52215.pdf.
36. U.S. Merit Systems Protection Board. 2008. "The Power of Federal Employee Engagement." http://www.mspb.gov/netsearch/viewdocs.aspx?docnumber=379024&version=379721.
37. U.S. Office of Personnel Management. 2012. "2012 Federal Employee Viewpoint Survey Results." *Employees Influencing Change, Governmentwide Management Report*. http://www.fedview.opm.gov/2012files/2012_Government_Management_Report.PDF.
38. Partnership for Public Service. 2012. "The Best Places to Work in the Federal Government." http://bestplacestowork.org/BPTW/analysis.
39. Braverman, Eric, Aaron De Smet, and Bill Schaninger. 2009. "Improving Worker Performance in the US Government." *McKinsey and Company*. http://www.mckinseyquarterly.com/Improving_worker_performance_in_the_US_government_2471.
40. Governing Issue Brief. 2012. "Driving Successful Employee Engagement: A Major Opportunity to Keep Public Sector Employees Connected and Committed." http://www.governing.com/papers/GOV-Paper-Elements-of-Sucessful-Organizations.html.
41. State of Washington, Office of Financial Management, Office of the State Human Resource Director. 2012. "2011 Washington State Employee Survey." http://www.hr.wa.gov/SiteCollectionDocuments/Strategic%20HR/State%20Employee%20Survey/2011WashingtonStateEmployeeSurveyReport1-24-12.pdf.

42. Society for Human Resource Management/Globoforce. 2012. "The Impact of Recognition on Employee Engagement and ROI." Employee recognition survey. Winter 2012 report. http://ebookbrowse.com/shrm-globoforce-survey-employee-recognition-winter-2012-pptx-d336836061.
43. Clarke, Nita, and David MacLeod. 2009. "Engaging for Success: Enhancing Performance Through Employee Engagement. A Report to Government." http://www.bis.gov.uk/files/file52215.pdf.
44. Jenkins, Linda. 1998. "Industry Commitment to Employee Training and Development." American Society for Training and Development 1998 study. http://www.gradview.com/articles/careers/commitment_to_training.html.
45. Clarke, Nita, and David MacLeod. 2009. "Engaging for Success: Enhancing Performance through Employee Engagement. A Report to government." http://www.bis.gov.uk/files/file52215.pdf.
46. Governing Institute Case Study. 2012. Unpublished.
47. Ibid.
48. Noel, Al. 2010. "Why Bother with Employee Engagement?" http://www.employee-engagement-surveys.com.
49. Ibid.
50. Byrne, John A. 1998. "How Jack Welch Runs GE: A Close-Up Look at How America's Number 1 Manager Runs GE." *Business Week*. http://www.businessweek.com/1998/23/b3581001.htm.
51. U.S. Merit Systems Protection Board. 2008. "The Power of Federal Employee Engagement." http://www.mspb.gov/netsearch/viewdocs.aspx?docnumber=379024&version=379721.
52. U.S. Office of Personnel Management. 2011. "Empowering Employees, Inspiring Change, Government Management Report." Washington, DC.
53. Hardrick, Julius, and Trudy Fernandez. 2012. "Every Employee Counts: Fostering Engagement on Shoestring Budget." *The Higher Education Workplace* 4(1).

CHAPTER 4

1. Pew Research Center. 2012. "Growing Gap in Favorable Views of Federal, State Governments." http://www.pewtrusts.org/our_work_report_detail.aspx?id=85899383082.
2. Stier, Max. 2012. "No Respect for Federal Workers." *Huffington Post*, March 29. http://www.huffingtonpost.com/max-stier/federal-workers_b_1379404.html.

3. Babcock, Pamela. 2011. "Public Employee Engagement in Peril." *Society for Human Resource Management.* http://www.shrm.org/hrdisciplines/employeerelations/articles/pages/engagementinperil.aspx.
4. Center for State and Local Government Excellence. 2012. "Survey Findings: State and Local Government Workforce: 2012 Trends." Washington, DC. http://slge.org/wp-content/uploads/2012/04/S-L-Govt-Workforce-2012_12-195_web.pdf.
5. Governing Issue Brief. 2012. "Driving Successful Employee Engagement: A Major Opportunity to Keep Public Sector Employees Connected and Committed." http://www.governing.com/papers/GOV-Paper-Elements-of-Sucessful-Organizations.html.
6. Partnership for Public Service. 2012. "Federal Leaders Face Challenges Attracting Top College Graduates to Government Service." http://ourpublicservice.org/OPS/publications/viewcontentdetails.php?id=170.
7. The White House, Office of the Press Secretary. 2009. "Remarks by the President in an AARP Tele–Town Hall on Health Care Reform." http://www.whitehouse.gov/the_press_office/Remarks-by-the-President-in-AARP-Tele-Town-Hall-on-Health-Care-Reform.
8. Applebaum, Binyam, and Robert Gebeloff. 2012. "Even Critics of Safety Net Increasingly Depend on It." *New York Times*, February 11, 2012. http://www.nytimes.com/2012/02/12/us/even-critics-of-safety-net-increasingly-depend-on-it.html?pagewanted=all&_r=0.
9. Wiseman, Paul. 2012. "Recovery Slowest Since WWII." *Wisconsin State Journal*, August 18.
10. Mayer, Gerald. 2011. "Selected Characteristics of Private and Public Sector Workers, July 1, 2011." Washington, DC: Congressional Research Service.
11. WAMU 88.5. "Stop Blaming Federal Workers: Commentary with Max Stier." March 8, 2010. http://wamu.org/news/10/03/08/stop_blaming_federal_workers_commentary_with_max_stier.
12. Ibid.
13. Center for State and Local Government Excellence. 2012. "Survey Findings: State and Local Government Workforce: 2012 Trends." Washington, DC. http://slge.org/wp-content/uploads/2012/04/S-L-Govt-Workforce-2012_12-195_web.pdf.
14. Losey, Steve. 2012. "Retirements Surged 24 Percent in 2011." *Federal Times*, February 9. http://www.federaltimes.com/article/20120209/BENEFITS02/202090303.
15. Losey, Stephen. 2013. "Retirement Wave Slows at Year's End." *Federal Times*, January 7.

16. Center for State and Local Government Excellence and ICMA-RC. 2012. "ICMA Conference Briefing: Local Government Employment, Benefits, and Retirement Issues." Washington, DC. http://www.icmarc.org/Documents/educomm/Briefing201210.pdf.
17. *The Wire*. 2010. "The Short, Strange Political Life of Craig Benson." http://www.wirenh.com/home-mainmenu-1/11-news-general/190-the-short-strange-political-life-of-craig-benson.html.
18. Eggers, Bill, and John O'Leary. 2009. *If We Can Put a Man on the Moon: Getting Big Things Done in Government*. Cambridge, MA: Harvard Business School Press.
19. Pfiffner, James P. 1999. "The Public Service Ethic in the New Public Personnel Systems." *Public Personnel Management* 28(4): 541–55.
20. Light, Paul C. 1999. *The True Size of Government*. Washington, DC: Brookings Institution.
21. Whitford, David. 2012. "Does Ray Kelly Have the World's Toughest Job?" *Fortune Magazine, CNN Money*. http://management.fortune.cnn.com/2012/10/12/ray-kelly-new-york.
22. Rothkopf, David. 2013. "Managing the Oval Office." *New York Times*, January 20, 2013.
23. Partnership for Public Service. 2008. "In the Public We Trust—Renewing the Connection Between the Federal Government and the Public." Washington, DC.
24. Chang, Kelly, David Lewis, and Nolan McCarty. 2001. "The Tenure of Political Appointees." Presented at the 2001 Annual Meetings of the Midwest Political Science Association, April 19–22, Chicago.
25. Cohen, David M. 1998. "Amateur Government." *Journal of Public Administration and Theory* 8(4): 450–97.
26. This and all other references to scores, rankings, and specific agency actions are taken from the Partnership for Public Service "Best Places to Work in the Federal Government" 2012 rankings: http://bestplacestowork.org/BPTW/index.php.
27. Seely, Ron. 2012. "DNR Appointee Resolved Massive Waste Violation Internally Instead of Referring Case to DOJ." *Wisconsin State Journal*, May 7. http://host.madison.com/wsj/article_07a64834-96e3-11e1-b4c6-0019bb2963f4.html.
28. Ink, Dwight. 2007. "Twenty-First Century Career Leaders." In *Transformational Trends in Government and Democracy*, edited by R. S. Morse, T. F. Buss, and C. M. Kinghorn. Washington, DC: National Academy of Public Administration.

29. *The Wire*. 2010. "The Short, Strange Political Life of Craig Benson." http://www.wirenh.com/home-mainmenu-1/11-news-general/190-the-short-strange-political-life-of-craig-benson.html.
30. Jenkins, Linda. 1998. "Industry Commitment to Employee Training and Development." American Society for Training and Development 1998 study. http://www.gradview.com/articles/careers/commitment_to_training.html.
31. Citizens for Responsibility and Ethics in Washington. http://www.citizensforethics.org/pages/state-ethics.
32. Mayer, Gerald. 2011. "Selected Characteristics of Private and Public Sector Workers, July 1, 2011." Washington, DC: Congressional Research Service.
33. Center for State and Local Government Excellence. 2012. "ICMA Conference Briefing: Local Government Employment, Benefits, and Retirement Issues." Washington, DC.
34. Washington State Workforce Report. 2010. "New Hire Age, Hiring Across Age Groups Has Leveled Since FY 2008." http://www.hr.wa.gov/SiteCollectionDocuments/Reports/2010WashingtonStateWorkforceReport/NewHireAge.htm.
35. Mayer, Gerald. 2011. "Selected Characteristics of Private and Public Sector Workers, July 1, 2011." Washington, DC: Congressional Research Service.
36. U.S. Bureau of Labor Statistics. 2012. "Economic News Release Union Members Summary." http://www.bls.gov/news.release/union2.nr0.htm.
37. Norcross, Eileen. 2011. "Public-Sector Unionism: A Review." Working Paper No. 11-26, The Mercatus Center, George Mason University, Fairfax, Virginia.
38. Brandeis University, Lewis J. Brandeis Legacy Fund for Social Justice. http://www.brandeis.edu/legacyfund/bio.html.
39. Killman, Emily A. n.d. "The Innovation Equation." *Gallup Management Journal.* http://businessjournal.gallup.com/content/27145/innovation-equation.aspx.
40. U.S. Office of Personnel Management. 2012. "Federal Employee Viewpoint Survey Results. Employees Influencing Change, Governmentwide Management Report." Washington, DC.
41. Partnership for Public Service. 2011. "Snapshot: What Drives Innovation in Government." http://ourpublicservice.org/OPS/publications/viewcontentdetails.php?id=163.
42. Lavigna, Bob, and Laurie E. Paarlberg. 2010. "Transformational Leadership and Public Service Motivation: Driving Individual and

Organizational Performance." *Public Administration Review* 70(5): 710–18.

43. Crewson, Philip E. 1997. "Public-Service Motivation: Building Empirical Evidence of Incidence and Effect." *Journal of Public Administration Research and Theory* 7(4): 499–518.
44. Pattakos, Alex. 2004. "The Search for Meaning in Government Service." *Public Administration Review* 64(1): 106–12.

CHAPTER 5

1. Public Sector People Managers' Association and Chartered Institute of Personnel and Development. 2012. "Leading Culture Change: Employee Engagement and Public Service Transformation." London.
2. Center for State and Local Government Excellence. 2012. "Survey Findings: State and Local Government Workforce: 2012 Trends." Washington, DC. http://slge.org/wp-content/uploads/2012/04/S-L-Govt-Workforce-2012_12-195_web.pdf.
3. The Conference Board. 2010. "CEO Challenge 2010: Top 10 Challenges." http://www.executiveconnectionsllc.com/pdfs/CEO Challenges_2010.pdf.
4. U.S. Merit Systems Protection Board. 2008. "The Power of Federal Employee Engagement." http://www.mspb.gov/netsearch/viewdocs.aspx?docnumber=379024&version=379721.
5. Partnership for Public Service. 2007. "Annual Report." Washington, DC.
6. Armey, Dick. 1995. *The Freedom Revolution*. New York: Regnery.
7. DeSeve, G. Edward. 2009. "Speeding Up the Learning Curve: Observations from a Survey of Seasoned Political Appointees." Washington, DC: IBM Center for the Business of Government and the National Academy of Public Administration.
8. The American Presidency Project. 1989. "Remarks to Members of the Senior Executive Service, January 26, 1989." http://www.presidency.ucsb.edu/ws/index.php?pid=16628.
9. Pattakos, Alex. 2004. "The Search for Meaning in Government Service." *Public Administration Review* 64(1): 106–12.
10. U.S. Merit Systems Protection Board. 2013. "Federal Employee Engagement: The Motivating Potential of Job Characteristics and Rewards." Washington, DC.
11. U.S. Office of Personnel Management. 2012. "2012 Federal Employee Viewpoint Survey, Employees Influencing Change: Report

by Demographics." Washington, DC. http://www.fedview.opm.gov/2012files/2012_Government_Management_Report.PDF.

12. Achievers and Experience Inc. 2012. "Class of 2012: Understanding the Needs of Your Future Workforce." http://images.experience.com/images2/fms/downloadcenter/class_of_2012.pdf.
13. Partnership for Public Service. 2007. "Back to School: Rethinking Federal Recruiting on College Campuses." Washington, DC.
14. Ibid.
15. Johnson, Jenna. 2011. "Teach for America 2011 Acceptance Rate: 11 Percent." *Washington Post,* August 3.
16. Teach for America, Press Release. 2012. "Teach for America to Bring a Record 10,000 Teachers to Nation's Highest-Need Classrooms in 2012." http://www.washingtonpost.com/blogs/campus-overload/post/teach-for-america-2011-acceptance-rate-11-percent/2011/08/03/gIQAqX8bsI_blog.html.

CHAPTER 6

1. Gallup Consulting. 2011. "Employee Engagement: A Leading Indicator of Financial Performance." http://www.gallup.com/consulting/52/employee-engagement.aspx.
2. Harter, J., F. Schmidt, E. Killham, and J. Asplund. 2006. "Q12 Meta-Analysis." Washington, DC: Gallup Consulting.
3. Governing Issue Brief. 2012. "Driving Successful Employee Engagement: A Major Opportunity to Keep Public Sector Employees Connected and Committed." http://www.governing.com/papers/GOV-Paper-Elements-of-Sucessful-Organizations.html.
4. Partnership for Public Service. 2012. "Beneath the Surface: Understanding Attrition at Your Agency and Why It Matters." Washington, DC.
5. Partnership for Public Service and Booz Allen Hamilton. 2008. "Getting On Board: A Model for Integrating and Engaging New Employees." Washington, DC.
6. Rubin, Ellen. 2011. "Appraising Performance Appraisal Systems in the Federal Government: A Literature Review, Preliminary Findings, and Prospects for Future Research." Presented at the Public Management Research Conference. http://www.maxwell.syr.edu/uploadedFiles/conferences/pmrc/Files/Rubin_Appraising%20Performance%20Appraisal%20Systems.pdf.

7. U.S. Merit Systems Protection Board. 2009. "Managing for Engagement—Communication, Connection, and Courage." Washington, DC.
8. Ellis, Christian M., and A Sorensen. 2007. "Assessing Employee Engagement: The Key to Improving Productivity." *Perspectives* 15(1). http://www.sibson.com/publications/perspectives/Volume_15_Issue_1/ROW.cfm.
9. Bradley, Mike. 2012. "The Cheap Climate Survey." http://mikejbradley.wordpress.com/2012/11/08/the-cheap-climate-survey.
10. Quantum Workplace. "Employee Engagement: Increase Engagement for Increased Business Success." http://www.quantumworkplace.com/your-challenges/employee-engagement.
11. U.S. Merit Systems Protection Board. 2008. "The Power of Federal Employee Engagement." Washington, DC.
12. Partnership for Public Service. 2010. "Best Places to Work in the Federal Government." http://bestplacestowork.org/BPTW/rankings.
13. Harter, J. K., F. L. Schmidt, and E. A. Killham. 2003. *Employee Engagement, Satisfaction, and Business-Unit-Level Outcomes: A Meta-Analysis.* Washington, DC: The Gallup Organization.
14. United Kingdom Cabinet Office. 2011. "Civil Service People Survey 2010: Initial Findings." http://www.civilservice.gov.uk/wp-content/uploads/2011/09/CSPS-2010-background_tcm6-38336.pdf.
15. Nisbet, Jody. 2010. "Employee Engagement Interjurisdictional Initiative." Presented at the Institute for Citizen-Centred Service Conference, Toronto.
16. U.S. Postal Service. n.d. "Safety and Employee Engagement." http://about.usps.com/publications/annual-report-comprehensive-statement-2011/html/ar2011_perfmnce_010.htm.

CHAPTER 7

1. "The *Fortune* Interview: Herb Kelleher." *Fortune*, January 14, 2013.

CHAPTER 8

1. Ellis, Christian M., and A. Sorensen. 2007. "Assessing Employee Engagement: The Key to Improving Productivity." *Perspectives* 15(1). http://www.sibson.com/publications/perspectives/Volume_15_Issue_1/ROW.cfm.

2. Tarran, Brian. "Postal Workers Union Urges Boycott of Employee Surveys." Research. August 17, 2010. http://www.research-live.com/news/news-headlines/postal-workers-union-urges-boycott-of-employee-surveys/4003381.article.
3. Clarke, Nita, and David MacLeod. 2009. "Engaging for Success: Enhancing Performance Through Employee Engagement. A Report to Government." http://www.bis.gov.uk/files/file52215.pdf.

CHAPTER 9

1. U.S. Office of Personnel Management. 2012. "Federal Employee Viewpoint Survey Results, Employees Influencing Change, Governmentwide Management Report." Washington, DC.
2. Ibid.
3. Ibid.
4. Partnership for Public Service. 2011. "The Best Places to Work in the Federal Government: Staff/Manager Alignment Scores, Agency Guide." Washington, DC.

CHAPTER 10

1. Lavigna, Robert. 2012. "Harnessing the Power of Employee Engagement, Part 2: Free Pizza and Coke on Friday Afternoon Is Not an Engagement Strategy." *Government Finance Review* 28(1).
2. Bernardy, Charles. January 3, 2013. Personal communication.
3. Ibid.
4. Public Sector People Managers' Association and Chartered Institute of Personnel and Development. 2012. "Leading Culture Change: Employee Engagement and Public Service Transformation." London.
5. Partnership for Public Service. n.d. "Best Places to Work: Action Planning." *Action Planning Facilitator Guide*. Washington, DC.
6. Caroselli, Marlene. 2000. *Leadership Skills for Managers*. New York: McGraw Hill Professional.
7. Partnership for Public Service. 2011. "Profiles of Notable Movers." http://bestplacestowork.org.
8. U.S. Merit Systems Protection Board. n.d. "The Survey Results Action Guide." Washington, DC. http://www.fedview.opm.gov/2012files/2012_Government_Management_Report.PDF.

CHAPTER 11

1. Rowe, Mary. n.d. Personal email communication. October 1, 2012.
2. Rosenberg, Alyssa. 2009. "OMB to Use Workplace Rankings in 2011 Budget Process." *Government Executive.* http://www.govexec.com/pay-benefits/2009/05/omb-to-use-workplace-rankings-in-2011-budget-process/29201/.
3. Partnership for Public Service. 2011. "Profiles of Notable Movers." Washington, DC.

CHAPTER 12

1. United Kingdom Civil Service. 2010. "Employee Engagement in the Civil Service." http://www.civilservice.gov.uk/about/improving/employee-engagement-in-the-civil-service.
2. Fox, Tom. 2012. "Improving the Department of Transportation: A Conversation with Ray LaHood." *Washington Post,* December 19.
3. City of Minneapolis. n.d. "Minneapolis Goals & City Direction." http://www.minneapolismn.gov/council/council_goals_index#P59_3204.
4. Rowe, Mary. n.d. Personal communication. October 1, 2012.
5. Local Government Employers. 2008. "Best Councils to Work For 2008." http://www.lge.gov.uk/lge/core/page.do?pageId=606186.
6. Clarke, Nita, and David MacLeod. 2009. "Engaging for Success: Enhancing Performance Through Employee Engagement. A Report to Government." http://www.bis.gov.uk/files/file52215.pdf.
7. United Kingdom Civil Service. n.d. "Embedding Engagement, Engagement Best Practice: Case Studies, Back to the Floor Initiative Launched by the Department for Work and Pensions." http://www.civilservice.gov.uk/about/improving/employee-engagement-in-the-civil-service/embedding.
8. Public Sector People Managers' Association and Chartered Institute of Personnel and Development. 2012. "Leading Culture Change: Employee Engagement and Public Service Transformation." http://www.cipd.co.uk/binaries/6010%20Leading%20Culture%20Change%20(WEB).pdf.
9. Robison, Jennifer. n.d. "Transforming Government." *Gallup Business Journal.* http://businessjournal.gallup.com/content/1159/transforming-government.aspx.
10. Ibid.

11. U.S. Office of Personnel Management. n.d. "Recruitment and Selection, Executive Core Qualifications (ECQs)." http://www.opm.gov/ses/recruitment/qualify.asp.
12. U.S. Merit Systems Protection Board. 2009. "Managing for Engagement—Communication, Connection, and Courage." Washington, DC.
13. United Kingdom Department of Health. "Engaging Your Staff: The NHS Staff Engagement Resource." http://www.nhsemployers.org/SiteCollectionDocuments/Staff%20engagement%20toolkit.pdf.
14. Partnership for Public Service. 2010. "On Demand Government: Deploying Flexibilities to Ensure Service Continuity." Washington, DC.
15. CPS HR Services. 2012. "HR Survey Series: Public Sector Telework Perceptions, Policies and Practices." Sacramento, CA.
16. Losey, Stephen. 2010. "'Snowmageddon' Drives Call for More Telework." *Federal Times*, February 21. http://www.federaltimes.com/article/20100221/PERSONNEL01/2210308/-8216-Snowmageddon-drives-call-more-telework.
17. Partnership for Public Service. 2010. "On Demand Government: Deploying Flexibilities to Ensure Service Continuity." Washington, DC.
18. United Kingdom Civil Service. n.d. "Embedding Engagement, Engagement Best Practice: Case Studies, Staff Engagement Recruitment Exercise." http://www.civilservice.gov.uk/about/improving/employee-engagement-in-the-civil-service/embedding.
19. McGee, Lucy. 2006. "How to Interview for Engagement." *People Management*, July 27. http://www.workinfo.com/articles/interview_for_engagement_109.htm.
20. Partnership for Public Service. 2008. "Getting On Board: A Model for Integrating and Engaging New Employees." Washington, DC.
21. Ibid.
22. Ibid.
23. Ibid.
24. United Kingdom Civil Service. n.d. "Embedding Engagement, Engagement Best Practice: Case Studies Health, DVLA Wellbeing & Sickness Absence." http://www.civilservice.gov.uk/about/improving/employee-engagement-in-the-civil-service/embedding.
25. Local Government Employers. 2008. "Best Councils to Work For 2008." http://www.lge.gov.uk/lge/core/page.do?pageId=606186.
26. Kenexa, an IBM company. 2008. "Employee Engagement, Stories of Success." New Zealand.
27. Pattakos, Alex. 2004. "The Search for Meaning in Government Service." *Public Administration Review* 64(1): 106–12.

28. Kenexa, an IBM company. 2008. "Employee Engagement, Stories of Success." New Zealand.

CHAPTER 13

1. International Public Management Association for Human Resources. 2002. "Workforce Planning Resource Guide for Public Sector Human Resource Professionals." Alexandria, VA.
2. International Public Management Association for Human Resources. 2010. "Competencies." Alexandria, VA. http://dev.ipma-hr.org/professional-development/certification/competencies.

APPENDIX 1

1. Partnership for Public Service. n.d. "Action Planning Guide." Washington, DC.

APPENDIX 2

1. U.S. Merit Systems Protection Board. n.d. "The Survey Results Action Guide." Washington, DC.

Index

Note: The letters *f*, *t*, and *n* indicate that the entry refers to a page's figure, table, or note, respectively.